CORPORATEERING

CORPORATEERING

How Corporate Power
Steals Your Personal Freedom . . .
and What You Can Do About It

JAMIE COURT

JEREMY P. TARCHER / PUTNAM
a member of Penguin Group (USA) Inc.
New York

Jeremy P. Tarcher/Putnam
a member of
Penguin Group (USA) Inc.
375 Hudson Street
New York, NY 10014
www.penguin.com

Library of Congress Cataloging-in-Publication Data

Court, Jamie, date.
Corporateering : how corporate power steals your personal freedom . . .
and what you can do about it / Jamie Court.
p.   cm.
Includes bibliographical references.
ISBN 1-58542-228-2
1. Corporations—Corrupt practices—United States.   2. Consumer protection—
United States.   3. Freedom of information—United States.   4. Privacy, Right
of—United States.   5. Social responsibility of business—United States.   I. Title.
HV6769.C69   2003   2002041372
364.16'8—dc21

Printed in the United States of America

1   3   5   7   9   10   8   6   4   2

This book is printed on acid-free paper. ∞

Book design by Lee Fukui

FOR MICHELLE,

WHO SHOWS ME EVERY DAY

WHAT IS REAL,

AND INSPIRES ME DAILY WITH

WHAT IS RIGHT.

ACKNOWLEDGMENTS

THESE PAGES are the essence of the thinking and struggles of my friends and colleagues who fight for the needs and interests of individuals against powerful enemies and daunting odds. This is their book, not mine, and I am forever grateful for all they have shared with me and all they do for the world.

My wife and partner, Michelle Williams Court, worked through these pages with me at every stage and gave selflessly of her insight, her struggles against injustice, and her epiphanies, which are the better part of my voice. My publisher and friend, Jeremy Tarcher, developed this book with me over two years' worth of breakfasts, and I am deeply indebted for his invaluable teaching. Jeremy's endless patience, brilliant mind, and boundless generosity make him the father of the movement to challenge corporateering. My friend and mentor Harvey Rosenfield has shown me and the world how to fight back and actually win. His unyielding commitment to justice, generosity with his spotlight, and support for every fight worth fighting, no matter what it costs, make him a true American hero. His personal friendship and unwavering support for me, no matter who I anger, has saved me from another career more than once.

My colleague Doug Heller is the future of the consumer movement in America. He was this book's eyes, ears, and voice during the California energy crisis. His 24/7 passion, commitment, and labor have prevailed over the most experienced and well-paid industry lobbyists and have saved ratepayers and policyholders billions of dollars. My thanks also to my other colleagues at the Foundation for Taxpayer and Consumer Rights, present and past, for their support, dedication, and inspiration: Carmen Balber, Pam Pressley, Jerry Flanagan, Margaret Strubel, Janine Hamner, Joe Newlin, Emmy Rhine, Mark Reback, Kathy Olsen, Gina Calabrese, Bill Gallagher, Paul Herzog, Phil Roberto, Andrew Pontious, and the volunteers of the Oaks Project.

My gratitude as well to those who shape justice so much in ways too few appreciate: Sara Nichols, Lea-Ann Tratten, John Richard, Linda Peeno, Joanne Doroshow, Frank Smith, Harry Snyder, Andy Court, and Suzanne Wierbinski.

My editor, Mitch Horowitz, has enlivened this book with his insight, passion, and wit. His careful eyes and challenging comments are responsible for the unearthing of some of the most powerful facts and evidence in the text. Mitch's support for this and other projects in the public interest help to make the world a safer place. Ralph Nader has done the same in so many ways that not even his staunchest critics can deny it. His pioneering advocacy and research on the issue of corporate accountability continue to teach, inspire, and challenge us.

CONTENTS

PART THREE
Counter-Corporateering

FOREWORD

IF CORPORATIONS WERE PEOPLE, this would be the time of their rehabilitation.

Unfortunately, there is no Betty Ford Clinic for corporations. No company has ever gone to San Quentin or any other prison for its crimes. Or received the death penalty. The possibility of Ken Lay calling me for a golf date is more likely than his ever making license plates in prison.

As of this writing, there's privacy for the corporation, not the individual; full legal rights for Corporate America, not the consumer; bankruptcy protection for Enron, but not for the average investors who lost their life savings by investing in Enron's stock.

Instead of being forced into detox, the U.S. corporation got Botox. Cosmetic answers to Enron-like, loophole-riddled accounting problems. But corporate accountability cannot end with corporate accountants. Easing investors' worries so that the public can sink billions more into the next generation of socially irresponsible corporations is not a real response to the growing power of corporations. The modern corporation is after more than your money.

Voice mail hell, credit card rate bait-and-switches, television commercials playing at the urinal. In this book, Jamie Court shows how such everyday "corporateering" springs from the same assumptions and strategies that led to the fire sales on stock at Enron, Global Crossing, WorldCom, and so on. This book teaches you how to see the invisible hand of the corporation, and the finger is pointing at you.

Now is the moment to prepare and take back the cultural turf lost to corporations during the last decades. *Corporateering* is a road map and a battle plan.

Want to see a CEO blush? Start using the word CORPORATEER-ING every day; write it on billing mistakes, suggestion cards, and credit card solicitations that you can send back incomplete in the business reply envelope. (Guess who is charged then!) If you want to understand the influence of corporate culture on American culture—and the growing power of the corporation to impose its goals on every other sector of society—this is the book to read. Pick it up, pass it on, and send it marked C.O.D. to the irresponsible corporations in your lives.

—Michael Moore
January 2003

INTRODUCTION

I HAD NOT VOTED many times in my life when I voted for California Proposition 103 in 1988, a sweeping insurance reform that made auto insurance premiums more reasonable. I was 21, about to graduate from college, and I could not afford car insurance, simply because I was under 25. Proposition 103 was the first thing I ever voted for that would have an immediate impact on my life. It was empowering to vote for something like that, to vote to lower *my* car insurance premiums. It became a symbol of my power to change things that seemed unchangeable.

From the day after the election, however, the insurance industry was defiant. After spending more than $80 million in a failed effort to defeat the ballot initiative, the industry vowed to spend many more years and millions of policyholder dollars challenging every provision in court. I was shocked. Naïvely, I believed that the industry could do nothing but comply with the will of the voters and their law. This was my first taste of the real power of corporations, their ability to use their vast resources to drain the time, energy, money, and hope of people ad nauseam, to disregard the collective will and individual desires. Over the last decade, I have found that most Californians who voted for Proposition 103 had a similar response. At first, they reacted with outrage, later with disillusionment.

My first job after college was canvassing door to door in order to raise money for the Proposition 103 Enforcement Fund. Every night from 4 P.M. until 9 P.M., I walked neighborhoods across Southern California collecting personal checks. I can still hear my rap: "That's why your neighbors are fighting back by writing tax-deductible checks for thirty-five dollars or more," I'd say. The doors, as we called them, were good to me. On average, I raised nearly two hundred dollars each night. The secret of my success was that I believed passionately that what my colleagues and I were doing was the only way to respond, to go one door at a time. Jackie, an older canvasser, during my first week on the job, put it this way : What you are doing is bringing people together so they can have power that they lack on their own. It was the kind of obvious statement that only becomes meaningful when you have to put it to use. The perspective was everything, and it has been an infectious urge ever since.

During the last thirteen years, I have worked, in various ways, to maintain a reasonable balance of power between individuals and large institutions that claim to be responsive to them. After wearing out many pairs of shoes on the canvass, I went to work for a public interest organization that was dedicated to fairer housing and health policy, then for a shelter for homeless families. In 1994, Proposition 103 author Harvey Rosenfield and I co-founded a patients' rights project at The Foundation for Taxpayer and Consumer Rights, our consumer group, which works with patients whose medically necessary treatments have been delayed or denied by HMO corporations. Our group sponsored one of the first HMO patients' bill of rights, which we put on the California ballot in 1996. Proposition 216 failed after a $10 million HMO campaign against it, but most of its provisions were enacted by the California legislature in 1999 and have since become the model for a national patients' rights movement.

The hard lessons learned by physicians, patients, and nurses about how quickly and decisively individual rights and privileges are eviscerated when corporations take over an enterprise like medicine have resonated with me. During the last few years, I have heard too many doctors' regrets that the leaders of the medical establishment ever let HMOs or managed care companies take a single step into the doctor-patient relationship. Organized medicine did not draw boundaries early or clearly enough, and it has been a bare-knuckles fight to force HMOs to relinquish even the smallest ground. I know from other battles with other industries that HMOs are far from alone in this.

During the last eight years, I have also advocated against abuses of law and ethics by manufacturers, oil companies, securities firms, banks, the accounting industry, and energy companies. In all these industries, I have learned that corporate power not only concedes nothing without demand but that it also takes every bit of new ground that it is not denied. I have witnessed how, in both subtle and not-so-subtle ways, corporations increasingly have strained and drained people's most vital resources, including their money, energy, time, health, safety, rights, and, most significantly, their belief in their own power.

There are telltale patterns to the corporate takeover of individual and societal space. This book investigates them. Most shocking to me in recent years is the lack of barriers individuals have drawn in their relationship to corporations, given the unprecedented, aggressive nature of the corporate interloping into their private lives. Like the disillusionment felt by the supporters of Proposition 103, it is almost as though individuals have forgotten that there can be another way, that they can demand boundaries to protect their resources.

It may be harder to fight corporations than it is to fight city hall, but the rewards can be worth it. Fourteen years later, Proposition 103's regulation has produced over $23 billion in savings for California consumers, and the industry has lost almost every legal challenge.

The first step to resisting unwarranted corporate intrusions into individual and societal space is recognizing how seemingly innocuous inconveniences by corporations are collectively far more emblematic and significant. Corporations test not only products, but attitudes. If individuals accept the attitude, then it becomes practice.

While there exist many kinds of corporations, there are certain types of invasive behaviors that are becoming increasingly common to the corporate form and deeply troubling. Most disconcerting is that the influence of corporations has grown well beyond the stream of commerce to infiltrate and manipulate cultural standards. When I told an editor at the *San Francisco Chronicle* about the concept for the book, she said, "Corporations are not impacting culture, they *are* culture." Corporate perspectives are becoming the prevailing perspectives, and these entities are changing the values of the individual and of society, as well as of the life of the mind. Corporations' growing power is allowing them to redefine the basic rules of society, law, and ethical custom to the detriment of traditional rights and freedoms of the individual. These are the trends traced in *Corporateering*.

While seeking to draw lines between the good and the bad, I use the term "corporation" to refer to large corporations, not small businesses, which often face the same imbalance of power with large companies that individuals do. Of course, some small companies are run by greedy people and the heads of some large corporations are wonderful individuals. At the point that a corporation becomes a large institution, however, it tends to adopt certain assumptions, strategies, and logic. These are the focus of this book.

It is often difficult for people not engaged daily in a struggle with corporate power to see beyond the surface of seemingly superficial changes in corporate influence. In fact, corporations' greatest powers reside precisely in their ability to hide from individuals substantive shifts in the individual-corporate compact.

Corporateering offers a prism through which to view the dramatic changes in the relationship between individuals and corporations. It is the prism my colleagues and I have developed in order to understand corporate power in its many dimensions. I hope it proves useful to you.

—Jamie Court
Santa Monica, California

PART ONE

MEET
THE
INVISIBLE
HAND

5 000127 052093 >

SEEING CORPORATEERING

cor•po•ra•teer v. *to prioritize commerce over culture*   n. *one who prioritizes commerce over culture*

- When an individual's private medical and financial information is bought and sold by corporations without the person's permission, have the corporation's commercial priorities changed ethical custom?

- When corporate stock is valued based on "share of mind," "consciousness occupied," and the number of "engaged shoppers," has the individual's attention and consciousness become a corporate possession?

- When an individual can no longer order a "small" coffee at Starbucks because the smallest cup is called a "tall" and the medium is a "grande," what is the corporation teaching society about making hyperbole and deception a commonplace part of existence?

- When people are charged a fee for access to information about their own credit history, have the commercial echoes of the individual's own behavior become corporate property?

- When a company makes a mistake, why is the burden on the individual to spend as much of their time fixing it as needed without ever being reimbursed for the value of that lost time?

- When cola companies adopt schools, and a student is suspended for wearing a Pepsi T-shirt on class picture day at a Coke school, what are children being taught about the relative value of the corporation and the individual?

- When corporate consolidation has left only a handful of corporations in each industry, do consumers really have more meaningful choices?

- When a customer who has been mis-billed calls a company to complain and is automatically forced on hold to listen to advertisements, what does it say about how corporations value the individual's time and attention?

- When an Internet "cookie" tracks a person's behavior on-line and the data is sold between corporations, has the individual's identity become a bar code?

- What are the consequences when a corporation encourages employees to lie on its behalf?

- When the average person experiences an estimated 16,000 corporate advertisements daily (including logos, labels, and announcements),[1] can an individual see the world without looking through a filter provided by corporations?

- When corporations cheat individuals in their billing statements, how does that impact the integrity with which people treat one another?

- If the corporation did not believe that economic gain was more important than people's lives, why did tobacco maker Philip Morris report to the Czech Republic that tobacco use was good because it resulted in "health-care costs savings due to early mortality"?[2]

- What were the corporation's priorities when fatal defects were exposed in the Ford Explorer's safety during 2000, but Ford paid its CEO 19 percent more than the previous year, or $12.1 million?[3]

- Do the needs of corporations outweigh those of children under 2001–2002 legislation, passed by both the U.S. House of Representatives and the U.S. Senate, requiring the bankrupt to give the same priority to paying off credit card bills as to continuing child support payments?

- Did the record number of 3.54 billion credit solicitations mailed out just in the United States during the year 2000 have any role in putting the average American in debt for the first time since the Great Depression?

- Are corporations seeking to buy commercial exposure, or cultural respect once reserved only for individuals, through the increasing sums they are paying for naming rights to nonprofit hospitals, museums, and zoos, such as $25 million for Mattel Children's Hospital at UCLA?

- When a corporation forces the individual to agree to binding arbitration in order to rent a car, buy a house, or have a credit card, is it purchasing the person's right to trial?

- When a supermarket chain makes an individual reveal personal information on a "club card" application in order for the individual to save money, is it buying the right to privacy?

- Has aggressive corporate marketing to children, which began with commercial television in the classroom two decades ago, contributed to the first college freshman class of the millennium wanting to make money more than anything else, including more than influencing social values and helping others?[4]

- Has the individual's increased reliance on the stock market for retirement caused a requisite cultural investment in corporate privilege?

- Why did no one suspect, until the fall of Enron, that Andersen, WorldCom, Global Crossing, Qwest, Kmart, Rite Aid, Tyco, and Halliburton would ever be dishonest?

- Is corporate control in American culture more than innocuous and inconvenient?

- Are corporations increasingly showing a disregard not only for individuals' privacy, time, energy, money, and personal space but also for their fundamental freedoms?

- Is the backdrop of what Americans see daily increasingly filled with corporate values, messages, logic, and assumptions?

- Do corporate-generated values govern American life today as only religion has in the past?

People across the world have been captivated by the corporate spirit's resilience and ingenuity. Major corporations serve individuals' needs in far more ways—from physical to financial to cultural—than any other large institutions in American life ever have. To their credit, large corporations have greatly expanded standards of comfort and convenience, putting within the average person's reach services and products that were available only to millionaires just a decade ago.

Many Americans enjoyed unprecedented material prosperity at the turn of this century due largely to the corporation's role in fueling Americans' economic well-being, through surging stock prices and innovation in sectors such as technology. More individuals owned homes than at any time in history. More goods and services were more readily available to a greater number of people than ever before. An increasingly sophisticated service standard could deliver almost any good or service overnight with the click of a computer mouse. Unemployment and inflation, typically at odds, both held steady at among their lowest rates in the previous century. The atypical forces and extraordinary productivity, fueled by the technology sector, caused the world's most powerful economist, Federal Reserve chairman Alan Greenspan, to ordain that the economy was "one that none of us has ever seen before, and indeed it may be unprecedented in our history."[5]

What the visible hand of the corporation provided was obvious to most witnesses. By century's end, the majority of Americans were accustomed to putting their savings in unsecured corporate stock rather than in insured savings accounts.[6] The counter-culture's day-trippers had become successful day-traders. "Pro-business" became a badge of honor in Washington, D.C., and across the nation.

Two-thirds of Americans gave the corporation credit for their economic prosperity in a major poll halfway through 2000. However, nearly three-fourths of the same group believed that the corporation had too much power over other parts of their lives.[7] While one hand of the corporation gave to the individual, another hand overreached and took something away. The hand that provided economically and commercially was easy to see in the phalanx of corporate boasts radiating from the most remarkable spaces, including supermarket floors and urinal traps, and in the flourish of twenty-four-hour financial channels that charted its every reflex. By contrast, the hand that took was almost invisible. Even *BusinessWeek*, which conducted the poll and dedicated its September 2000 cover to the question, "Too Much Corporate Power?" could not adequately define the feeling of unease. The magazine could only show a slipping grip on customer service, a squeeze on workers, and the heavy hand of HMOs, Big Tobacco, Big Oil, and pharmaceutical companies. Of the two hands of the corporation, the one that gives and the other that takes, only the former has been well understood. That is the greatest power of the other hand, which has been largely invisible.

What You See and What You Don't

Individuals have typically seen of the corporation what it has wanted them to see. That is the end product of the more than $1 trillion spent annually on marketing by U.S. corporations since the mid-1990s.[8] About $240 billion of marketing money was spent on advertising in America in 2001 and about $460 billion was expended on global corporate advertising.[9] The United Nations reported in 1998 that global advertising growth outpaced global economic growth by more than one-third.[10] Corporations have spent more money, energy, and time than they—or any other sector of any society—ever have to persuade individuals about how to view them. American corporations spend annually roughly as much on marketing as the United States of America spends on its entire health-care system—one of every six dollars of the Gross Domestic Product (GDP).[11] The typical American sees about thirty-five-thousand television commercials each year.[12] The average American child spends forty hours every week engaged with media, most of which is advertising-based.[13]

Corporate marketing messages are the results of carefully crafted polling, focus groups, and increasingly creative feats of cultural anthropology. For instance, not only do corporations now employ anthropologists, but corporate "cool hunting" is a new form of scholastic espionage. Marketing agents actually enter high schools under cover to spy out "cool" trends in order to better market to children. Similarly, the individual's perspective on the corporation is shaped not just by ubiquitous traditional marketing but also increasingly by corporate political campaigns on "issues" and candidates; by corporate purchases of "naming rights" to hospitals, museums, parks, arenas, towns, and schools; and by the media's elevation of Wall Street analysts and corporate scions to the new class of societal opinion leaders. The popular projection of the corporation does not just communicate about specific products and services, it also presents a larger worldview about the corporation and the individual that is remarkably consistent.

A trillion-dollar annual communications budget is the societal power to bring into focus and to blur, to promote fictions or facts that are beneficial for one's interests, and to fade out facts that are not. This is the force to advance not only the individual's identification with a particular brand but also their empathy with the corporate form. In the marketers' Oz, individuals typically see the corporation's individuality, not corporations' commonality. Corporations are presented as independent, competing entities, each having its own "personality" and distinct values. Individuals engage personal characteristics of the corporation, personifications of human values that imply a person or personality is there for you. McDonald's loves to see you smile. You're in Allstate's good hands. Like a good neighbor, State Farm is there. Avis is trying harder. AT&T puts things within your reach. GE brings good things to life (and, as of 2003, is "Imagination at work"). The job of marketers is to distinguish corporations, but during the past two decades this has translated to giving corporations a living soul and personality, "meaning" in the cultural sphere rather than just the commercial one.

"'Brands, not products!' became the rallying cry for a marketing renaissance led by a new breed of companies that saw themselves as 'meaning brokers' instead of product producers," according to journalist Naomi Klein, who explored the phenomenon in her book *No Logo*. "The old paradigm had it that all marketing was selling a product. In the new model, however, the product always takes a back seat to the real product, the brand, and the selling of the brand acquired an extra component that can only be described as spiritual. Advertising is about hawking product. Branding, in its truest and most advanced incarnations, is about corporate transcendence."[14]

During the 1980s and 1990s, corporations sought to transcend their roles as impersonal bureaucratic institutions that an individual might fear and instead present themselves as transmitters and reflectors of cultural meaning—traditionally the individual's and the community's role. Could Starbucks peddle a three-dollar cup of coffee if, as its CEO Howard Shultz stated, people were there for the java and not "the romance of the coffee experience, the feeling of warmth and community people get in Starbucks stores"?[15] Nike shoes are made in third-world sweatshops, but teenagers shoot each other over them[16] because owning the brand means being a revolutionary through sports. Driving Nissan's Xterra is sold as getting close to nature—"get out into the air no one else breathes"[17]—while SUVs harm the environment. CEOs have embraced the tactic across industry lines. By imbuing the corporate brand with the illusion of cultural meaning, the company can sell many products. The corporation is peddling the meaning, not the goods, and an effective corporation can then sell any good or service in the glow of the brand's meaning.

Individuals today see the corporation compete to reflect human cultural meaning that transcends a commercial profit motive. This brings the marketed face of the corporation into focus but blurs well-established facts about how the corporation actually functions. In recent years, the individual has been presented in their public and private life with a cast of corporations that have faces and personalities as diverse as the characters of Oz. The manifestations of marketing effectively communicate a desired view of the corporation—that it subscribes to human values. For example, a Harvard researcher found in 1999 that adult Americans equated corporate brand names with values in personal relationships nourished by the corporation's marketing messages. AT&T equaled Mother. Apple Computer equated with Close Friend. McDonald's corresponded to Childhood Buddy. IBM meant Teammate. Harley-Davidson signified Best Friend.[18] Such corporate marketing can also erase from the individual's consciousness undesirable truths about the corporation as an institution. Isn't it easier to trust, and harder to be angry at, one's mother, best friend, teammate, or childhood friend? The characters of Oz each teach their own lesson, but they also keep Dorothy from seeing what's behind the curtain. The trillion-dollar-per-year illusion of the corporation conceals the corporations' motivations, thinking, and strategies—which are still as uniform in bottom-line orientation as business schools teach and, as such, can be a threat to the individual.

The Memo Behind the Curtain

What the individual sees of the corporation is inextricably linked to what the corporation does not want it to see. For example, as one of America's older corporations, General Motors has had its fair share of scandals. In the 1930s and '40s, General Motors led the destruction of electric rail systems in the United States to make way for the automobile homogenization of American transportation. "By 1949, GM had been involved in the replacement of more than 100 electric systems with GM buses in more than 45 cities including New York, Philadelphia, Baltimore, St. Louis, Oakland, Salt Lake City, and Los Angeles," wrote Russell Mokhiber in his book *Corporate Crime and Violence*. "In April of that year, a Chicago grand jury indicted and a jury convicted GM, Standard Oil of California, Firestone and R. Roy Fitzgerald, among others, for criminally conspiring to replace electric transportation with gas- and diesel-powered buses and to monopolize the sale of buses and related products to transportation companies throughout the country."[19]

Thanks to one of the nation's first perception management specialists, Bruce Barton, the public does not see *this* General Motors Corporation—one ready to disregard societal priorities for its own commercial ones. In the 1920s, Barton invented the visible hand of General Motors, "GM," which turned the impersonal corporation into the old trusted family friend who one might call by his initials.[20] Barton's contribution, as one of his agency's campaign objectives stated, was "to personalize the institution by calling it a family."[21] His 1924 advertising campaign was titled "Facts About a Famous Family: Mothers, sisters, wives." GM's signature was added to advertisements, using simply "General Motors" without the impersonal "Corporation."[22] GM's advertising in *The Saturday Evening Post* from 1924 to 1925 identified the corporation with human characteristics: the service of a preacher ("Through the eyes of faith"); the prompt arrival of a doctor (". . . that the doctor shall arrive *in time*"); and the family picnic ("The whole family enjoys life much more").[23] Barton used the same tactic to transform the bureaucratic General Electric Company, later to become one of the world's largest producers of nuclear arms, into GE, which Barton's own copy in the 1923 *Literary Digest* proclaimed: "The initials of the friend. You will find these letters on many tools by which electricity works. . . . Hence the letters G-E are more than a trademark. They are an emblem of service—the initials of a friend."[24]

The illusion of the family-friendly GM soul has helped to obscure how the corporation's commercial calculations have put its profits above the health of the people who drive its vehicles. For example, recent legal evidence against General Motors shows that the company failed to fix known fatal defects in its vehicles and that money was the key value.[25] Consider the following excerpt from an internal memo written by General Motors engineer E. C. Ivey, entitled "Value Analysis of Auto Fuel Fed Fire Related Fatalities," which was made public in a Los Angeles lawsuit brought by burn victims against General Motors that culminated in 1999 with a record-setting verdict. This confidential memo explored the cost effectiveness of doing nothing to fix General Motors' cars with defective gasoline tanks that led to fuel-fed fires:

The following assumptions can be made:

1. In G.M. automobiles there are a maximum of 500 fatalities per year in accidents with fuel fed fires where the bodies were burnt.

2. Each fatality has a value of $200,000.

3. There are approximately 41,000,000 G.M. automobiles currently operating on U.S. highways.

Analyzing these figures indicates that fatalities related to accidents with fuel fed fires are costing General Motors $2.40 per automobile in current operation.

$$\frac{500 \text{ fatalities} \times \$200,000 \text{ / fatality}}{41,000,000 \text{ automobiles}} = \$2.40 \text{ / automobile}^{26}$$

In this Ivey calculation, the expected number of annual fatalities from the defect (500) was multiplied by the expected cost of each lawsuit over the fatality ($200,000) and divided by the number of GM automobiles (41 million). This determined the cost per car of doing nothing about the defect. The attorneys for those individuals trapped and burned when the gas tank of their automobiles exploded claimed that installing a safer fuel system would have prevented 300 to 500 injuries per year. Evidence the lawyers produced in the case showed that it would have cost GM $8.59 per car to fix the problem (as opposed to the $2.40 per car to simply pay off lawsuits). The burn victims' attorneys successfully argued in court that the automaker chose not to warn the public of such defects because the cost of recall exceeded the potential costs from lawsuits.[27] "GM has no regard for the people in their cars, and they should be held responsible for it," said jury foreman Coleman Thorton after issuing a $4.9 billion verdict for the plaintiffs.[28]

General Motors has claimed that Ivey's memo had no relevance on its decision not to notify the public of the problems with fuel-fed fires or to change its vehicles' design to stop such fires. Ivey, who by the time of the 1999 verdict was General Motors' director of chassis engineering, had written the document nearly thirty years before as a young engineer. The company has consistently claimed in legal filings that the memo was not company policy and that Ivey did not distribute it but that the engineer merely was engaged in an intellectual exercise. However, handwritten notes taken by a General Motors lawyer in 1983 after a debriefing with Ivey about the document stated, "Purpose: how much money could we spend on each car to prevent it? . . . Did not do it on his own."[29] In the end, for whatever reason, corporate, not human, values prevailed to keep information from individuals that was vital to their safety. Ivey's personal elevation within the corporation also reflects the same type of corporate values.

The Ivey memo, and "smoking gun" documents like it, reveal a hidden hand of the corporation that has privately weighed and decided matters of the greatest societal import based on commercial standards.

Another recent example is a handwritten corporate note produced in 2002 litigation against the makers of the drug Rezulin that reads "monthly sales/deaths" when referring to the marketing of the drug.[30] Though the visible hand of the corporation presents the individual's and corporation's interests as identical, the invisible hand will advance the corporation's interests without regard for the individual's. The visible hand shows us the subjective portrait of "GM, the family friend." The invisible hand can treat the individual like an expendable object that has only a commercial worth.

At the end of his memo, Ivey qualified his analysis, stating that it must "be tempered" with the thought that "it is really impossible to put a value on human life. This analysis tried to do so in an objective manner, but a human fatality is really beyond value, subjectively." Unfortunately for the burn victims and their families, the "objective" analysis won out over the "subjective" concern.

When corporate commercial calculations obliterate societal mores and customs, commerce becomes a conspiracy of things over people. At its worst, the hidden hand of the corporation redefines the individual as an "object" or "thing" in a commercial calculation. Such corporate thinking makes the individual and his rights disposable and has become a powerful subtext in society with profound ramifications for individual freedom. This subtext is not simply one of materialism playing out in markets, it is also a social and cultural attitude with power to impact law, policy, politics, education, arts, science, and other aspects of culture.

Treating the Individual as Object

In many markets, corporations now routinely assign a code to a customer based on his or her profitability for the company. The code determines how a customer call is routed (only the most valuable customers get speedy access to a live person), which promotions exist, and what level of service the customer service representative offers.[31] The customer is no longer always right by definition, no longer the focus of the corporation's attentions. The customer is an object that accumulates commercial value, and only when attaining the status of a "corporate level" spender does she receive extraordinary attention. The message for individuals is: Spend like a corporation and be treated like a person. Not surprisingly, from 1994 to 2000 overall customer satisfaction with products and services from airlines, banks, stores, hotels, personal computers, and phone companies plummeted.[32]

At a societal level, by reversing the roles of person and thing, corporations have been able to claim the mantle of cultural freedoms that traditionally belonged to individuals. For example, secrecy is a privilege that corporations have increasingly appropriated even while taking extraordinary liberties with the individual's privacy. The financial scandals of 2002 were largely born from the corporation's opaqueness. GM's secret settlements with burn victims prevented the public from viewing the Ivey memo and its revelations for twenty-five years. In legislatures and courts, I have seen tobacco companies, drug manufacturers, insurers, energy traders, oil companies, stock brokerages, and banks all claim the same entitlement to secrecy by taking on the characteristics of people, describing their fragility and susceptibility to damage if confidential information is revealed. Across industry lines, the corporation has successfully argued that if damaging information is revealed it will face litigation and a loss of protection for the corporation's intellectual and other property rights. The corporation's right to think, its intellectual property, has trumped the individual's right to know.

In the corporate case for secrecy, the individual and society are inanimate, entitled to nothing more than what the corporation is ready to offer because of the potential damage to the corporation, which is the subject of concern. In their arguments against greater privacy protections for individuals, as discussed further in Chapter 2, corporations similarly describe people only as objects in their relationship to the company. Corporations claim that they should be allowed to share financial information about individuals without consent because it allows companies to better offer customers commercial opportunities. After all, if companies do not share personal data, how can the corporation then code its computer files to determine which are the best customers to receive the best discounts? The corporation recognizes no inherent harm to the individual from a violation of the individual's privacy, because, absent the relationship to the company, the corporation increasingly does not recognize the individual and his societal rights.

The Invisible Hand Overreaches: Commerce and Culture Clash

Culture has been a human possession, but the next decades could change that. The difference between culture and commerce is blurring. The American Heritage Dictionary defines culture as "the totality of socially transmitted behavior, patterns, arts, beliefs, institutions and all other products of human works and thought."[33] Commerce is the buying and selling of goods. Culture is about people, their uniqueness and the better angels of their nature. Increasingly, corporations confuse culture, the rules of people, and commerce, the rules of things. The corporation, at its worst, applies the priorities of things to the institutions, behavior, and beliefs of people. Individuals ultimately hold the societal power to invest in such corporate priorities or to divest them of worth. Unfortunately, such shifting priorities are often hard for the individual to see.

Western society has consistently exerted itself to prevent commerce from limiting the individual's cultural freedoms. The abolition of slavery, prohibition of child labor, and new worker rights during the industrial revolution were all societal reactions to unrestrained commerce's offense of social mores. In the last decade, however, the corporation's invisible hand has endangered a far more subtle litany of the individual's cultural freedoms. These include freedoms of privacy, of personal security, of legal recourse, of association, of the press, of intellectual property rights, and of speech. The following table shows new corporate assumptions about each freedom that have, in discourse and policy, challenged the individual's schoolbook understanding. The invisible hand's assumptions commodify the individual's freedoms by making them relevant only to the corporation's commercial interest, not to society's cultural interest in freedom. The assumptions are about the growth of commerce, the traffic in things, not the growth of people. For instance, privacy is redefined for commercial convenience, or freedom of speech has meaning only in a commercial context—only individuals who "speak" through their purchases can speak to a live human being at a corporation. These types of corporate assumptions are now vying with long-defended cultural standards to determine the shape of freedom in the individual's public and private life.

Individual Freedom	Schoolbook Assumption	Corporate Assumption	Corporate Application
Personal Privacy	Privacy is a fundamental right of every person, even enumerated in the Constitution as protection from search and seizure.	Individual privacy does not exist innately because it defeats the ability of corporations to know about consumers and, thus, serve them better by proposing new commercial opportunities. Privacy can only be manifested when explicitly asserted.	Banks, credit card companies, and insurers share individuals' personal financial and medical information without permission.
Personal Security	Human life and health are priceless.	Every human life has an exact price—the financial cost to the corporation of saving it versus not protecting it.	Manufacturers, pharmaceutical companies, and HMOs have often claimed that the commercial needs of "the many" to afford a product outweigh the social obligation to "the few" (continues on next page)

Individual Freedom	Schoolbook Assumption	Corporate Assumption	Corporate Application
			to recall a defective product or pay for a lifesaving treatment covered under a health contract.
Legal Recourse	Every individual has the right to hold wrongdoers accountable and be made whole for his or her injuries.	Legal accountability of corporations to individuals must be limited if product costs are to be contained and "frivolous" lawsuits are to be avoided.	Most industries lobby to cap the amount of compensation that a consumer can recover in personal injury cases, regardless of the severity of the injury or egregious nature of the company's conduct.
Enjoyment of Public Space and Events	Individuals should be able to enjoy public spaces and cultural events freely and without commercial requirement.	There is almost no space, time, or event that is inappropriate for the promotion of commercial opportunities that vie for an individual's attention.	Schools, cultural events, art festivals, sidewalks, civic arenas, and restaurant tables have ceased to be commercial-free zones.
Right to Trial	Every individual is entitled to the right to trial under the Seventh Amendment of the Constitution.	As a condition of commerce, individuals may be required to sign away their right to trial in favor of mandatory "binding arbitration" should a dispute arise. There is no appeal, public exposure, or judge, and decision-makers (continues on next page)	Credit card companies, car dealers, and HMOs have required that, as a condition of buying their product, individuals relinquish their right to trial in the event of disputes.

Individual Freedom	Schoolbook Assumption	Corporate Assumption	Corporate Application
		can receive repeat business from the corporation.	
Press and Expression	The press serves the public interest in informing. The more diverse the voices, the richer the public debate and the society. The airwaves are publicly owned.	The commercial interest of the corporation's profit is greater than the public interest in informing.	The media increasingly serves the corporation's commercial needs to entertain and capture consciousness rather than society's informational needs.
Association for Individuals and Workers	Government is the vehicle of the collective will of the people and can be a force to protect the individual from oppression. Unions allow workers to associate for common goals.	Government is the enemy of progress because it impedes corporations' ability to serve individuals. Its only appropriate role is to encourage business and salvage markets that fail. Unions undermine efficiency and threaten worker loyalty to the corporation, which is needed for global competitiveness.	Corporate-funded think tanks and issue-oriented advertising campaigns have successfully vilified government and government regulators. Industries have successfully diluted the number and power of labor unions.
Ownership of Time and Attention	Individuals should reasonably be able to control their own time and attention.	There should be no limit to the corporate appropriation of an individual's time and attention because it helps the person to (continues on next page)	Corporations have increasingly bombarded individuals with commercial messages, intrusive phone calls, and (continues on next page)

Individual Freedom	Schoolbook Assumption	Corporate Assumption	Corporate Application
		better make commercial choices.	advertising aimed at children.
Professional Integrity	Individuals have a duty to one another and society to be ethical and adhere to standards of moral conduct.	The individual employee's first and only duty is to the corporation that employs her and to its commercial needs.	Corporate analysts, accountants, auditors, and lawyers have often been forced to choose between telling the truth and protecting their employers' pecuniary interests.
Care and Nurturing of Children	Raising children in a safe, ethical environment is the duty of each individual, the school system, and the culture as a whole.	Children are a valuable "market share" with increasing amounts of discretionary income.	Products that have traditionally been seen as adult, such as high fashion and makeup, are marketed to younger and younger children. Schools are beset with commercial vending machines and televised advertisements. Children are encouraged to identify with labels, consumer products, and entertainment by corporate campaigns.

Such corporate assumptions about the individual's public and private life have gained momentum in society because of the corporation's newfound power to transmit cultural messages. Exploring the tactics and strategies that corporations employ to this end is the focus of this book. Making visible the corporation's invisible hand and making audible the corporation's subliminal voice is the first step toward erecting new rules for what, when, and how much the invisible hand can touch.

REMOVING ACCOUNTABILITY TO THE INDIVIDUAL

cor•po•ra•tion n. *a body that is granted a charter legally recognizing it as a separate legal entity having its own rights, privileges, and liabilities distinct from those of its members*
per•son n. *a living human being*

THE AMERICAN HERITAGE DICTIONARY, THIRD EDITION

Traditionally, corporations were a means to a commercial end for individuals. From the chartering of the first European corporations in the late 1500s, the silent social contract between individuals and corporations was rooted in the recognition that corporations were artificial entities created to serve human beings' commercial needs. If corporations exceeded those boundaries or abused that responsibility, they would cease to exist. Corporations were servants, not masters.

Monarchies began granting corporate charters in the age of European exploration for specific purposes related to serving individuals, such as providing transportation, importing spices, manufacturing steel, or constructing canals. The East India Company was chartered to serve the British appetite for tea and spices, as well as for exploration. In 1629, a royal charter from Charles I created the Massachusetts Bay Company

for the purpose of establishing a colony in the New World. Puritan em-
igrants bought stock from other investors and set sail from England in
1630 with seventeen ships and 1,000 people, the largest such migration
in the seventeenth century.[1] Charters were a means of the corporation's
accountability to both the individual and his government. Charters articulated a specific commercial role for the corporation that could be revoked, and they specified an internal system of corporate governance
that assured stockholder control. In the European Old World, the corporation was accountable to the king. In the New World after Independence, the corporation was accountable to the state, the stockholder,
and the individual through the legal system. Individuals threatened by
abusive or excessive corporate power could petition their government
for a charter revocation. Until the nineteenth century in Western nations,
individuals could take legal action to hold investors fully liable for the
total cost of damage from abuses by publicly held corporations, whether
or not it exceeded the value of the shares held by the investor. The law,
at least in this respect, recognized that the individual's needs outweighed
the corporation's. Such accountability to the individual helped to keep
corporations small, closely held, and responsible to investors.

Such societal controls grew out of a widely held recognition that
without such accountability to the individual, the corporation would
be prone to value things more than people. As a Congressional representative from Virginia, James Madison told his colleagues in 1791 that
corporations "are powerful machines which have always been found
competent to effect objects or principles in great measure independent
of the people."[2] An 1830 editorial in the *Trenton Emporium and True
American* clearly foreshadowed the dilemma of individuals today when
it warned that the "Legislature ought cautiously to refrain from increasing the irresponsible power of any existing corporations or chartering new ones," because individuals might become "mere hewers of
wood and drawers of water to jobbers, bankers, and stockbrokers."[3] For
such reasons, the United States Supreme Court ruled in 1855 that the
people of the states had not "released their powers over the artificial

bodies which originate under the legislation of their representatives."[4] As late as 1906, the U.S. Supreme Court observed, "The corporation is a creature of the state. It is presumed to be incorporated for the benefit of the public."[5] Unfortunately, legal changes were already underway that relieved corporations of much of their accountability to individuals and the government.

By the late 1880s and 1890s, most industrialized nations, including the United States, had enacted "limited liability" laws that restricted an individual investor's losses to the value of the stock the shareholder owned. This removal of full accountability to the individual enabled the growth of the big modern corporation with its need for larger pools of capital to finance more sophisticated machinery.[6] The new, practical terms of the corporation's growth made it accountable to the capital it could muster rather than to the individual and his community. Not surprisingly, the railroad barons and industrialists of the age did not merely abuse their economic power to create trusts and cartels that fixed prices, restricted production, and cornered markets. They also sought, and obtained through the courts, changes in a corporation's legal status that limited the ability of the government to revoke a corporation's charter. In a key ruling, the 1886 *Santa Clara County v. Southern Pacific Railroad Company* decision, the U.S. Supreme Court ruled, without hearing any oral arguments, that for the purposes of law, corporations had the same rights as people and were protected under the Due Process Clause of the Fourteenth Amendment, a civil-rights amendment designed to safeguard newly emancipated African-Americans. Fifty percent of the Fourteenth Amendment cases thereafter related to the defense of corporate business, as opposed to one-and-one-half percent for African-Americans' status.[7] The disadvantaged status of people vis-à-vis corporations today springs from this ruling by the Supreme Court.

As a de facto individual, the corporation would acquire the right to life, liberty, and association independent of its state charter—the public's greatest authority over it. In one of the last charter revocations,

New York's highest court withdrew, in a unanimous 1890 decision, the charter of the North River Sugar Refining Corporation for combining with another corporation illegally, which stopped North River's sugar refining operations. The court's reasoning about the corporation's accountability to the state would eventually vanish under a string of legal victories by corporate lawyers over the next century. In June 1890, the New York Court of Appeals ruled the following:

> The judgment sought against the defendant is one of corporate death. The state which created, asks us to destroy, and the penalty invoked represents the extreme rigor of the law. The life of a corporation is, indeed, less than that of the humblest citizen. . . . The abstract idea of a corporation, the legal entity, the impalpable and intangible creation of human thought, is itself a fiction, and has been appropriately described as a figure of speech. . . . The state permits in many ways an aggregation of capital, but, mindful of the possible dangers to the people, overbalancing the benefits, keeps upon it a restraining hand, and maintains over it a prudent supervision, where such aggregation depends upon its permission and grows out of its corporate grants. . . . [I]f corporations can combine, mass their fortunes in a solid trust or partnership, with little added risk to the capital already embarked, without limit to the magnitude of the aggregation, a tempting and easy road is opened to enormous combinations, vastly exceeding in number and strength and in their power over industry any possibilities of individual ownership; and the state, by the creation of the artificial persons constituting the elements of the combination and failing to limit and restrain their powers, becomes itself the responsible creator, the voluntary cause, of an aggregation of capital which it simply endures in the individual as the product of his free agency. What it may bear is one thing; what it should cause and create is quite another. . . . [T]he defendant corporation

has violated its charter, and failed in the performance of its corporate duties, and that in respects so material and important as
to justify a judgment of dissolution. . . . [8]

The legal rulings expanding corporate rights beyond such public
control generally occurred either between 1880 and 1900—the so-called
Gilded Age—or since the late 1970s, when transnational corporations
sowed their oats across the globe and cemented their constitutional
equivalence to individuals. Legal scholar Carl Mayer explained, in the
March 1990 *Hastings Law Journal*, "Twenty years ago the corporation
had not deployed Bill of Rights provisions successfully. . . . [A]s an historical matter, the Supreme Court only recently conferred Bill of Rights
guarantees on corporations."[9]

The following U.S. Supreme Court decisions, all since 1976, show
the impact of modern corporations gaining title to the first ten amendments of the Constitution.

- First National Bank of Boston's First Amendment right to speak
  through money stops state limits on corporate spending for
  political referendums (1978's decision in *First National Bank of
  Boston v. Bellotti*). Supreme Court Justices White, Brennan, and
  Marshall wrote in dissent: "The State need not let its own creation consume it."

- A corporation's Fourth Amendment right to be free from unreasonable search and seizure prevents the IRS from seizing a corporation's assets to fulfill obligations to the taxpayer (1977's *G.M.
  Leasing Corp. v. United States*). The Fourth Amendment allows an
  electrical company to avoid federal inspections under the Occupational Safety and Health Act (1977's *Marshall v. Barlow's Inc.*).

- A corporation's commercial speech is protected under the First
  Amendment and does not require the consent of the "listener"
  (1980's *Central Hudson Gas & Electric Corp. v. Public Service Com-*

mission of New York and 1983's *Bolger v. Young's Drug Product Corp.*). Corporations use these rulings to justify junk faxing, telemarketing, and door-to-door solicitation.

- The Fifth Amendment's Double Jeopardy Clause protects a textile corporation from a government retrial in a criminal antitrust action (1977's *United States v. Martin Linen Supply Co.*).

- Corporations have a right to speak through money and to associate with national political parties—as well as their connected Political Action Committees—through unlimited contributions (1976's *Buckley v. Valeo*).

- Corporations have a First Amendment right not to speak when government tells them to. A public utility has won a right to be silent and not follow a regulation requiring that a notice from a ratepayer advocacy group be put in ratepayers' bills (1986's *Pacific Gas & Electric Company v. Public Utility Commission*).

From this legal reasoning rises the inability of the individual and his government to hold the corporation accountable for widely acknowledged problems. For example, Americans have recently been very concerned about the privacy of their financial records. Privacy advocates sought protections for individuals in about two dozen statehouses between 2000 and 2002. Banks, financial services corporations, and insurers successfully argued, however, that the corporation's free-speech rights under the United States Constitution trumped the individual's right to privacy.[10]

In my home state of California, the state constitution guarantees in Article I, Section I, "All people are by nature free and independent and have inalienable rights. Among these are enjoying and defending life and liberty, acquiring, possessing, and protecting property, and pursuing and obtaining safety, happiness, and privacy." As in many statehouses, legislation was introduced during the past few years seeking to preclude any corporation from sharing private financial information about consumers without their prior, written consent. By late 2002, no state in the nation had enacted the protections, because banks, credit card companies, and other corporations have defeated bill after bill in state after state. In the market, corporations put the system of shared private financial information into practice without asking permission. They effectively forced every individual to automatically "opt in" to the system, placing the burden of time and energy on individuals to know enough to "opt out" by writing a letter specifically asking for an exemption from the sharing of their personal information. Privacy advocates simply wanted a standard requiring that corporations receive written permission from an individual indicating that she really wants to "opt in" before the corporation can share private information with other companies. The assumption underlying the corporation's "opt out" perspective is a powerful example of the corporate worldview taking hold in other quarters. The individual is not a subject of the law with an innate privacy right that the corporation must recognize. Societal rights of the individual can be voided when commercial necessities arise. Instead, all the world is a commercial market of shared information from which a person must exclude himself in order to exercise his privacy. Most remarkably, the corporations claimed that the law backed them up.

At a California statehouse hearing in 2000, corporate opponents of the privacy bill, representing major industries, argued in their joint analysis, "The 'opt-in' system of managing customer information creates an unjustifiable burden on commerce. . . . [T]he broad application of 'opt-in' rules may be unconstitutional. The use of 'opt-in' requirements in situations where no clearly defined, significant harm is threatened may violate the First Amendment."[11] In other words, the corporation's free-speech rights, never articulated in the First Amendment, outweighed the individual's explicit right to privacy under the California constitution. The bill's opponents reminded legislators, "The Supreme Court has declared unconstitutional many ordinances that would require affirmative consent, for example, before receiving door-to-door solicitations (*Martin v. Struthers*), . . . even before receiving 'patently offensive' cable programming (*DAETC, Inc. v. FCC*)."[12] Such arguments have been effective because of the legal constitutional equivalence of corporations to people and a coordinated national lobbying campaign by insurers, banks, and the securities industry. The Financial Services Coordinating Council, formed by five leading financial services trade groups, toured the nation to successfully assert the corporation's constitutional equivalence.[13] I personally witnessed the anti-privacy testimony delivered in California by dozens of corporate lobbyists from nearly every major industry, standing in a long line that stretched from the front of the large hearing room to the rear. Watching each lobbyist defend the corporation's right to speech and association, I had a profound sense of how, in the future, the corporation's freedoms would be advanced at the expense of the individual's through even more potent assumptions spoken in unison by industry after industry.

As the opponents of the California privacy protections proved, modern corporations aggressively promote their rights to out-shout human beings on their own doorsteps, over the telephone lines, and without deference to the individual's constitutional right to privacy of information. Corporations may have legal standing equivalent to individuals, but they are not bound by the same social ties individuals have to one another. They are not limited by time (are not born/do not die), are not socialized to distinguish right from wrong, nor can they be imprisoned. Modern corporations are not subject to human rules of social conduct, nor are they the beneficiaries of human social development.

Corporations can be fined, but often have reserves of money. They can be sued, but their legal defense teams can deplete the resources of nearly any individual that challenges them. They can be punished, but they can appeal their punishment in the courts for a very long time, and their managers are almost never jailed. The impact of the legal redefinition of the corporate form made it a sovereign entity with the power to dominate people and, increasingly, the public institutions that collectively represent individuals. This outcome was no accident. It was the result of a concerted public-education, judicial, and political strategy first hatched in a confidential 1971 memo by a senior partner at the Richmond, Virginia, law firm of Hunton & Williams named Lewis F. Powell, Jr., whom President Nixon appointed to the U.S. Supreme Court that same year. Before leaving Hunton & Williams in 1971, Powell represented clients such as Philip Morris (as a board member, Powell started smoking at photo opportunities), Colonial Williamsburg, and Ethyl Corporation, for which Powell engineered what is widely believed to be the first leveraged buyout.[14] Seven years later, Powell would be writing the legal decisions protecting these and other corporations under the Bill of Rights, beginning with *First National Bank of Boston v. Bellotti.*

The Powell Memo and The "Counter-Attack"

The "Confidential Memorandum" sent by Powell in August 1971 to the leadership of the U.S. Chamber of Commerce sounded an alarm with its title, "Attack on the American Free Enterprise System." The previous decade had seen the regulation of many industries and, as Powell argued, "The most disquieting voices joining the chorus of criticism came from perfectly respectable elements of society: from the college campus, the pulpit, the media, the intellectual and literary journals, the arts and sciences, and from politicians."[15] The Powell memo first articulated what was to become a three-decade-long plan by corporate America to take cultural and societal power from those who would regulate, criticize, and reform the corporation. In an extraordinary prefiguring of the social goals of business that would be felt over the next three decades, Powell wrote:

> One of the bewildering paradoxes of our time is the extent to which the enterprise system tolerates, if not participates in, its own destruction.
>
> The campuses from which much of the criticism emanates are supported by (i) tax funds generated largely from

American business, and (ii) contributions from capital funds controlled or generated by American business. The boards of trustees of our universities overwhelmingly are composed of men and women who are leaders in the system.

Most of the media, including the national TV systems, are owned and theoretically controlled by corporations which depend upon profits, and the enterprise system to survive. . . .

American business [is] "plainly in trouble"; the response to the wide range of critics has been ineffective, and has included appeasement: the time has come—indeed, it is long overdue—for the wisdom, ingenuity and resources of American business to be marshalled against those who would destroy it. . . .

The day is long past when the chief executive officer of a major corporation discharges his responsibility by maintaining a satisfactory growth of profits, with due regard to the corporation's public and social responsibilities. If our system is to survive, top management must be equally concerned with protecting and preserving the system itself. This involves far more than an increased emphasis on "public relations" or "governmental affairs"—two areas in which corporations have long invested substantial sums.

A significant first step by individual corporations could well be the designation of an executive vice president (ranking with other executive VP's) whose responsibility is to counter—on the broadest front—the attack on the enterprise system. The public relations department could be one of the foundations assigned to this executive, but his responsibilities should encompass some of the types of activities referred to subsequently in this memorandum. His budget and staff should be adequate to the task.

But independent and uncoordinate activity by individual corporations, as important as this is, will not be sufficient. Strength lies in organization, in careful long-range planning

and implementation, in consistency of action over an indefi-
nite period of years, in the scale of financing available only
through joint effort, and in the political power available
only through united action and national organizations.

Moreover, there is the quite understandable reluctance on
the part of any one corporation to get too far out in front and
to make itself too visible a target.

The role of the National Chamber of Commerce is therefore vital. Other national organizations (especially those of
various industrial and commercial groups) should join in the
effort, but no other organizations appear to be as well situated
as the Chamber.

Changing how individuals and society think about the corporation, the government, the law, the culture, and the individual became,
and would remain, a major goal of business. By capturing the means of
societal control that Powell proposed next in his memo, the corporation would be in a position to revise social custom, ethics, and the rule
of law to the corporation's advantage. Among the initial targets Powell
identified were:

- "The Campus." Powell astutely noted that students who mistrusted
  corporations would graduate to pivotal roles in the news media,
  particularly television; government, as staffers, elected officials or
  regulators; and in higher education, as writers and lecturers. He
  proposed establishing a network of pro-business scholars; creating
  a staff of speakers who "exert whatever degree of pressure—publicly and privately—[that] may be necessary to assure opportunities
  to speak"; "urging of the need for faculty balance upon university
  administrators and boards of trustees . . . a long road and not
  one for the fainthearted"; and evaluating textbooks to assure fairness to the corporation in the same manner as "we have seen the
  civil rights movement insist on rewriting many of the textbooks
  in our universities and schools."

- "Graduate Schools of Business." Powell recommended that the memo's material become the subject of specific business school courses. "This is now essential training for the executive of the future."

- "Secondary Education." The local chambers of commerce were urged to begin action programs tailored to high school students. The modern result is the national network of "Jaycees," or Junior Chamber of Commerce members.

- "[T]he Public." To influence it, "[t]he first essential is to establish the staff of eminent scholars, writers and speakers, who will do the thinking, the analysis, the writing and the speaking. It will also be essential to have staff personnel who are thoroughly familiar with the media, and how most effectively to communicate with the public."

- "Television." "The national television networks should be monitored in the same way that textbooks should be kept under constant surveillance. . . . Complaints—to the media and to the Federal Communications Commission—should be made promptly and strongly. . . . Equal time should be demanded."

- "The Scholarly Journals" and "Books, Paperbacks and Pamphlets." The Chamber's "faculty scholars" should publish and submit articles to popular and intellectual magazines, while efforts also should be made to put business literature in drugstore and airport newsstands "filled with paperbacks advocating everything from revolution to erotic free love."

- "Paid Advertisements." "If American business devoted only 10% of its total annual advertising budget to" advocating not just products but the corporate system, "it would be a statesman like expenditure."

- "The Neglected Political Arena." To counter "the stampede by politicians to support almost any legislation related to 'consumerism' or to the 'environment,'" corporations must learn the lesson that political "power must be assiduously cultivated; and that when necessary, it must be used aggressively and with determination—without embarrassment and without the reluctance which has been so characteristic of American business."

• "Neglected Opportunities in the Courts." Given his next job, it's not surprising that Powell would advocate that the corporation seek influence over the judiciary because, "[u]nder our constitutional system, especially with an activist-minded Supreme Court, the judiciary may be the most important instrument for social, economic and political change."

Powell's vision became real within a decade. Corporate-financed think tanks, trade associations, lobbying groups, academic programs, and political action committees proliferated to change both the individual's view of the corporation and the balance of power between the corporation and society. The U.S. Chamber of Commerce heeded most of Powell's recommendations. Chambers have become aggressively engaged at the federal, state, and local levels as political lobbyists, grassroots campaigners, campaign contributors, media buyers and spinners, judicial critics, and academic patrons to bolster the corporation's position. The Business Roundtable, an organization of chief executive officers committed to the aggressive pursuit of political power for the corporation, was founded in 1972 and has been a major roadblock to popularly sought reforms ever since through aggressive lobbying, campaign giving by its CEO members, and media campaigns.[16] This includes, in recent years, opposing HMO reform, a Medicare prescription drug benefit, and corporate accountability measures.

Consumer advocate Ralph Nader—described by Powell in his memo as "perhaps the single most effective antagonist of American business"—observed, "It took a while to entrench this counterforce."[17] Nader also stated:

If I had to pick a date for the beginning of the latest cycle of giant business's big-time resurgence, it would be in the last eighteen months of the Carter administration [1979–1981]. . . . Emboldened corporations on the ascendancy observed their opponents inside and outside of government moving from resistance to retreat, losing even the sense of trumpeting their successes of the prior fifteen years in making America a better and safer place to live. . . . Historians often describe the engines of such ebbs and flows between contesting constituencies to be the rise of new ideas, dogmas, ideologies or perceptions. In this case, it was more a flood of propaganda repeated with daily determination by business-sponsored institutions (the American Enterprise Institute, the Heritage Foundation) through reports, conferences and media programs attacking regulations and other allegedly 'failed' government programs while touting so-called free-market solutions for what traditionally have been public responsibilities. . . . In the eighties, Washington Post and New York Times reporters started responding to our reports and testimony exposing business abuses by saying, 'We don't cover reports.' That was not entirely accurate. They did cover the reports and studies of the Heritage Foundation and the American Enterprise Institute because these right-wing groups had allies in the White House and Congress. Unlike previous years, our consumer and environmental associations did not have such governmental support. Therefore, the major press deemed them not newsworthy.[18]

Acquiring "Mind Share"

The sophisticated apparatus that corporations created sought to change how individuals and society thought—to acquire "mind share." In his 1967 study of power in America, *Power,* Columbia law professor A. A. Berle explored the economic, political, judicial, international, and personal spheres of power. "Power," he wrote, "cannot control a man's mind."[19] In the 1980s and 1990s, corporate power strived for just such control in markets and beyond them.

At the dawn of the information age in the late 1970s, persuading people to remember the corporation fondly became the corporation's primary commercial goal—be it a cola company, bank, or perfume. The trend's perils became clear about twenty years later when truth itself was revealed as a casualty of an ever-escalating contest among corporations to capture public consciousness. The cause of the accounting scandals of 2002 was a widespread effort to profit from illusion. Similarly, Wall Street bankers/brokerages made billions in the late 1990s by taking profitless "dot coms" public, based exclusively on their popular "mind share" and "consciousness occupied." Technology companies that never earned a profit experienced stock values greatly exceeding blue-chip companies. Enron built its inflated stock value not on energy production but, as explored in Chapter 3, on an illusory energy brokering system that, in the end, had no real value.

The mental control that late-twentieth-century corporations sought to exert over individuals about more than their purchases—about their own customs, laws, ethics, rights, and freedoms—was an unprecedented power grab. Given corporate resources, the sum of the diverse parts of the apparatus to achieve this cultural control might be described as a "mind machine." The 1980s provided important opportunities for corporations to expand on Powell's blueprint.

- In the Reagan era, a dramatic drop in tax rates freed corporate capital for the massive financial investment required to create an infrastructure that could impact societal laws and customs to the advantage of corporations.

- The transition from factory-driven production by corporations to an information-based, service-sector orientation sparked a corporate interest in communicating more frequently and persuasively with individuals because the advantages of services such as

financial planning were not as obvious as those of goods like vacuum cleaners. Corporations needed to create a "milieu" to peddle
many of their services.

- The demise of communism in the 1980s permitted the boosters
  of global business to claim the spoils of the Cold War in American culture—the victory of capitalism and of capitalist corporations over governmental systems that regulated them.

In the post–Cold War world of the Reagan-Gorbachev era, a sophisticated corporate apparatus, utilizing the latest technologies, evolved
to build a drumbeat in America life promoting corporate rights. Such
promotion came at the expense of traditional notions about the corporation's accountability to the public and, often, to the detriment of the
individual's rights. The underlying argument was that the American
free market had been responsible for winning the Cold War and should
be sovereign not only in commerce but other areas of American life as
well. Politics was about protecting business and its freedoms, too. Government should turn control of sanitation, electricity, water, education,
prisons, and hospitals over to private corporations. Children need not
be so protected by the government from commercialism in their television programming. The rights of workers, such as air traffic con-
trollers, to unionize was not as important as the rights of industries to
operate as they see fit. The corporation should be free from regulation
and taxation, while receiving public subsidization. These, and other
similar messages, reverberated through the corporate apparatus as it
grew significantly beyond Powell's vision.

By the early 1990s, more than 1,000 think tanks existed in America.[20] Although there is no way to know how many were corporate-
controlled—because funding sources are typically not disclosed—it
has been revealed that many of the largest and most influential think
tanks receive generous corporate contributions and support industry
positions. "Documents, obtained by the Washington Post, provide a
rare look at think tanks' often hidden role as a weapon in the modern

corporate political arsenal," investigative journalist Dan Morgan reported at the turn of the millennium. "The groups provide analyses, TV advertising, polling, and academic studies that add an air of authority to corporate arguments—in many cases while maintaining the corporate donors' anonymity."[21]

"Technology companies give to think tanks that promote open access to the Internet," explained Tom Brazaitis in a similar investigation in the Cleveland *Plain Dealer*. "Wall Street firms donate to think tanks that espouse private investment of social security funds."[22] The mission statements of some of America's most widely quoted think tanks— such as the Heritage Foundation, the Cato Institute, and the American Enterprise Institute—state their dedication to freer corporate markets and more limited government, the corporation's twin cultural goals.

Corporations alter public perception by having such groups deployed on various fronts with common themes. The first line of attack on any given issue consists of opinion leaders—legislators, regulators, judges, media. The public "learns" the arguments on the specific issue and the greater mantra of market sovereignty by hearing those opinion leaders speak to them on talk shows, in the newspapers, in the legislature, and through the courts.

Perhaps the most troubling development during the last decade is the growth in deception by corporate groups who hide their identities from the public. The corporate-funded groups I continually battle with all claim to represent individuals, not corporations. My colleagues and I call them "astro-turf groups" because of their impersonation of grassroots organizations. For example, Citizens Against Lawsuit Abuse, whose role will be explored in Chapter 4, fights to limit the individual's legal rights to challenge corporations in court, and this astro-turf group, which exists in many states, is backed by big corporations. It places letters to the editors in local newspapers and lobbies legislators under the banner of a "citizen's" organization. Similarly, when my colleagues and I placed an HMO patients' rights initiative on the California ballot in 1996, the coalition of HMOs and other big corporations against Proposition 216 called themselves "Taxpayers Against Higher Health Care Costs." When we fought for a utility company reform initiative in 1998 (Proposition 9), to save Californians billions of dollars on their electric bills by blocking a deregulation law, the utility companies banded together to form "Californians Against Higher Taxes and Higher Electric Rates." Another group I often tangle with, the California Tort Reform Association, recently found its name too big business–like and changed it to the Civil Justice Association. Its only goal is to limit liability for large corporations. It also intervenes in lawsuits on behalf of large corporations to help change the law and limit corporate liability. Such groups operate under the principle enunciated by Neil Cohen, the grassroots consultant to the corporate-funded American Tort Reform Association, and recorded on tape at a big-business gathering in 1994 at a Florida resort: "You need to have credibility. And that means when you pick people to join your coalition make sure they're credible, and if they're not credible, keep 'em away. In a tort reform battle, if State Farm is the leader of the coalition, you're not gonna pass the bill. It is not credible. Okay?"

When communicating to their backers, however, think tanks can be quite explicit about their role in the corporate apparatus. For instance, the Manhattan Institute, whose donors include a roll call of Fortune 500 companies from State Farm to Philip Morris, bragged in its solicitations for contributions from corporations that it has shaped the debate to limit liability for big corporations by mass mailings to judges with the corporate perspective. The think tank claimed to make "the rhetoric of liability reform incorporate transcending concepts like consumer choice, fairness and equity"; and ensure that the "terms of debate remain favorable" by paying scholars to write books that articulate the corporate position and are then read by judges, commentators, and talk-show hosts. The think tank boasted, "Journalists need copy, and it's an established fact that over time they'll 'bend' in the direction which it flows. If, sometime during the present decade, a consensus emerges in favor of serious judicial reform, it will be because millions of minds have been changed, and only one institution is powerful enough to bring that about. . . . We feel that the funds made available will yield a tremendous return at this point—perhaps the 'highest return on investment' available in the philanthropic field today."

The implications for an independent judiciary and free press are obvious, and the results are nearly inevitable. Enough drumbeats always produce some kind of song. Not surprisingly, one of the biggest targets of the invisible hand's war drums has been government, and, at least as a partial result, there has been a precipitous drop during the last two decades in Americans' faith in their government.

Greater Than Government

Government has never been the model of efficiency. The founding fathers acknowledged its power for evil and provided the Bill of Rights to protect against abuses. Nonetheless, the collective power of individuals to challenge corporate abuses resides in government—in its powers to legislate new laws and to enforce existing ones. Historically, government has been the most effective countervailing power for individuals seeking to limit corporations' power:

- Charters could be revoked.

- New laws could be legislated.

- Regulations could be imposed.

- Taxes could be assessed.

- Prices could be fixed.

- Monopolies could be busted.

During the last few decades of the twentieth century, however, many of these governmental powers, with respect to the corporation, have been frustrated or abandoned at the time they were most needed.

Richard Nixon was the last U.S. president to apply wage and consumer price controls. Ronald Reagan dismantled the corporate regulatory and tax structures. President Clinton championed governmental partnership with private industry rather than viewing it as an entity to be regulated on behalf of the public. At the same time that Clinton declared the death of social programs for individuals—"the era of big government is over"—he encouraged the era of big corporations. Under the Clinton Administration's permissive consolidation policies, each year from 1994 through 1998 set a new national record for the biggest merger year in history.[23] No significant industry was left unconsolidated. My colleagues and I, who watch most domestic areas of consumer concern, consider it a rule of thumb that no more than six to eight corporations control most major industries in America.[24]

The shrinking role of government in American life, at precisely the moment an activist government was needed to regulate larger corporations, would not have been possible without the corporate apparatus's daily harangue of government and glorification of unregulated markets. Powell identified this need in his 1971 memo: "As every businessman knows, few elements of American society today have as little influence in government as the American businessman, the corporation or even the millions of corporate stockholders. If one doubts this, let him undertake the role of 'lobbyist' for the business point of view. . . . [I]n terms of political influence with respect to the course of legislation and government action, the American business executive is truly 'the forgotten man.'" In March 2001, Robert Reich, President Clinton's first Secretary of Labor, described in *The New York Times* the dramatic turnabout:

> There is no longer any countervailing power in Washington. Business is in complete control of the machinery of government. . . . The Business Roundtable, comprising the chief executives of large American corporations, typically establishes at the start of a new Congress a legislative agenda reflecting

what its members consider the most important issues. The United States Chamber of Commerce . . . also develops a strategy. The National Association of Manufacturers weighs in with its wish list. And the National Federation of Independent Business, composed of small firms, sets its goals. These groups do not always see eye to eye, but under normal circumstances they understand that legislative success requires coordination. . . . The trade associations representing specific industries [ ] play supporting roles. Their own parochial legislative goals can't interfere directly with the priorities of business as a whole because the industries often depend on the larger business groups to be heard. Specific firms may retain their own Washington lobbyists, but they, too, have to work with others in order to have a significant effect. . . . Every trade association must demonstrate to its members large returns from their investments. . . . [T]he pressure only ratchets upward: Every time one company or one industry receives its rewards, other Washington lobbyists, representing other firms or industries, come under even more pressure to score victories.[25]

By 1998, *The Commanding Heights*, a book by Daniel Yergin and Joseph Stanislaw, had chronicled the global victory of corporate markets over the government, which thirty years before occupied the "commanding heights" over the economy. In the first episode of the 2002 PBS series "Commanding Heights," derived from the book, former Clinton Administration Treasury Secretary Lawrence Summers, the President of Harvard University, summed up the new status quo: "The old debates were about what the role of the market was, what was the role of the state," Summers said. "I think it's now generally appreciated that it's the market that harnesses people's initiative best. And the real focus of progressive thinking is not how to oppose and suppress market forces but how to use market forces to achieve progressive objectives."[26]

Late-twentieth-century corporations, for the first time in history, became bigger than government. Fifty-one of the largest 100 economies in the world were corporations, when measuring gross corporate revenue against gross national product.[27] The gross annual revenue for the six largest corporations in America combined was greater than the government budget of every nation in the world except the United States.[28] Corporate consolidation, globalization, and internationalization of capital greatly diminished the ability of national governments to hold corporations accountable to the individual.

The little-told story of the true balance of power in American politics has been that even when big corporations lose legislatively, they get another bite at the apple by using their money and might in the regulatory process to foil already enacted laws. My colleagues and I, who work regularly with regulators, can attest that litigious corporations and their lawyers have often been the forces that have given government bureaucrats a bad name. Regulations proposed by President Clinton for greater medical privacy were gutted by industry lobbying before they were finalized during President George W. Bush's Administration.[29] Due to industry pressure, it took the Food and Drug Administration more than twenty-five years to ban cancer-causing red dyes in food, including twenty-eight postponements.[30] Automobile makers were first directed to install air bags in cars by the Nixon Administration in 1970. Auto manufacturers, through bureaucratic and legal maneuvers, managed to stall implementation for twenty years, until 1990.[31] As Robert Reich noted in 2001, with the growing corporate power over government, "Demands for regulatory relief are growing louder, and most will have to be met. Corporate welfare will flow ever more freely; . . . corporate tax breaks will blossom like the cherry trees."[32] Through such strategies, corporations have not just obstructed the countervailing power of government but have actually brought the government into service of the corporation's commercial needs. As the next chapter shows, the invisible hand has enlisted government in helping it socialize corporate risk and privatize corporate gain.

By the new millennium, corporate power had not only overtaken the three branches of government but other significant checks on its abuses as well. The strength of labor unions was diminished by the corporate machine's drumbeat against corrupt labor bosses and by antiunion tactics in many workplaces, which are discussed in Chapter 5. Less than 10 percent of the private workforce was unionized at the turn of the millennium, the lowest percentage in sixty years.[33] As revealed in Chapter 7, the muckraking media's new rules often put the corporation's interest above the public interest. Taken in its totality, the invisible hand's power grab during the last three decades of the twentieth century put the corporation in an unprecedented position to limit the individual's traditional freedoms for its own advantage.

The Terms of the Individual's Freedom

Corporations and the moneyed class that invested in them always posed a threat to good government. Thomas Jefferson, who drafted the Declaration of Independence, decried the manufacturers of his time whose politicking threatened his vision of an agrarian society that avoided the social decay and political corruption of British industrial development. Jefferson wrote in 1816 to his political supporter George Logan, "I hope we shall . . . crush in its birth the aristocracy of our moneyed corporations, which dare already to challenge our government to a trial of strength and bid defiance to the laws of our country."[34] The activities of the invisible hand have challenged not only government but also the very assumptions and institutions that keep individuals free and for which the American nation was founded. The corporate investment in cultural control has grown exponentially in recent years. Its targets have also become increasingly personal, such as the cultural values of our children and their constitutional rights, which are vital to the continued transmission of our cultural heritage as a sovereign people. Remarkably, there is only one parallel in American history for such attempts by an unaccountable power to change the rules of law, ethics, and social custom. These are the actions by which King George III provoked the colonists who founded this nation.

The standard for individual freedom in American life has always been the Declaration of Independence. The Declaration defined the key pillars of a free and sovereign American people. What the hand of the king took away—the freedoms of self-determination—the people of America would build a free nation upon. The Constitution took thirteen years of deliberation to finalize in 1789, but the Declaration of Independence was born from an instinct of human worth and a consciousness of what true justice should be. The Declaration describes both the world as it was and the world as it should be. It's remarkable that many of the tactics used by the monarch to redefine the basic rules of society, law, and ethical custom to the detriment of individuals are the same as the modern corporation's. Many of the grievances against King George in the Declaration of 1776 also apply to the invisible hand. In fact, the Declaration of Independence could be rewritten today, with corporate-funded and -inspired efforts to undermine individual rights and freedoms replacing the list of grievances enumerated against the king of Britain.

- The Powell-inspired mind machine fits the bill of having "erected a multitude of new offices, and sent hither swarms of officers to harass our people, and eat out their substance."

- When its corporate lawyers stonewall government regulations and its astroturf groups seek to undo laws protecting individuals, the sovereign corporation has "refused his assent to laws, the most wholesome and necessary for the public good."

- Through its various satellite operations, like Citizens Against Lawsuit Abuse and the American Tort Reform Association, the corporation has tried "depriving us in many cases of the benefits of trial by jury."

- Through obstreperous litigation tactics, corporations have "obstructed the administration of justice." At the same time, groups like the Chamber of Commerce and Manhattan Institute seek to have "made judges dependent on his will alone," as has increasing corporate financing of judicial elections for candidates who support limited liability for corporations.

- Think tanks, academics, and social scientists paid for by corporations too often determine the public record on an issue, and they—instead of affected individuals—control the timing, testimony, and terms of legislative debate. Their capacity to tie up government with studies, statistics, and other information that makes the corporate case is no match for the average citizen and less well-funded public interest groups. This is the modern-day equivalent of the colonists' grievance against King George of having "called together legislative bodies at places unusual, uncomfortable, and distant from the depository of public records, for the sole purpose of fatiguing them into compliance with his measures."

- Rather than showing a primary allegiance to individuals whom they serve as customers, corporations since the 1970s have often colluded with other corporations to further an industry's rights at the expense of the individual's, as discussed by Robert Reich and explored further in Chapter 6. This corresponds to the colonists' complaint of having "combined with others to subject us to a jurisdiction foreign to our constitution, and unacknowledged by our laws."

The king was not allowed to capture American culture and neither should the corporation. James Madison wrote, in his retirement, "The People of the U.S. owe their Independence & their liberty, to the wisdom of descrying in the minute tax of 3 pence on tea, the magnitude of the evil comprised in the precedent. Let them exert in the same wisdom, in watching agst every evil lurking under plausible disguises, and growing up from small beginnings."[35] Small evils quickly become large ones when nourished by institutions as powerful as modern corporations and not responded to by individuals. The price of commercial convenience should never be an individual's cultural freedom. Yet this is a Faustian bargain that the invisible hand has offered and that American society is being asked to accept daily in subtle yet significant ways. Individuals have not established clear rules and boundaries for corporations' cultural intervention, possibly not just because the hand of the corporation that takes is largely invisible. Most Americans now have an investment in the stock market and naturally bestow their economic confidence in corporations. We are all reminded daily about the importance of consumer confidence to a fragile economy and the growth of our retirement savings. The Dow Jones Industrial Average has become the scoreboard for all of society, not simply the market. However, investing in the stock market does not necessitate allowing corporations the latitude to change the rules of society.

Ironically, Madison uttered his admonition about "every evil lurking under plausible disguises" in a letter lamenting the lack of public consciousness regarding the perils inherent in the corporate institution from the chartering of religious corporations. Years earlier, out of similar concerns, he had been a fierce opponent of chartering a national bank.

> Are the U.S. duly awake to the tendency of the precedent they are establishing, in the multiplied incorporations of Religious Congregations with faculty of acquiring and holding property real as well as a personal property. Do not many of these acts give this faculty, without limit either as to time or as to amount? And must not bodies perpetual in their existence, and which may be always gaining without ever losing, speedily gain more than is useful, and in time more than is safe?[36]

Madison's warning is prophetic. Preventing corporations from abusing their form to capture culture requires facilities that make the invisible hand and its power grabs visible, as well as better boundaries for corporate conduct. The main strategies by which the invisible hand has overreached during the age of the corporateer, the last two decades, are discussed in the coming chapters. Steps for opposing the power grab are discussed in later chapters, but the first step is to develop a vocabulary that describes it.

There is no word in the American vocabulary that defines the moment when corporations exceed their marketplace role and dominate culture. This suggests the lack of societal attention to the proposition itself, and therefore its potential for abuse.

- Is the loss of cultural traditions and liberties for individuals that have served this nation well a necessary or acceptable consequence of American fascination with corporate commercial ingenuity?

- How much of its cultural heritage has America already lost to an increasing corporate power, and how did it happen?

- How can individuals recover their time, energy, money, rights, and power by restructuring the individual-corporate compact?

- Are the individual's only freedoms to be commercial ones?

This book explores these questions by proposing a new word for the American vocabulary that is a yardstick by which to measure them.

cor•po•ra•teer *v.* to prioritize commerce over culture   *n.* one who prioritizes commerce over culture

corporateering: When corporations exceed their traditional role in a marketplace to dominate the cultural sphere and compromise individuals' rights, freedoms, power, and the democratic systems that protect them. The act implies corporations vying with a democratic people for sovereignty over their society and societal rights by redefining the basic rules of society, law, and ethical customs to the detriment of individuals.

THE LOGIC OF MAKING CORPORATIONS COUNT MORE THAN INDIVIDUALS

Sin has many tools, but a lie is the handle which fits them all.
—OLIVER WENDELL HOLMES

Control how a society reasons and you control that culture. Kings and queens maintained their positions for centuries through the logic of divine sovereignty, which held that God entrusted royalty with handling mortals' affairs because they were God's messengers on earth. Socialist regimes' logic—the needs of the many outweigh the needs of the few—put the state above the individual to rationalize elimination of individual freedoms. Fascist rulers frequently relied on nationalism and eugenics for their power: Extraordinary measures had to be taken to root out the enemies of a people and their nation. Prevailing logic has the power to subtly rearrange the hierarchy of societal values that serve as checks and balances on inappropriate personal and institutional authority. It controls how people relate to one another and to the institutions in their lives. The corporation has today rearranged prevailing logic to advance the corporation's freedoms, often at the expense of the individual's.

The problem with logic is that it multiplies. If one buys into a single socially questionable premise, then all the rational outcomes of that premise are accepted as reasonable. The growing social power of corporations from the 1980s onward is advancing a new logic that emphasizes the commercial over the social, the corporation over the individual, the thing over the person.

In campaign after campaign to reform corporate abuses, I have seen the same logic relied on by corporations in defending the status quo or in advancing on new social frontiers. I hear it again and again, but it's always amazing to see the power of this same troubling logic take hold over government in times of crisis, to change jurisprudence, and to also come out of the mouth of a friend at a dinner party: "That will kill the business climate. . . . The confidence of investors is at stake. . . . It's just how business works. . . . Do you know what that will do to the economy?" The mantras have credibility because of the power of the logic that underlies them—that the good life is an unregulated commercial transaction. This is the freedom of things, not people. Nonetheless, such logic is quickly becoming a sieve for individuals' private and public lives, as well as public policies and public strategies that once protected those domains from commercial incursions.

Nearly every industry my colleagues and I have ever tried to reform has raised the same logical objections to protect corporate freedoms that injure people:

- the increased costs will be astronomical and put the product beyond the reach of customers;

- corporations will stop doing business or leave the state;

- the free market will be crippled;

- massive layoffs will ensue and many jobs will be lost.

The industries' arguments are that commercial concerns—a.k.a. economic advantages—always trump social considerations, such as the quality of health care, the availability of electricity, and the affordability of insurance. Beyond policymaking, corporations use the same paradigm to replace social standards and ethical rules benefiting the individual with corporate rules and logic that emphasize the commercial. Increasingly, the goal of the invisible hand is to have individuals live in a commercial world instead of a public and private one. At its worst, the logic of corporateers does not even acknowledge the individual's public and private needs as distinct from the needs of the commerce.

- Privacy for an individual's medical information and financial records can be rationalized out of existence because there should be no privacy from the market and its commercial opportunities. Secrecy about even the corporation's financial health can be guaranteed because individuals are not entitled to anything that does not lead to a commercial transaction.

- Fundamental needs of the individual's existence once protected by a regulated public domain, such as health care and electricity, are now delivered by unregulated, for-profit corporations. HMOs and independent power producers have applied commercial standards of judgment to the delivery of such necessities of life.

- The individual can no longer say "no" to commercial companionship in her private life. Corporations leave computerized commercial pitches on personal answering machines, spam e-mail ads, send unsolicited junk faxes, and, in the case of the television network ABC, have planned computerized promos from prime-time celebrities to greet diners in restaurant restrooms.[1]

- Movie theaters ceased to be commercial-free zones because corporations have come to view all individuals' time, attention, and space as the market's time and space to promote commercial opportunities.

- In the market itself, social mores and taboos that had prohibited certain once-socially-unacceptable products, pricing structures, and practices have largely vanished. This helps to explain how kids can buy the ultra-violent children's video-game series "Mortal

Kombat" and the video game "BMX XXX," which features topless female bicycle racers and video clips of strippers. It also sheds light on how societal abhorrence of price gouging gave way to the creation of the Coca-Cola machine with a built-in thermometer that automatically upped the price of the drink with rising outdoor temperatures.[2] And it answers the question of how so many denizens of Wall Street played so fast and loose with the truth about their finances. ("It's as if the line between right and wrong, legal and illegal, acceptable and unacceptable, was so little enforced that it became blurred," said U.S. Senate Majority Leader Tom Daschle.)[3]

Tensions between the interests of society and the market have always existed. The math to weigh them has radically changed. Government commissions and panels have long had to balance the costs and benefits of approving development plans that will aid an area economically but hurt it environmentally. The mathematical principle was simple:

$$\text{Economic Advantage} > \text{Social Cost}$$
(Economic Advantage is greater than Social Cost)
OR
$$\text{Economic Advantage} < \text{Social Cost}$$
(Economic Advantage is less than Social Cost)

Increasingly, however, corporations have succeeded at silent mergers of social and commercial values that seek to make the interests of the market and society synonymous. The corporateers' new computation for critical societal decisions, becoming widely accepted, is:

$$\text{Market} = \text{Society}$$
(The Market equals The Society)

The equation accomplishes through reason what corporateers have increasingly done by sleight of hand since the bull commercial culture of the 1980s—making social costs, already subtle, magically vanish while inflating economic advantages into miracle cures. Fundamentally, the "market = society" equation skews the scale of any cost-benefit analysis.

When the only unit of measure is dollars, as it is in the market, social costs cannot fully be counted. If society is the market, then social costs are always less than economic advantages. This logic has justified extraordinary corporate tax breaks, stymied social reforms in statehouses and in Congress, impacted legal outcomes in the courts, and greatly diminished the power of the individual to have the social means to object to abusive corporate practices. The even-greater danger for the individual's freedom is that this logic has the power to redefine the individual in terms of his or her relationship to the corporation only—which is the status of a thing.

- Will individuals measure life only in dollars?

- Will the quality of life in the future be determined only by the quality of one's commercial transactions?

- If "market = society" determines great societal questions, will life-saving resources be allocated only to the best consumers, who can fully participate in the market, and not all individuals?

- Will widespread acceptance of this commercial logic erode the societal basis for resistance to further market expansions into cultural space, such as giving corporations naming rights to museums, schools, and even towns?

Socially, when the market is society, the corporation can be implicated in all aspects of the individual's life because it is the market's agent. If "market = society," then there can be no limit on commercialization of schools, publication of private information, or privatization of public functions of government. The individual cannot exist without the market's presence in every aspect of his public and private life.

The real craft of the logic is that any adjective modifying the word *market* will then also apply to society.

Free Market = Free Society
Good Market = Good Society
Bad Market = Bad Society

The connotations of the phrases employed give these types of equations tremendous power to infect the vocabulary with their logic. If "the free market = the free society," then the fewer restrictions corporations face the freer all individuals are. If "a good market = a good society," then the importance of the government making certain the market endures, expands, and thrives is no less than the future of society itself. Ensuring that markets do not go bad is tantamount to ensuring that society does not go bad. This logic is not mere semantics, but represents widely held assumptions underlying critical decisions in cultural life. For instance, Congressional proposals to privatize the social security system by investing funds in the stock market could not have even been contemplated without the underlying logic "free market = free society."

Other words can then be implicated based on these notions. If "free market = free society," then "free market = free choice." To buy is then to choose. Traits associated with the individual become attributed to the consumer. This gives corporations seeking greater power new terms to rationalize their expansion. Regulators may not be convinced that it is in the individual's interest for corporations to have too much power or market share. However, they are often swayed by the argument that corporate consolidations produce "economies of scale" that allow the consumer to enjoy savings, and "to save = to choose." "Choice" has become a powerful selling point in corporate interests' bid to subject individuals to greater corporate power. For example, AT&T won governmental approval for its 2002 MediaOne purchase—making it the nation's largest provider of cable television, long-distance telephone service, and high-speed Internet access—by promising greater consumer choices, despite shrinking competition to produce them. "This merger will mean a real choice and lower prices in local phone service, faster Internet access, and better cable TV," said C. Michael Armstrong, AT&T's chairman. "For consumers, that's a home run in any ballpark."[4] Similarly, as *The New York Times* reported, AOL and Time Warner responded to government approval of their 2000 merger "by calling the agreement 'a win for consumers' and predicted that other cable companies would follow the lead of Time Warner, the country's second largest cable operator, in making a 'commitment to consumer choice.'"[5]

To have commercial choices, individuals often must relinquish social or personal ones. For example, to choose to save the most money in a supermarket with a club card that tracks purchases, an individual must sacrifice his personal privacy. Similarly, to have AT&T as a cable operator in your area is to choose to have the company leave a message on your home answering machine touting its broadband Internet service.[6]

Who Serves Whom?

Corporateers claim that it is the individual's appetite that dictates to the market and to the corporation. This is the logic for tearing down boundaries between the market and society. What do individuals have to fear from corporations that only want to serve them better? In reality, corporations serve the economic appetites of consumers far better than the social needs of individuals. This explains the widespread social criticism of HMOs, which apply commercial concepts to the social services of medicine; of the entertainment industry, which ignores social taboos on violent and sexually explicit marketing to youth; and of the aggressive corporate financing of politics. Even in the purely economic realm, society's lack of power over modern corporations has led many to ignore popular sentiment. Certainly, consumers can move markets based on their tastes and impact the general direction of commercial product development. However, while consumer tastes may have provoked the general high-tech boom, they were hardly responsible for Microsoft's notorious efforts to require use of its web navigator with Windows software, the use of Internet cookies to track web surfers, ubiquitous Internet pop-up advertising that freezes computers, and shrink-wrapped software that precludes any liability for the corporation once the seal is broken. The "market = society" logic, when broken down, is fundamentally a tautology—an empty statement composed of simpler ones in a manner that makes it logically true whether the simpler statements are factual or not.

"Society should serve the market because the market serves individuals' appetites, and individuals make up society." Hence, "if society serves the market, the market will serve society." How can the corporation serve society if it has so little responsibility to the individual and her society?

Increasingly, the corporation only acknowledges the consumer, not the individual or her society. This is why those individuals who do not like all that advertising, junk mail, tele-soliciting, spam, and other marketing and intervention in their private space do not matter to the corporateer. The corporation is not talking to them. If "the market = the society," then individuality and the values associated with it do not exist. In the market, there are no individuals, only consumers. This equation is a critical part of the corporateer's math.

$$Individual = Consumer$$

It has become a cliché to say that corporations are trying to turn all individuals into consumers. Imagine, though, what the literal loss of individuality would entail. What would happen if economic savings/profit became the only responsibility in society? Commercial values, such as accumulation and domination, would outweigh communal values such as nonviolence and cooperation. Truth and honesty would disappear, as they did for Enron, Arthur Andersen, and WorldCom. The social consequences from the preeminence of commercial logic are not the responsibility of the corporation but of society and the individual.

In the corporate mind, a consumer is a rational actor in a market in search of products, not an individual in society whose complexity and personal expression must be accommodated. To the corporation, the consumer is predictable and marketable, while the individual is unpredictable and demanding. For example, the rationale behind "no choice" customer service voice mail "options" is just one expression of this logic. The corporation distills the consumer to predictability and ignores the individual who cannot be predicted. Of course, corporations would like to distill the consumer in all of us to maximize their profits and disregard the economically irrational individuals (as well

as the society and government they have built). That is why social responsibility is generally predicated on a duty to individuals, not to consumers as they are viewed by corporations. Even failure to disclose a
product's defect to the consumer can be rationalized away when the
world is peopled by corporate consumers rather than individuals.
More consumers will benefit from lower costs for the product if the
corporation does not have to recall the marginally defective product
that affects only a small number of consumers. And shareholders
would needlessly have to sacrifice profits as well, the fundamental no-no
of management. Internal Ford memos from as early as 1987 show stability problems with the Explorer prototype, and internal Firestone
memos dating back to 1989 discuss problems with "severe tread separation."[7] It was not until 1999, however, after more than fifty lawsuits
were filed alleging injuries from tread separation, that either company began notifying customers that it would replace Explorer tires.
The "market = society" equation and its corollary, "individual = consumer," are principally a recipe for relieving corporations of a duty and
responsibility to individuals and their society, as distinct from consumers and their market. When all society is a market and all individuals are consumers, corporations can make the logic of social responsibility
disappear.

Doing the Math of Efficiency

"Efficiency" has been the manifest destiny of the corporation, its strategic reason for expansion into new societal frontiers.

Corporation = Efficiency

This rationale has been a catalyst during the last two decades for
making individuals and their social needs less important than the corporation and its commercial needs.

Under this logic, corporate power has grown to a position of un-
paralleled dominance in society.

- Corporate lobbyists justified deregulation of electricity, banking, gasoline, air-travel, and telecommunications industries by claiming that flexibility in the market, freedom from government intervention, would result in greater efficiencies and consumer choice. For example, the claim that consumers "will be able to purchase a brand of natural gas and electricity in much the same way they do their long-distance telephone service" was how Enron's CEO Kenneth L. Lay sold electricity deregulation to America. "The end user buys the commodity from competing suppliers at an unregulated price. . . . While the BTU content may be the same, its price will reflect whether it is firm or interruptible, or whether it is peak or off-peak."[8]

- Massive mergers were rationalized under the notion that greater size meant greater efficiency because redundant operations could be eliminated and a bigger corporation had better purchasing power ("economies of scale"). Seeking government approval for the 1996 merger of Aetna and U.S. Healthcare, U.S. Healthcare chairman Leonard Abramson argued that giving the insurer control over one of every ten American patients would provide the "mass we needed, the power to negotiate with the physicians, the hospitals, the drug companies" and to drive down their charges so the insurer could lower its premiums.[9] In an editorial entitled "When Big Is Good," *The New York Times* wrote that the merger "would create a health plan of forbidding size. . . . But in health care, size is probably necessary to create the extended networks and information systems that improve quality."[10]

- Efficiency was the rationale for privatizing in the corporation traditionally public functions, such as running schools, policing communities, and delivering electricity and medicine without regulation.

Often corporateers have used the mandate of cost-cutting for "efficiency" to rewrite social rules and standards that are unrelated to saving dollars for the consumers but are tied to making more money for the corporation. The growth of HMO medicine is a good example of how the push for efficiency defied cultural trust and standards and in the end was anything but cost-effective. Large, for-profit corporations took over community HMOs and the health-care system in the 1990s with the promise of efficiency, i.e., high-quality health care at an affordable price. Such "managed care" medicine has mostly meant cost-cutting by the company to make more money for itself. By late 2002, Americans were facing a crisis of cost, quality, and access in medicine. While the federal government spent less than 2 percent of Medicare dollars administering the program,[11] HMOs spent twenty to thirty cents of every health-insurance-premium dollar on their own administrative costs and profits.[12] My book *Making a Killing: HMOs and the Threat to Your Health*[13] documented more than one hundred cases where HMOs were penurious with patients in need of access to basic treatment like second opinions, specialists, and high-cost drugs. Yet managed care executives have been lavish with the corporation's needs. For example, in the $9 billion merger of U.S. Healthcare and Aetna in 1996, U.S. Healthcare chief Leonard Abramson took home more than $900 million for himself.[14]

The mantle of "efficiency" allowed HMO corporations to transform medicine from an imperfect, wasteful system controlled by the judgment of individual doctors and the needs of patients to one controlled by corporations insensitive to the needs of patients. *Making a Killing* showed that the less doctors do for patients, the more they are paid, promoted, and lauded. Sick children suddenly become unacceptable liabilities if they do not meet the national cookie-cutter guidelines for hospital discharge one day after diabetic coma, two days after osteomyelitis, and three days after contracting bacterial meningitis.[15] After the discharge time elapses, the consumer to serve becomes the individual to deal with. The Seattle-based accounting firm Milliman & Robertson that publishes these ubiquitous guidelines acknowledged, "We do not base our guidelines on any randomized clinical trials or other controlled studies, nor do we study outcomes before sharing the evidence of the most efficient practices with colleagues."[16] In other words, it's business, not science.

The logic that permitted the medical takeover was much the same as that used in other spheres to take power from individuals and rewrite hierarchies of values.

The Corporation > Accountability > The Individual

Corporations step in to define efficiency and its terms, which necessarily places them hierarchically above both accountability and the individual. The logic that the invisible hand brings to such endeavors is this: Economic accountability is greater than the individual. The corporation is greater than economic accountability because it is naturally accountable in the market. Therefore, the corporation is greater than the individual, and the individual is accountable to the corporation's logic of efficiency. Under this strategy, corporateers often argue that the corporation and the market were brought in to do the job that the individual, government, and society could not do on their own. For instance, one of the HMO industry's favorite retorts to problems with quality has been, "You can't buy a Chevy and expect a Cadillac." The job of diminishing a healing art like medicine to an assembly line, and reducing the patient to the status of a thing, is a job corporations have been proven uniquely qualified to do. However, there was never a public mandate for such thinking, which explains the broad public support in recent years for an HMO patients' bill of rights in order to swing the pendulum back to society's side. To the degree there was a mandate for corporate intervention of some kind, the HMO and insurance industry manufactured it.

In medicine and other traditional social spheres, the invisible hand has created a unique place for the corporation above the individual through a conscious strategy of disenfranchising its only real competitor, government, which the public has come, through conditioning and inclination, to fear. How could individuals really believe that HMOs would deliver on what they promised—high-quality health care at an affordable price? HMOs and insurers used their economic and political might to convince the society that there was nowhere else to turn. The public was looking for such a simple answer in the aftermath of the failure of the Clinton health-care plan in 1994. HMOs filled a vacuum that they created when the industry torpedoed the Clinton universal health-care proposals with the now infamous "Harry and Louise" television advertisements, which stoked the specter of government bureaucrats rationing health care. Ironically, the corporate bureaucrats turned out to be far crueler. In the vacuum of the Clinton plan, however, corporations appeared to have the only solution—since government had failed—to a health-care crisis that had resonance for most Americans and even helped to elect Clinton president. The insurers hijacked an issue of deep emotional concern for the public after using their political power to thwart the government from enacting a genuine solution. The public passively gave HMOs and managed care companies the license to fill a void that they believed government could not deal with. By the mid-1990s, the majority of Americans with insurance were enrolled in an HMO or managed care plan that restricts access to medical care. What first allowed HMOs and managed-care companies to multiply and then dramatically alter the rules of medical conduct was public consent that they had tacitly manufactured in order to meddle in the makeup of the medical care system. Corporations made themselves necessary in medicine, then used the artificial mandate as a wrecking ball to long-established social principles of medical care delivery. In the same way, corporateers have made the corporation necessary in all aspects of life.

The logic of efficiency has been the justification for "deregulation" of America's essential resources and major industries during the last twenty-five years. As with HMO medicine, however, the promise of efficiency from deregulation has often failed to live up to the reality, as the chart below details.

Industry Deregulated	Promise of Deregulation	Reality of Deregulation
Airline (1978)	More competition, better service, cheaper prices.	Rapid consolidation, more delays, higher prices, restricted service in smaller markets, and poor security counter the benefits of more capacity in some major markets.
Electricity (1990s)	Lower prices, better access, greater environmental sensitivity.	Price spikes, blackouts, removal of environmental regulations on plants.
Gasoline (1982)	More competition, increased supply, lower prices.	Consolidation, artificially low inventories (see Chapter 6), $2.00-per-gallon gasoline.
Banking/Insurance/ Stock Brokerages (1999). Ending depression-era walls between industries so each could sell others' products.	Greater convenience, more innovative financial investment choices, more financial security.	More privacy violations, conflicts of interest in investment recommendations that affect affiliates, more financial losses on riskier unsecured investments, more ways to conceal debt and insider deals.
Natural Gas (1985)	Increased supply and access resulting from competition.	A handful of companies control distribution, resulting in shortages, higher prices and pipeline safety problems.

Bailout Boom

The corporation's role as the guardian of efficiency led to the late-twentieth-century conclusion that saving the corporation from others, or even itself, was a social imperative. The reasoning naturally follows from "market = society."

Market Benefit = Societal Benefit

The corporation has used such logic for taxpayer bailouts, public subsidies, other forms of corporate welfare, and basic rewrites of core economic rights for shareholders and consumers.

Corporations are the preeminent foe of big government, except when they want to be saved from mismanagement, cash shortage, or other natural or manufactured threat. Then, the government's job is to rescue the corporation to save the consumer, even when it comes at great financial or cultural peril to the taxpayer and the individual. This paradox has tremendous power today. Society has invested so heavily socially in corporations that when they fail or are in danger of failing—even if it is due to their own inefficiency—the public must bail them out in order to "restore confidence."

The corporation asks to be put above the public. The required sacrifice—be it tax dollars, undiminished social space, or environmental prosperity—is to guarantee that the market be maintained, that the corporation not die, because too much is at stake. The logic gaining ground in the individual's public and private life has been that the corporation counts more than the individual.

Corporation > Individual

This cultural assumption has led to corporate welfare programs that siphon off taxpayers' resources and dollars for the corporation's benefit. These depend on the brute political force of corporate lobbies but could not succeed without some level of cultural assent. No official figure exists for the government's corporate welfare budget, but one can see the progression in costs soaring into the hundreds of billions of dollars simply by adding up the major bailouts of the corporateer's age: the 1974 Lockheed bailout ($250 million), the 1979 Chrysler bailout ($1.5 billion), and the savings-and-loan bailouts of the late 1980s and early 1990s (more than $500 billion).[17] The ultimate proof of the effectiveness of the logic that "the corporation > the individual" is that a whole host of corporate attributes become more meaningful than those of individuals precisely when the corporation fails to be efficient. This shows that corporate dominance has in many ways outgrown the reasoning that established it. The government would not rescue the family-owned business that failed. The large corporation, however, secured a cultural status that prevented its demise and promoted a logic that could be modified to protect it against its own inefficiency. Among the most significant modifiers:

Corporate Pain > Individual Pain

Since corporate pain is more significant than individual pain, the taxpayer could be asked to pay more than $500 billion to clean up the savings-and-loan scandal rather than the financial industry that created the problem. The S&L industry papered over the problem for years, with politicians, bankers, and accountants turning a blind eye, until the scandal grew so big that the industry did not have the resources to fix the problems it created. Big accounting firms, without whose complicity the S&Ls could not have succeeded in their swindles, should have paid a price, but didn't. Commercial banks designed the bailout plan especially so they would not incur costs. Wall Street brokers, who made a killing marketing both the S&Ls' junk bonds and the government's new taxpayer debt, did not pay. Instead, individuals were forced to.[18] Ironically, the S&L industry had created the conditions of its own demise by successfully lobbying on Capitol Hill for deregulation in the early 1980s. The absence of strict governmental controls permitted the excesses and abuses that led to the savings-and-loan industry's financial failures.

Corporate Risk > Individual Risk

The current tax structure considers corporate risk as greater than the individual's risk. During the booming economy at the end of the 1990s, Goodyear, Texaco, Colgate-Palmolive, MCI WorldCom, and eight other of America's largest corporations took in more than $12.2 billion in profits but none owed corporate income taxes.[19] Over the five-year period from 1996 to 2000, Enron, at the height of its profitability, received a net tax rebate of $381 million. The company paid no income taxes in four of the five years, even though its profits during the period were $1.8 billion.[20] A single worker at any of the companies bore more tax risk than their behemoth employers. These corporations made use of tax loopholes that guaranteed the risk of their business endeavors were limited. Overall, corporate profits jumped from 23.5 percent from 1996 to 1998, but corporate taxes grew just 7.7 percent.[21] The lost tax revenue would have paid for better education, more child care, and other social necessities. While major corporations continue to advocate for bigger tax breaks than individuals have, *The Wall Street Journal* reported that in 2001, corporate income tax revenues accounted for only 8 percent of all IRS collections while individuals' income tax collections made up 53 percent.[22]

Corporate Gain > Individual Gain

When the consumer is not served by the corporation, as with HMOs, the market still must be maintained. Rational solutions to pressing social problems that displace the corporation and market are simply taken off the table. For example, a universal-health-insurance system that does not include corporate overhead and profit is seen as an unacceptable solution, despite the fact that the rest of the industrial world has lower cost, higher quality health care because of it, according to a 2001 World Health Organization report.[23]

Such logic endangers not just the individual's money and services, but also their societal freedoms. California's electricity crisis, a national fiasco during 2001, when the lights repeatedly went off in the world's fifth largest and most technologically advanced economy, was caused by this line of reasoning. The crisis was not precipitated by the supply of and demand for electricity, but by a growing market for the new logic.

The Real Power Crisis: The Market Must Be Maintained

There had been no forced statewide blackouts in California since World War II until the winter of 2001. By January of that year—three years into a four-year transition to full statewide electricity deregulation—California's so-called "utility restructuring" law had largely phased out public controls over the wholesale price and supply of electricity. Although only eight months earlier the law was being touted by utilities as a powerful consumer tool, the deregulated electricity system was falling apart.[24]

That Californians' electricity might be deregulated in the first place would hardly have been fathomable to previous generations of public leaders. They understood better than this generation that there were certain necessities of life that the market should not control because its vicissitudes can endanger individuals' basic needs, such as keeping traffic lights working or keeping the lights on in an operating room. During the last two decades of the twentieth century, however, that social philosophy of an inviolate public domain protecting the individual's right to security—and maintaining immovable barriers to interfering with it—was rewritten by the new logic of corporate efficiency. The rationale for deregulation of electricity was that the unregulated market could reduce prices and increase access to supply through innovation. Standards that secured legal obligations to the public for reasonable electricity pricing and reliable supplying—such as price controls and government mandates for producers to keep electricity flowing—were replaced with new market incentives for both.

As part of the transition to deregulation, a new sector of independent energy producers, Wall Street–backed corporations, emerged to buy the conventional power plants from the regulated utility companies. The regional utility, in the deregulated market, still delivered the power to homes and businesses but had to buy it on the market from the independent energy producers that now owned the old utility plants. Under deregulation, the legal obligation of energy-producing corporations to supply affordable electricity was replaced with no more than a market incentive to do so. Unlike their utility counterparts, neither the prices these power generators could charge nor the amount of power these plants would produce were regulated by the state. As a result, almost as soon as it started, the system went haywire with artificial shortages and unprecedented profiteering. Some generators saw as much as 600 percent increases in profit.[25]

San Diego, which was the first region to fully deregulate in California, saw electricity rates quadruple during the summer of 2000.[26] Small businesses and restaurants were threatened with closure. Seniors could not afford to turn on their air-conditioning despite the heat. However, defying the economic logic proposed to explain these price spikes, the summer demand for electricity was actually lower than the previous year.[27] The new power producers had no consideration for the societal need to keep seniors cool and small businesses open. They charged whatever the market would bear, not what society needed or deemed reasonable. The situation was so grave that my colleagues and I were forced to go to the legislature for a temporary rate freeze in the autumn of 2000, which was enacted, though San Diego ratepayers will likely be forced to absorb the utility's costs over time.

Our consumer group entered the deregulation debate two years prior with an unsuccessful ballot effort to undermine a massive utility-company bailout contained in the original deregulation law. The power of the logic "corporation risk > individual risk" was clear under California's 1996 electricity deregulation scheme. In exchange for the public receiving the benefits of a private market, residential and small business ratepayers were required to pay off the utilities' "stranded assets." These were debts from dirty, economically unsound power plants, including nuclear, which were bad investments for the utilities. By 2001, a $23 billion bailout of bad corporate debt had been paid off by rate-payers.[28] The promised benefits of the private market, however, never materialized. By Christmas of that year, all Californians faced a growing crisis of access and price as the profits of independent power generators under deregulation skyrocketed. The less supply available, the higher the price spiked. The market incentives were precisely for power producers to keep plants off-line, which created artificial shortages that sent the speculative price of electricity sky-high. An unprecedented number of power plants were suddenly shut down for "maintenance problems" at the height of the crisis—246 percent more megawatts off-line in November 2000 than in November 1999, and 348 percent more in April 2001 than in the previous April. Workers at one of these power plants later testified before a state Senate committee that equipment to repair the operation was delivered, but disappeared.[29] On some temperate December days, the price of energy was more than 3,000 percent of the actual costs of producing it.[30] Such price gouging was later confirmed by the findings of state and federal regulators. The chairwoman of the California Public Utilities Commission testified before Congress that Enron's subsidiaries had engaged in sham transactions during the crisis to artificially inflate the price of electricity.[31] At the same April 2002 hearing, the head of the California Power Authority, David Freeman, concurred that "the so-called invisible hand of Adam Smith was Enron and their fellow gougers picking the pockets of Californians to the tune of billions of dollars."[32] Internal Enron memos released by federal regulators in May 2002 confirmed that California's energy crisis was artificially created by power-company manipulation through strategies dubbed by Enron "Death Star," "Fat Boy," and "Get Shorty." Ironically, the Enron memos were written in December 2000 at precisely the moment our consumer group was calling for an end to deregulation because of the very gaming of the system acknowledged in the internal Enron memo from December 6, 2000.

- Enron created apparent shortages in order to get paid for unnecessary power. According to the memo, "The answer is to artificially increase ('inc') the load [the demand] on the schedule submitted to the ISO [Independent System Operator]." In other words, Enron artificially "congested" the system in order to raise the price of energy.

- Enron created real shortages by temporarily moving power out of state to increase prices. "Such exports may have contributed to California's Stage 2 Emergency yesterday."

- Enron got paid by the state "a congestion fee" for relieving the artificial congestion that it created. "Enron gets paid for moving energy to relieve congestion without actually moving any energy or relieving congestion."

- Enron worked with other power companies to game the system. "Enron's traders have used these nicknames with traders from other companies to identify these strategies."

While California's private utility companies had to pay exorbitant wholesale prices to companies like Enron for power that was no longer regulated, the rates they could charge customers were still frozen until certain thresholds for the retirement of utility debt were achieved. This turns out to be the chief irony of the California energy crisis: The utility-crafted deregulation froze consumer rates above 1996 market rates to protect the utilities from the downward price pressure of a competitive electric market, which worked brilliantly for two-and-a-half years. The power companies, however, exposed the utilities' hubris in the end by creating not a market-driven price war but cartel-driven price spikes. This left the utilities exposed to—and the ratepayer, at least temporarily, protected from—the unregulated marketplace.

Just days before Christmas 2000, one of the state's newly deregulated utility corporations announced that it would turn the holiday lights out on 11 million people unless it immediately received a double-digit rate increase. For the first time in history, a corporation was about to hold Christmas hostage.

That the plug would be pulled on Christmas, when businesses were closed and demand for energy was low, was hardly a coincidence, or a product of the law of supply and demand. The company, Southern California Edison, said it would take the step to save money, which it claimed to be running out of in California's newly deregulated electricity market, even though it had just paid out dividends on its stock, spent two years on an international buying spree of power plants, and kicked back $4.8 billion to its parent corporation.[33] In fact, the announcement was a tactical move. Turning on a Christmas tree is a potent symbol of freedom in the American way of life. By threatening to turn off the holiday lights, Edison no doubt believed it had the ultimate leverage over California governor Gray Davis and other politicians, who would not want to be remembered for a dark Christmas. A *Los Angeles Times* report just before Christmas showed that the power crisis was about not just money but core freedoms of access to a necessity of life that was once a public possession. "[Governor] Davis could direct the National Guard and California Highway Patrol to seize power plants within the state borders and order that they supply electricity," the *Times* reported four days before Christmas, evoking a scene more reminiscent of a civil-rights struggle than a price dispute.[34]

The logic of the corporateer had created the standoff. The belief that private corporations like Enron would be the engines of efficiency was so fervent that not a single state legislator voted against giving them control over electricity when the deregulation law was approved in 1996. Although the utility companies claimed in 2000 that they were the victims of the deregulation law, they actually lobbied for it and spent $40 million to maintain it by opposing the 1998 California Proposition 9, which was authored by my colleague Harvey Rosenfield to stop parts of the deregulation law. Deceived by the utility companies' advertising, three-quarters of California voters chose the vicissitudes of the market and a $23 billion bill of bad corporate debt for themselves rather than Prop 9. What the public did not understand was that the market would not operate for society, because the corporation had every incentive to make it work only for itself. For the same reasons that generators had no incentive to bring existing plants back on-line, private generators had no market incentive to build new plants, because the less power there was, the more they could charge for existing power.

Although rate increases were not immediately granted, the lights stayed on at Christmas. Three weeks later, however, the day the first tax-payer bailout package was to be heard in the legislature, rolling blackouts darkened much of the state. On the second day of rolling blackouts, the legislature approved (this time with two dissenting votes) what my colleague Harvey called "an $800 million ransom to keep the lights on, blackout blackmail." From then on, the public spigot was open and $2 billion flowed out before Valentine's day. The state of California—that is, the taxpayers—began paying the cost of electricity on behalf of the private utility corporations. This was the most inefficient system imaginable. At the height of the crisis, Californians were paying on average 1,000 percent more for electricity than the previous year, even though Californians, already second in the nation in conservation, month after month demanded less energy than the previous year.[35] In the first six months of 2001, California's treasury bled approximately $10 billion dollars.

Throughout the crisis, sensible solutions advocated by my colleagues Harvey Rosenfield and Doug Heller confronted the logic that "corporate pain > individual pain."

- Anything and everything would be done to keep the utilities out of bankruptcy because the market had to be saved, even if it meant the second taxpayer bailout in five years.

- Any solution had to be acceptable to Wall Street, the utilities, and the power producers, even if they had caused the crisis.

- While public audits showed that the parent companies of the state's two major utility companies received billions of dollars from their subsidiaries, and paid the money out in dividends, the parent companies would not be responsible for returning those dollars. Indeed, the regulatory decision that authorized the creation of a parent company required that the "capital requirements of the utility . . . shall be given the first priority" by the new parent company, but the local utility subsidiaries were laid to waste, with the public left to clean up the mess.[36]

- Without a public bailout of the private market, a domino effect would occur, and first California's economy then the national economy would go down the toilet.

That the logic was inefficient economically mattered little. Profitability was to be the private realm of the corporation, and risk would be the social responsibility of the public. Only under this logic could the governor's spokeswoman justify the state hiring consultants also under contract with Edison to develop a public bailout of the company: "Edison and the Governor's Office have the same goal."[37] The logic mandated a public bailout because, absent the market, the private power producer, and the utility corporation, there was no alternative. The discredited government would have to assume the function of producing and distributing electricity. As Davis told the *Los Angeles Times,* "It's very important that utilities not go into bankruptcy, primarily because they know best how to keep the lights on."[38] (This ignored the fact that while lights were going out under the private utilities' watch, municipally owned public utilities like the Los Angeles Department of Water and Power faced no blackouts or price spikes during the crisis.) Governor Davis had tough public talk for the profiteering energy producers in his 2001 State of the State speech, but he ultimately conceded, paying the power companies' price in the short term and, in the long term, signing contracts that locked Californians into above-market prices for a decade (and, in one contract, twenty years). Davis subscribed whole-heartedly to the "domino" theory perpetuated by the energy industry and Wall Street. He stated:

> I reject the irresponsible notion that we can afford to allow our major utilities to go bankrupt. Our fate is tied to their fate. Bankruptcy would mean that millions of Californians would be subject to electricity blackouts. Public safety would be jeopardized. Businesses would close. Jobs would be lost. Investment would flee the state. And our economy would suffer a devastating blow.[39]

The death of the corporation would not be allowed. Other options were available: The state could take over the power producers' plants under eminent domain or through temporary, emergency commandeering, and the public would only have to pay a fair and reasonable price to the company for the plant. If the utility companies did go through bankruptcy, the ratepayers may have paid nothing for their debts and the lights would stay on via court order. However, under both scenarios the power producers would not have been paid according to their demands, the utility corporations would look very different, and the Wall Street banks that held the utility debt would not have recovered all their money. Letting the corporation and market die was, therefore, unthinkable.

This logic aligned every major player in the capital markets against a tiny group of consumer advocates, led by Harvey and Doug, who were trying to stop the bailout. To safeguard the market they financed, Wall Street was complicit in what amounted to economic blackmail of the state of California—claiming it would not lend money to utilities to buy California's energy without rate increases being approved. This was dubbed a "capital strike," where money, rather than labor, stops working. Wall Street demanded that taxpayers bail out the utilities and pay off the power generators or the state's economy would be brought down. At the same time, Standard & Poor's, the Wall Street rating service, downgraded the utilities' credit rating so that they could not borrow money to buy power without immediate rate relief. The day after the first 9 percent rate increase was approved by the Public Utility Commission, Wall Street analysts claimed it was simply not enough.[40] Only a huge rate increase would keep the lights on. Wall Street took its case to the state capitol in Sacramento. As the governor and legislators crafted a long-term solution to the energy crisis, the statehouse became "Wall Street West," with an invasion of New York investment bankers playing pivotal roles. Reasonable solutions to the power crisis, such as stringent public controls over price and supply, public ownership of power, or a windfall profits tax (similar to the federal tax imposed on oil companies' excessive profits twenty years earlier) suddenly collided with the logic "the corporation > the individual" in every corner of the state capitol.

Every decision maker in the process had a financial incentive to maintain the market. This included the advisors to Governor Davis who negotiated long-term contracts with the power producers while holding significant stock in the energy industry. Goldman Sachs, an early advisor to the governor on electricity, was also financially tied to the industry and the California crisis.[41] Credit Suisse First Boston had on its client list power generators that sold electricity to the state, yet its investment bankers drafted industry bailout legislation for California Assembly speaker Bob Hertzberg. The bank was also awaiting repayment of a loan defaulted on by Southern California Edison. Remarkably, it was a Credit Suisse analysis that first revealed the smoking gun of California's manufactured energy crisis. It informed its investors that the rolling blackouts plaguing California were simply a negotiating tool and that the California electric grid was not in real trouble. According to the Credit Suisse analyst:

> [T]he rolling blackouts in California are more likely intended
> to soften up the Legislature and the voters to the need for a rate

increase than they are indicative of a permanent "when the lights went out in California" scenario. (Parenthetically, during the New York City fiscal crisis 25 years ago, we once came up against a Friday deadline when the City would not have cash to make some welfare payments and some police and fire department payrolls on the same day. That prospect helped energize some legislative and banker concessions that got us over the hump. The "unthinkable" rarely will be permitted to happen.)

Relatively soon, some cash infusion to the California public utility system will be accomplished to restore an ongoing flow of power. The alternative is in the category of the "unthinkable."[42]

The corporation was suddenly defining what was "thinkable" and "unthinkable" based on commercial logic, not society's—the ultimate cultural power.

In 1998, Kenneth Lay, then chairman of Enron, which profited greatly from Californians' pain, claimed, "Under open-access restructuring, the end user buys the commodity from competing suppliers at an unregulated price. . . . [T]he reward will be significantly lower rates—as much as 30 to 40 percent below what consumers are paying today."[43] Three years later, in the midst of the California crisis, Lay warned simply that ratepayers "need to see the price signals [a.k.a. pay more] and start modifying behavior to reduce demand until we get new supply."[44] Individuals just had to keep paying more or using less until the corporations got it right. Individuals keep giving and corporations keep taking, because the alternative—regulation or public control—is "unthinkable" for society. What had been this industry's modus operandi for a century became unacceptable in less than a decade.

In the end, when the legislature refused to bail out the utilities, the Davis Administration entered into a legal settlement with one utility that could cost the California ratepayers $4.9 billion.[45]

Even as deregulation was crumbling, big business—Wall Street, generators, and the utilities—retained the power based on the reality they colluded to create. Regardless of the audacity of their request, there would be a bailout simply because they could challenge the perception that California's economy was strong. They could do damage because their cultural status allowed them to shatter "confidence." Confidence is a cultural currency, and the ability to manipulate it is a potent cultural weapon. In California's energy crisis, key players exploited the confidence quotient for their own ends. For instance, restoring confidence in California demanded environmental sacrifice. Suddenly, polluting power plants were brought back on-line, and the state agreed to pay their fines. It never mattered whether the utility corporations really were in trouble, or whether the energy producers would stop doing business with the state if they were not allowed to price gouge, only that the energy industry and its Wall Street bankers contended that this was so. All that mattered was the potential to shatter confidence and do damage.

Even as Californians rebuked the corporations' explanations for the power crisis—throughout the year, *Los Angeles Times* headlines read, "Most Californians Think Electricity Crunch Is Artificial,"[46] and "Power Shortage Not Real, Most Californians Say"[47]—the corporate truth prevailed because it was accepted by opinion leaders and policymakers as incontrovertible.

The position of corporations above the individual in this line of logic gave them the ultimate cultural power—to generate social knowledge and, therefore, "truth."

Corporate Knowledge > Individual Knowledge
Corporate Truth > Individual Truth

Defining cultural knowledge and truth is the ultimate ability to act. By the turn of the twenty-first century, such logic led many of America's largest corporations to believe that they could redefine truth by "cooking their books"—lying about their finances. In California's electricity crisis, the public's representatives allowed proven liars to define the "truth," based on cultural confidence in the corporation. The power to do so resides in a new vocabulary created by the invisible hand to make the corporation's "truth" more real to individuals than their own. When corporations capture language, as they increasingly have, they can change societal "truth" to suit their needs. This is a key element of their cultural control.

Trojan Horses in the Vocabulary

"The great enemy of clear language is insincerity," George Orwell noted. "When there is a gap between one's real and one's declared aims, one turns as it were instinctively to long words and exhausted idioms, like a cuttlefish squirting out ink."[48] The invisible hand has placed many such terms, used to conceal and control, into common parlance. Orwell recognized that "if thought corrupts language, language can also corrupt thought." He saw that a "speaker who uses that kind of phraseology has gone some distance toward turning himself into a machine. The appropriate noises are coming out of his larynx, but his brain is not involved as it would be if he were choosing his words for himself."[49] When individuals use the invisible hand's language, particularly opinion leaders such as reporters, judges, and politicians, the individual—whether knowingly or not—becomes a tool of the corporation.

The invisible hand's language embodies a logic that turns accepted hierarchies of social values on their head, subtly putting the commercial above the social, the corporation over the individual. For instance, in the HMO context, "medical loss ratio" denotes the percentage of every premium dollar paid to an HMO that is used to deliver medical care as opposed to that used to pay for marketing, administrative costs, profits, and CEO compensation. In other words, money spent on medicine is a "loss." The parlance perfectly represents, and transmits with each usage, the corporate-medicine philosophy.

In broad ways, corporateers deploy language that gives them greater possession of cultural knowledge and truth. The types of laden terms that follow allow corporations to appropriate credibility and recourse for their point of view. They are like Trojan horses in our vocabulary. Most of these terms have been invented and promoted through the billions of dollars spent on corporate-fed public relations and political campaigns. When you hear these words, watch out:

Big government. Corporations know that the public often sees the appropriate role of government as protecting the weak from the strong. To label government as "big" is to discredit it as the bully and undermine its role as the protector—the countervailing power to the corporation.

Business climate. Islands and land masses have climates. Businesses have markets. To conjure a business climate is to project the corporation as a ship on a dangerous sea of society. Inappropriate cultural weather can send the business ship adrift, and the right barometric environment can keep it on course. Business becomes the protagonist of the story and society the helper figure or villain depending upon the climate it creates. This changes the order of social value. When necessary, the culture must change for business to thrive. Usually this means tax breaks, removing regulatory protections, or limiting legal liability for the corporation.

Business incentive. Read tax reduction, tax loophole, or tax credit for corporations to have an incentive to continue to make more profit.

Chilling effect. This is the climatic curse for corporations. The freeze is usually said to be caused by taxes, regulatory protections for the public, or the public's right to legal remedies for unfair business practices. Removing these mechanisms has its own "chilling effect" on the public's safety, powers, and bank account (because other taxpayers pay more when corporations pay less), but these are never spoken of in such terms.

Choice. This is *the* buzzword that the early-twenty-first-century corporateer uses to rationalize the most choice-less policies. For example, the "drive-thru" baby delivery, where newborns and their mothers were discharged as early as eight hours after birth, was lauded, in an internal memo from the nation's largest HMO to its staff, entitled, "Positive Thoughts Regarding the Eight Hour Discharge."[50] The benefits were enumerated as giving mothers the choice of "unlimited visitors at home," better food because "hospital food is not tasty," and "better quality sleep at home in familiar bed and environment," despite the significant health risks of jaundice and dehydration to the baby. Mothers were given no choice, of course. A Newt Gingrich–controlled Congress ultimately had to act, to prevent HMOs and hospitals from giving consumers so much "choice," by placing a forty-eight-hour floor on discharges. Similarly, telecommunications giant AT&T used the "choice" rationale to keep high-speed, broad-band Internet hookups owned by the company closed to other Internet providers. The highly successful AT&T rap, which was targeted at local governmental bodies dealing with the cable industry in Los Angeles and elsewhere, was that the Internet had grown precisely because regulators had not directed its growth and created "forced access."[51] The Hands Off the Internet campaign literature called upon the public to: "Encourage local officials not to regulate access to the Internet; instead they should allow consumers to choose the winners and losers of the high-speed Internet market." In other words, keep the market closed, by allowing access only to the network of services that owns the hookup, to keep it free. "Choice" is not really what the individual thinks it is—access to any provider—but what the corporation redefines it as.

Cost of business. Read, the justification for huge profits, lavish executive compensation, extravagant junkets, as well as unexpected service fees. (As former chief executive Al Dunlap said, "Most CEOs are ridiculously overpaid, but I deserved the $100 million I took away when Scott merged with Kimberly-Clark."[52])

Deep pocket. This has become a buzzword used to turn the tables on an individual injured who seeks legal redress against a big corporation. No longer is the corporation the wrongdoer, but the "deep pocket"— taken to court for their money, not their conduct.

Economic growth. Encouraging economic growth has been the justification for promoting socially questionable policies—such as tax credits for oil companies to find oil so they can make private profits from it. Economic growth has become so equated with progress of all kinds—social, technological, personal—that it is encouraged often at significant social costs, such as suburban sprawl, toxic dumps, dishonesty in accounting standards, and economic inequities. "The economic accounting system by which economic growth is measured makes no comparable adjustment for the depletion of social and natural capital," writes David Korten in his book *When Corporations Rule the World.* "For example, the costs of cleaning up the Exxon Valdez oil spill on the Alaska coast and the costs of repairing damage from the terrorist attack in New York both counted as net contributions to economic output."[53]

Free market. The holiest dimension in which only the market's own forces command. No individual or their representative should dare challenge its whim. The cultural equivalent of The One Mind, Buddha, Adonai, Mohammad, and The Good Lord—beyond reproach.

Frivolous lawsuit. Many industries have spent lavishly to convince Americans that a "litigation explosion" has become burdensome for society. Sources such as the RAND Institute, however, chart the sharp decrease in civil lawsuits during recent years.[54] The theme has nonetheless resulted in decreased rights for individuals, which is investigated in the next chapter. Interestingly, business-to-business litigation is rarely ever characterized as "frivolous," and corporations never work to curb their own rights to take anyone to court.

Government takeover. This is the standard tag line for disguised campaigns against legislating better business practices. For instance, the notion that a Medicare prescription drug benefit would put "big government in your medicine cabinet" was the tag line for the Pharmaceutical Research and Manufacturers of America's successful 1999 television campaign to stop the benefit.[55] The industry operated under the name

"Citizens for Better Medicare." Another group, "Taxpayers Against a Government Takeover," is an insurer-funded political action committee I have battled with over health care reform in California. The demonized government bureaucrat may not be the model of effectiveness, but it is usually far more benign than the corporate bureaucrat.

Job killers. Industry lobbies have used this bullet to stop reforms that create better business practices, such as upping the minimum wage, creating greater workplace safety, and even putting restrictions on HMOs. "Lost jobs" is always the reason given for maintaining the status quo in the business climate, no matter how far removed from reality this claim is.

Liberal media. You rarely hear the terms "corporate media" or "conservative media." That may be because corporations and politicians with strong corporate contributions and connections have stigmatized a "liberal media." The corporate owners of the most media, however, exercise the most control over its agenda, as we will explore in Chapter 7.

Pro-business politician. Public acceptance of the phrase has legitimized the notion that corporations are entitled to the same democratic representation as individuals, even though corporations do not vote and are not citizens.

Restructuring. Be it in a company or industry, this is code for major bloodletting and change—be it massive layoffs or changes in established practices, such as cutting production and boosting marketing. Restructuring is the real job killer. "Creative destruction" is the oxymoron often used to rationalize the blood, because only by destroying today's job will tomorrow's be born.

Shareowner value. In fact, the average investor *holds* shares, not *owns* them, since they have little input into the corporation's decision-making. Shareowner implies ownership rights that do not exist. Why did "value for the shareowner" become the buzz of the 1990s among executives instead of the interests of the shareholder? If small shareholders were the real owners, why did they not have control? Holding shares was once regarded as an entitlement to control, however illusory. But since the 1990s, "value for the shareowner" has been the sole object of business. The shareholder is not guaranteed a right to be heard at the annual meeting or to access all the information about corporate dealings. They own money rather than holding a proxy for control. The shareowner can sell the share, but they will be hard pressed to find a corporation that operates differently. The chairman and CEO of The Coca-Cola Company, Robert Goizueta, asked and answered the question, Why shareowner value? "Increasing shareowner value over time is the job society demands of us. . . . I believe it would be wrong, perhaps even arrogant, for a business to think it can be all things to all people. We have one job: to generate a fair return for our owners, who have entrusted their assets to us."[56] This presumption reflects a larger shift in the belief that corporations have no social duties, only economic ones.

Union bosses. Labor unions, as among the most powerful countervailing forces on corporate practices, are being transformed in our language from heroic representatives of the weak, who coalesce for strength through unions, into corrupt bullies. Other corporate opponents are similarly smeared. Attorneys representing the injured become "ambulance chasers" and conservationists become "elitist environmentalists." As discussed in more detail in Chapter 5, workers themselves are being redefined as corporate loyalists through new assignments as "cast members" at Disney, "team members" at other companies and compensation programs, such as bio-tech company Monsanto's move to tie all 27,000 employees' pay to the rise in its stock price. The experts from Price Waterhouse who interviewed the nation's top corporate executives explain, "Management has a new freedom to demand that workers intimately identify with their corporations and commit themselves completely to its goals, thus freely producing and creating to the maximum."[57]

These types of labels have grown beyond mere terms into forces that shape individuals and their society, as the next chapters explain. The vocabulary has helped create structural remodeling of basic societal institutions that now increasingly reflect the corporateer's priorities rather than serve the individual and protect his or her freedom.

PART TWO

THE
MEANS
OF
CONTROL

CAPTURING JUSTICE, EDUCATION, AND COMMUNITY

Like an answer, the three slogans on the white face of the Ministry of Truth came back at him:

WAR IS PEACE
FREEDOM IS SLAVERY
IGNORANCE IS STRENGTH
—GEORGE ORWELL, *1984*

During the last two decades, the invisible hand of the corporation has sought to capture and control the most pivotal institutions in the determination of culture, consciousness, and individual freedom. Among these are the justice system, the educational system, and the public spaces that define community. Until the 1980s, these areas were strictly the province of a civic culture determined by individuals and their works. The individual was not routinely asked to waive her legal rights as a condition of commerce, as mandatory binding arbitration agreements demand today. Corporations did not interject commercial messages into the public school classroom, as a September 2000 U.S. General Accounting Office report documented,[1] or into the home, with marketing messages on answering machines. Public space was the individual's and society's, not the market's—a philosophy resulting in bans on billboard advertising on highways inspired by Lady

Bird Johnson and in parks, art festivals, and museums being free from commercial sponsorship. No more.

The global triumph of capitalism over communism in the 1980s emboldened corporateers to target key societal institutions that had previously been taboo. Ironically, these were the same societal pressure points exploited by George Orwell's fictional communist regime in *1984* to control national culture and subvert the individual's rights: justice, education, and community.

The corporateer takeover of justice, education, and community is far from complete, but it has created popular empathy for the corporation and its needs. As the next sections show, one consequence of the corporateer strategy has been to inanimate the individual so that individuals do not use their legal rights, do not value their civic community as much, and do not think of childhood education as separate from commerce. In many legislative battles I have fought, the corporation has often won support from key individuals for taking away the individual's legal right to hold the corporation accountable, the individual's right to join a union, and the government's right to regulate corporations for the individual's safety. If corporateers are able to turn the individual against the institutions that affirm his freedoms, then they can remake the individual into the corporation's image of him, just as Orwell portrayed the remaking of the individual in his fictitious communist state of Oceania.

The main difference has been that corporateers have proposed a forced purchase of the individual's rights. Framing the proposition of capturing justice, education, and community as a commercial exchange conceals the fact that it is a cultural power grab. The result has been the same. Individuals who wish to exercise their freedoms in these institutions are still bound by decisions made by a few judges, politicians, or executives that have adopted the corporateer logic. The framing of the capture as a purchase, however, implies free will, even if the individual really has no choice if she wants to send her child to public school, enjoy a public space, or have both health coverage and the right to trial.

That is why capturing the individual's consciousness about the key institutions became an integral part of the invisible hand's work. The individual's perspective had to be aligned with the corporation's if corporateers were to change society for their benefit.

Orwell understood that to conquer, one must first surround. *1984* showed the power of ubiquitous slogans and subtexts echoing through key societal institutions to change the individual and his culture. Corporateers have applied similar, though subtler, tactics. The invisible hand, subliminal voice, and mind machine have made these beliefs reverberate through the institutions and consciousness of modern society.

LEGAL JUSTICE IS FRIVOLOUS

CHILDREN ARE CUSTOMERS

THE CORPORATION IS THE COMMUNITY

The power of these concepts have fundamentally altered institutions at the heart of American democracy.

Frivolous Justice

The legal system has more than its share of problems. It can be time-consuming, frustrating, expensive, emotionally draining, and, at times, unreasonable. Still, the judicial branch has been the only remaining branch of government where the average person can reasonably expect to routinely succeed at taking on the rich and powerful. In many cases, the invisible hand has succeeded at limiting liability for corporations, taking the individual's right to trial and removing the person's right to recover damages against a corporation. For example, in 1987, the U.S. Supreme Court ruled, at the request of insurance-industry lawyers, that injured consumers who receive insurance through their job could not recover any damages from their insurer for denying a legitimate claim.[2] Such changes have removed the corporation's accountability to society and to the individual, confining corporate accountability to the market. Whatever the market bears, society also has to. Lawsuits have changed social policy. For example, without *Brown v. Board of Education*, Southern schools would not have been desegregated. The legal system has also been a primary protector of the individual's health and safety. One corporate-funded group found that the individual's right to recover damages against corporations for dangerous and defective products (called product-liability lawsuits) has changed corporate decision-making about the safety of its products. The Conference Board reported in a 1987 study of 232 risk managers of large American corporations that "[w]here product liability has had a notable impact—where it has most significantly affected management decision-making—has been in the quality of the products themselves. Managers say products have become safer, manufacturing procedures have been improved, and labels and use instructions have become more explicit."[3] The reason is what the public has already learned in court about corporate conduct, a scrutiny other corporations do not wish to face. The following cases reflect the power of legal exposure:

- The 1970 case of a four-year-old burned badly by highly flammable pajamas showed that the manufacturer knew more than ten years earlier that the fabric was flammable. At trial, the corporation argued that warning the public would curb sales by stigmatizing the product. A letter from a company official, exposed during trial, explained that the company would not treat the fabric with flame-retardant chemicals until federal law required it because it was not cost-effective.[4] After trial, the company stopped selling the pajamas, and Congress enacted tougher protections for flammable pajamas.

- The Dalkon Shield IUD was a birth-control device used during the 1970s that had a tendency to trap bacteria in the uterus and cause infections, spontaneous abortions, infertility, and death. The manufacturer, A. H. Robins, received dozens of reports of spontaneous abortions. It defended the product, even after the Food and Drug Administration ordered the device removed from the market in June 1974, until incurring eleven punitive-damage awards throughout the 1980s totaling more than $24.8 million. Then, the corporation urged doctors and women to remove the device, and even paid for its removal.[5]

- A lawsuit filed in 1998 on behalf of a worker who contracted leukemia after continual exposure to electromagnetic pulse radiation (EMP) showed that The Boeing Company knew since the 1970s that such prolonged exposure was lethal. Evidence demonstrated that Boeing had used employees in EMP radiation research for the Department of Defense. After settling the case, Boeing minimized employee exposure to EMP radiation, implemented an employee health-monitoring program, and warned employees of exposure risks.[6]

By discrediting the legal system, the corporateer can evade such societal accountability. That may be why the corporateer attack on the individual's legal rights has typically targeted "frivolous lawsuits," "trial lawyers," and "activist judges." For example, President George W. Bush adopted the HMO industry's argument in opposing 2001 patients' rights legislation passed by the U.S. Senate because business "should be shielded from unnecessary and frivolous lawsuits."[7] Similarly, Bush's 2002 plan to suspend laws requiring environmental review of logging projects was based on the timber industry's complaints about frivolous lawsuits.[8] One consequence, at least, of the corporate campaign against the legal system has been acquiescence to corporateer-backed laws that limit the individual's access to justice but do not restrict the corporations' trial lawyers and lawsuits.

Corporateer campaigns in statehouses, Congress, and the courts have resulted in tangible losses for the individual.

- Industries have been granted special immunity from legal accountability that no individual enjoys. For example, a California law gave immunity to the tobacco industry for all its misconduct between 1988 and 1998.[9] The cigarette makers' immunity was dubbed "the napkin deal" because politicians and lobbyists scrawled the details on a napkin at Frank Fat's restaurant in Sacramento. In twenty-six states, auto insurers have won immunity for not paying a legitimate claim (a practice called "bad faith") to an innocent accident victim hit by a company policyholder. The most notable example is the blanket protection from prosecution provided by the U.S. Supreme Court in 1987 for HMOs and insurers that deny legitimate claims if a private employer pays for coverage.[10] (By contrast, government-paid insurers are liable.) The epidemic of HMO abuses can be partially explained in this context, as can the bipartisan support in 2002 for an HMO patients' bill of rights to remedy the problem.

• The contingency-fee system has permitted injured individuals to obtain legal representation without hourly fees because the attorney takes a percentage of the recovery as a fee, typically one-third. If the individual does not win the case, the attorney receives nothing. Corporateers have legislated in some states strict limits on what percentage of damages an attorney can recover in fees, discouraging attorneys from taking many legitimate cases that do not have the potential for large damages. For example, in California and New York, an attorney's contingency fee is limited in negligence cases filed against hospitals.[11] It's an ironic position for corporations that have vigorously defended their absolute right to contract for anything and refused any cap on executive compensation.

• So-called "safe harbors" have been enacted by Congress and state legislatures for certain industries so that they cannot be held legally accountable. For example, in 1995 the U.S. Senate overrode President Clinton's veto to enact legislation giving accountants a "safe harbor" from liability to investors for securities fraud. The Senate ignored the warnings of my friend Jeri Mellon, head of the Lincoln Bondholders' Association, in the *New York Times* Op-Ed page days before Clinton's veto: "If this bill had been in

place when the bonds sold by Lincoln Savings and Loan Association turned worthless overnight, people like me—the victims of
Charles H. Keating and his professional accomplices—could not
have recovered most of our lost life savings."[12] The victims of
2002's corporate crime wave had to live with the consequences.

• Increasingly, corporations have advocated eliminating "non-
   economic" recovery in lawsuits, which is damages not for medical
   bills or lost wages but for an individual's pain and suffering from
   an injury that is not her fault. An example of "non-economic"
   damages is, if a woman lost her fertility due to the use of the
   Dalkon Shield, there would be no economic damages, only compensation for her "non-economic" loss, her physical trauma,
   emotional distress, and other pain and suffering.

Through Steven's Eyes

On this last point, the limited-liability movement has been about more
than just restricting the ability of individuals to have their day in court
and hold corporations accountable. Applying a one-size-fits-all limit to
non-economic damages objectifies and erases the person, considering
him as a fixed "thing" for the purposes of law so that there is no recognition of the uniqueness of his suffering. There is no quicker way to
strip an individual of his humanity than to fail to recognize his suffering. Corporateer legal maneuvers have accomplished just this. My personal bias on this point springs from the experiences of a friend who, at
the time of publication, is twelve years old. Steven Olsen is blind and
brain-damaged because, as a jury ruled, he was a victim of medical
negligence when he was two years old.[13] He fell on a stick in the woods
while hiking. Under the family's HMO plan, the hospital pumped up
Steven with steroids and sent him away, although his parents had asked
for a CAT scan because they knew Steven was not well. Steven returned
to the hospital comatose. At trial, medical experts testified that had he

received the $800 CAT scan, which would have detected a growing brain abscess, he would have his sight and be healthy today. The jury awarded $7.1 million in "non-economic" damages for Steven's avoidable life of darkness and suffering. The jury, however, was not told of a two-decade-old $250,000 cap on non-economic damages in the state. The judge was forced to reduce the amount to $250,000. The jurors found out that their verdict had been reduced only by reading about it in the newspaper. Jury foreman Thomas Kearns expressed his dismay in a letter to *The San Diego Union-Tribune.*

> We viewed video of Steven, age 2, shortly before the accident. This beautiful child talked and shrieked with laughter as any other child at play. Later, Steven was brought to the court, and we watched as he groped, stumbled and felt his way along the front of the jury box. There was no chatter or happy laughter. Steven is doomed to a life of darkness, loneliness and pain. He is blind, brain damaged and physically retarded. He will never play sports, work, or enjoy normal relationships with his peers. His will be a lifetime of treatment, therapy, prosthesis fitting and supervision around the clock. . . .
>
> Our medical-care system has failed Steven Olsen, through inattention or pressure to avoid costly but necessary tests. Our legislative system has failed Steven, bowing to lobbyists of the powerful American Medical Association (AMA) and the insurance industry, by the Legislature enacting an ill-conceived and wrongful law. Our judicial system has failed Steven, by acceding to this tilting of the scales of justice by the Legislature for the benefit of two special-interest groups. . . .
>
> I think the people of California place a higher value on life than this.[14]

When in San Diego, I often visit Steven and his family. Their struggles are unfathomable to me. In 2001, Steven had 74 doctor visits, 164 physical- and speech-therapy appointments, and three trips to the emergency room. And his parents say that was a good year because Steven was not hospitalized. Steven's mother, Kathy, had to leave her job because caring for Steven is a full-time job. She has to struggle constantly with the school district for Steven to receive special-education classes. One day, Steven ate a lightbulb, typical of the kind of problems faced by children with brain injuries. He has to be watched constantly. Corporate executives that seek to limit jury awards for the individual's pain and suffering claim society must do so to save money. Yet these executives typically make millions every year without any of Steven Olsen's pain and suffering. Limiting their responsibility for the pain of individuals reduces not only the corporation's accountability but also the worth of the individual to that of a mere object.

The language of the corporate campaign against the individual's legal rights itself conceives of the corporation's humanlike frailties and sensitivity to damage. The corporation must be protected from a "litigation explosion." The individual becomes a dangerous thing responsible for explosions. "Despite all the rhetoric about litigiousness, empirical research shows that Americans are not all that litigious," stated Deborah R. Hensler, director of the RAND Institute for Civil Justice—an arm of the RAND Corporation, which is funded heavily by corporate contributions—at a seminar for corporate lawyers in 1994.[15] The Institute conducted a comprehensive study of injured Americans in the 1980s and found that only 2 percent of those injured sought recovery through lawsuits. During the 1970s and 1980s, approximately 3 percent of those injured filed lawsuits. University of Wisconsin law professor Marc Galanter, a student of lawsuit patterns, observed that litigation rates were higher in colonial and pre-twentieth-century America than at the height of the so-called "litigation explosion."[16] In the late 1980s and 1990s, lawsuits over wrongful acts or injuries not covered by a contract, "torts" in legal parlance, declined precisely as corporateers were escalating their efforts to limit the individual's right to utilize the legal system. For instance, Galanter found that between 1985 and 1991 (excluding suits relating to asbestos exposure), the number of product-liability cases in federal courts fell by 40 percent, from 8,268 cases to 4,992. During the same period of time, nearly half of all federal lawsuits filed involved inter-business disputes.[17] The National Center for State Courts reported that in state trial courts in 1992, less than 2 percent of all cases were tort cases.[18] Such facts, however, have not deterred corporateers in seeking tort reform (or as my colleagues call it, "tort deform") or popular acceptance of the invention of a litigation explosion. Not surprisingly, none of the legal restrictions ever fall upon corporations, although business-to-business litigation is the highest growth area.

From my perspective of dealing with aggrieved consumers, one consequence of the corporateer's discrediting of the justice system has been the creation of a cultural stigma for individuals who choose to file lawsuits to fight corporate misconduct. The relatively small number of lawsuits during the 1990s may be directly related to a cultural climate in which individuals are more inclined to give up than to fight. Unfortunately for society, the cultural climate created by the invisible hand has become hostile to individuals who stand up for themselves and exercise their legal rights, a far cry from the spirit of the colonial period when Americans went to war over King George usurping their legal rights.

Buying Judges

Corporateers have begun targeting for electoral defeat judges who don't speak their language. In October 2000, the U.S. Chamber of Commerce announced it was spending more than $1 million for advertising in state supreme court races to educate voters about judicial candidates who "might overrule so-called tort reform legislation," according to *The New York Times*.[19] The Chamber said it would advertise in seven states and had already contributed to its Michigan affiliate's advertising campaign for the state's supreme court elections. Jim Wootton, president of the Institute for Legal Reform at the Chamber, refused to disclose the budget for such advertising by state affiliates, but said it was

less than $10 million. The U.S. Chamber advertised heavily for "tort re-
form" in pivotal states such as Ohio, where a state supreme court judge
who struck down a tort reform law as illegal was up for re-election.
Crossing a cultural divide that had always existed, the effort was the
Chamber's first intervention in state judicial politics. No activity in
modern times more closely mirrors the American colonists' complaint
of "making judges dependent upon his will alone."

Remarkably, the Chamber claimed its advertisements were simply
educational and not subject to election reporting requirements and
contribution limits. A federal judge in Mississippi disagreed. U.S. District Judge Henry Wingate ruled that the advertisements "offer thinly
veiled exhortations" to support candidates for the Mississippi Supreme
Court and, while not specifically calling for any judge's election, used
words viewers could not mistake as an endorsement by describing the
candidate as someone who "will use common sense, ensure prompt ad-
judication of death penalty cases and uphold victims' rights."[20] In response, a defiant Wootton claimed the ads "were clearly proper and
within the Chamber's constitutionally protected free speech rights."[21]
By April 2002, Wootton had won a victory in a federal court, which
overturned the decisions based on the logic that the corporation's federal free speech rights trumped Mississippi's elections law. "This is not
only a huge victory for the U.S. Chamber but for anyone who cares
deeply about protecting the constitutional right to free speech."[22]

In Ohio, state-based business groups spent considerably more than
the candidates for the judgeships themselves to influence the election.
Citizens for a Strong Ohio, a business group, spent $1.7 million to elect
Republican Judge Terrence O'Donnell, who spent only $500,000 but
was the opponent of Democratic Justice Alice Robie Resnik.[23] Resnik
authored the legal opinion that a state statute restricting victims' recovery violated the Ohio state constitution and was "an attack on the
judiciary as a coordinate branch of government." Resnick said the
Chamber's advertising threatened society with the proposition that "you
can buy a seat on the Supreme Court."[24] Fortunately, she withstood the

Chamber's attack ads and was re-elected. However, the Chamber knows that whether it wins or loses the specific race, such efforts always win the bigger battle by letting all judges know the extent big business is willing to go to defend its interests in a restricted judicial branch.

The Center for Justice & Democracy and Public Citizen, both public interest groups, charted such increasingly aggressive and deceptive corporate tactics to limit the individual's right to justice during the last fifteen years. The groups' November 2000 joint report examined an anti-litigation group called Citizens Against Lawsuit Abuse (CALA) that has chapters in eighteen states. Drawing from tobacco industry papers, which surfaced in national litigation, and other sources, the report revealed the corporate financing and arrangement of "the CALA campaign to manipulate the media, the legislative process, the electoral process and the American public."[25] Among the key findings:

- Since 1991, "'tort reformers' set up tax-exempt groups in at least 18 states to broadcast their mantra of 'lawsuit abuses' with 27 active groups. They claimed to speak for individuals, operating under names such as Citizens Against Lawsuit Abuse, Stop Lawsuit Abuse, Lawsuit Abuse Watch and People for a FAIR Legal System." However, "the money trail from many of these groups leads directly to large corporate donors, including tobacco, insurance, oil and gas, chemical and pharmaceutical companies, medical associations and auto manufacturers."

- Despite CALA's tax-exempt status, since the mid-1990s it has been working with local business associations to "exercise considerable electoral influence" and "to ensure the election of pro-industry state judges and to ensure the defeat of judges who typically support plaintiffs' verdicts or have voted to strike down state tort law restrictions as unconstitutional."

- CALA was born in South Texas in the early 1990s and, in a model that went national, had a "statewide support network that included the Texas Chamber of Commerce, the right-wing Texas

Public Policy Foundation and numerous corporations wishing to shield themselves from consumer lawsuits." Then-Governor George W. Bush was one of Texas CALA's biggest boosters and "raised more than $4 million in his gubernatorial races from organizations and individuals affiliated with Texas 'tort reform' groups."[26]

The Seventh Amendment for Sale

Amendment VII of the U.S. Constitution was the only article of the Bill of Rights unanimously ratified by all the states. It reads:

> In suits at common law, where the value in controversy shall exceed twenty dollars, the right to trial by jury shall be preserved, and no fact tried by a jury shall be otherwise reexamined in any court of the United States, than according to the rules of the common law.
>
> Proposed September 25, 1789; ratified December 15, 1791.

Without a constitutional convention, corporateers have effectively eliminated this right to trial for individuals in all kinds of commercial transactions. Contracts for credit cards, car purchases, health care, bank loans, and real estate transactions frequently contain a mandatory arbitration provision, usually in the fine print. Judges, influenced by the invisible hand's drumbeat and by Congress's enactment of the Federal Arbitration Act at the behest of industries, have shown a preference for mandatory arbitration. Repeatedly, lower court rulings hostile to arbitration have been "depublished" by the state supreme courts, while controversial arbitration clauses have been upheld.[27] In March 2001, the U.S. Supreme Court ruled that companies can force workers into binding arbitration as a condition of employment.

That a corporate contract, particularly one for employment, can now supersede the Seventh Amendment shows that even the founding fathers' most cherished principles have succumbed to the growing commercial needs of corporations to save money and to maintain secrecy. Because arbitrators depend on repeat business from corporate defendants, and some even own stock in defendants' companies,[28] the justice they dole out is rarely as costly as a jury's. Arbitrators know that to rule against a corporation in a significant way can end its relationship to a bread-and-butter client. Such repeat business appears to be the reason that First USA bank—having filed over 50,000 cases with one arbitration firm—has won 99.6 percent of them since 1998, a fact revealed only by data produced in an actual court lawsuit.[29] Most significantly, since the public cannot see corporate abuses in the secret arbitration process, as there is no public record, it cannot hold corporations accountable, or see future dangers.

Discovery, the legal right of an injured party to obtain evidence by which a case can be proven, is not even a right in arbitration, merely in the discretion of the arbitrator. An individual can be precluded from even asking for documents from a corporation that might prove her case. Since there can be no judicial review by a court of an arbitrator's legal errors in states like California, only of outright fraud, an individual can lawfully be denied other traditional legal protections, such as a decision based on legal precedent.

The reasoning in favor of forced arbitration has been that it is more cost-efficient and expeditious. The private justice system has certainly been more cost-effective for the corporation, which does not have to face a jury, and traditionally shares the cost with the consumer.[30] It has hardly been so for the individual, who has to pay for the $200- to $400-per-hour fee of the arbitrator. The *San Francisco Chronicle* reported that arbitrators "can make $10,000 or more a day, in comparison with a Superior Court judge's $133,000-a-year salary," and consumers in arbitration have to pay thousands of dollars in hearing-room and filing fees—compared to state superior court filing fees of between $90 to $185.[31] Nor are prevailing plaintiffs entitled to recover their attorney fees in arbitration, as they sometimes are in court.

There is evidence that arbitration is less expeditious than court as well, particularly when the corporation wants it to be. Individuals lack leverage in the process against large corporations and their well-paid defense attorneys. In one HMO case, in which our consumer group served as an amicus, or "friend of the court," Wilfredo Engalla claimed that doctors at Kaiser, the nation's largest HMO, misdiagnosed his lung cancer as colds and allergies. Engalla's family filed an arbitration claim against the HMO for medical malpractice. After waiting for more than six months for an arbitration hearing, they charged Kaiser with intentionally stalling. By stonewalling, Wilfredo might die and Kaiser could avoid liability for "non-economic " damages, since the dead can collect no money for their pain and suffering. Multi-year data for all Kaiser arbitrations surfaced in the court case Engalla's family pursued after his death. The data showed that Kaiser's service contract promised an arbitrator would be appointed within two months but, on average, it took more than two years. The California Supreme Court ruled, six to one, "There is evidence that Kaiser established a self-administered arbitration system in which delay for its own benefit and convenience was an inherent part, despite express and implied contractual representation to the contrary."[32]

Individuals should have the freedom to arbitrate a dispute, but should they ever be forced to waive the right to trial simply to participate in a market? The logic of "market = society" demands that the societal right be sacrificed for the market. Such lessons are taught today by the invisible hand beginning in early childhood, where the subliminal voices children hear typically do not distinguish between commercial and societal responsibilities.

Kids For Sale

The Judge Baker Children's Center, an affiliate of Harvard Medical School, and researchers at Wheelock College estimated that children influence the spending of about $400 billion annually and elementary school children spend $2.3 billion a year just on snack foods and beverages.[33] Not surprisingly, advertising money directed at children has grown twenty-fold during the last ten years. Corporations spend $12 billion per year marketing to children.[34] During the last two decades, modern corporations have targeted children of all ages with the most ambitious social stimulus-response campaign in American history. Children have been taught the logic of the invisible hand—that everything is for sale, corporations are your friend, and things can be valued more than people. Societal taboos that separated childhood development and the market have been forgotten. The child's consciousness has been put up for sale in schools, in the home, and in the community.

Academic researchers from across the nation contend that this change of social custom has contributed to significant physical and psychological problems among youth. These are among the broad societal consequences associated with the corporate capture of the consciousness of impressionable children who, unlike adults, are often unable to distinguish truth from fiction.

The Fattening of America

Childhood obesity has become a major public-health problem during the last decade. A 1998 study found that children's fast-food diets and immobility due to video games and television placed California teenagers at a greater risk of chronic disease and preventable health problems.[35] Two-thirds of those teenagers interviewed were overweight, half reported having no vegetable the day before, but one-third had at least one fast-food meal. The fast-food industry is the biggest advertiser on television, and McDonald's alone spends $600 million per year on advertising.[36] In 1999, American children accounted for $4.7 billion in candy sales.[37]

Video Violence Begetting Real Violence

U.S. Surgeon General David Satcher reported that young children's repeated exposure to graphic expressions of violence in television programming and video games causes more aggressive behavior throughout a child's life.[38] The lesson has not been heeded by the video traders who have made violence a ubiquitous presence in children's lives. Documents submitted to the Federal Trade Commission showed that major movie studios used underage children to test-market violent films with "R"—for "restricted"—ratings. Children too young to see the movie at a theater without their parents saw in test-screenings movies such as the R-rated *Judge Dredd* and the R-rated horror movie *Disturbing Behavior.*[39] A memo for the main market research group for the studios explained why children ages nine to eleven were interviewed about concepts for the sequel to the slasher film, *I Know What You Did Last Summer:* "There is evidence to indicate that attendance in the original movie dipped down to the age of 10," according to the memorandum from the National Research Group, Hollywood's largest market research firm. "Therefore, it makes sense to interview 10- to 11-year-olds."[40]

Undermining Parental Control

The United States General Accounting Office (GAO) reported in September 2000 that a pervasive corporate presence in schools has aroused community concern about the undermining of parental control and consent.[41] The report found that one-quarter of all middle schools showed Channel One in the classroom, a commercial television broadcast that includes advertising. Two hundred schools had exclusive contracts with soda companies to sell their products. In one case, students using computers in the classroom were given incentives to offer personal data that would then be sold to advertisers. An Internet company called Zapped Me gave schools personal computers with screens that included flashing advertisements and collected general information about students that it made available to its advertisers. The GAO found textbooks using consumer product names, including on their covers; Coke and Pepsi machines in hallways functioning as brand billboards; and a boom in in-school marketing through new school district contracts negotiated between savvy marketers and far more naïve district officials. U.S. Representative George Miller, a California Democrat who requested the report, said, "Not a lot of attention is being paid to whether parents agree with this or want their children to participate or not participate. Sometimes parents have a different opinion from that of the superintendent or the school board."[42] U.S. Senator Chris Dodd of Connecticut noted in reaction to the report, "There is a tremendous amount of information being solicited and used to market back to kids without administrative consent or parental consent. If you had an 8-year-old or a 10-year-old, would you allow someone to come into your house to do a survey on your child without consent?"[43]

Young children in reading groups are no longer hearing just stories that teach social mores such as the Grimm tales and Aesop's fables. Toddlers now learn to count using the "Kellogg's Froot Loops! Counting Fun Book." "It is a great way to get the Froot Loops brand equity into a different place, where normally you don't get exposure—taking it from the cereal aisle into another area like learning," said Meghan Parkhurst, a Kellogg spokesperson.[44] (Fortunately, the company is not sponsoring spelling bees, or "froot" might be a candidate for the dictionary.) Other baby books feature brand-name snacks such as M&M's, Reese's Pieces, Skittles, Hershey's, and Oreo. Such readers teach toddlers that the corporation is on a cultural par with literary characters such as Cinderella, Snow White, and Peter Pan. In fact, corporations like Disney and Burger King have even turned these types of characters into commercial counter-images that peddle their products. "Throughout the ages, the wisdom, knowledge and experience of culture has been passed along by stories, myths and symbols it provides its youth," observed Allen D. Kanner, Ph.D., of The Wright Institute in Berkeley, California. "Today, we are witnessing nothing less than an invasion of the

hearts and minds of our children with stories, myths and symbols cal-
culated to convince them that what they buy is who they are. The myth
that permeates these stories, the Big Lie that is presented as an unchal-
lenged article of faith, is that happiness can be bought. The symbols
that embody the myth take the form of corporate logos."[45] Kanner and
other academics who have studied the commercialization of childhood
find the cumulative impact of the commercial messages on children
particularly troubling. Kanner stated, "Research shows that teenagers
who adopt materialistic values are doing poorly in their lives, be it
emotionally (they're more depressed), academically or relationally."[46]

Undermining the role of parents has been a strategy marketers
have exploited to sell their brands through the development of "kids
only" products and marketing themes. For instance, Nintendo sought
to sell its video games to eight- to twelve-year-olds through a "Play It
Loud" television advertising campaign where the fictional youth characters, tired of adult control, were encouraged to find refuge in a video
game in order to "be heard" and "play it loud."[47] "To minimize the role
of paternal gatekeepers, corporations often seek to undermine the authority of parents," noted Linda Coco, who studied such marketing
campaigns in preparation for "A Parent's Guide to Fighting Corporate
Predators," published by the Washington, D.C.–based Corporate Accountability Research Group. "In their advertisements, corporations
portray parents, often in jocular veins, as stupid, out of date and out of
touch with the children's world, and they frequently ridicule parental
concerns for health and safety."[48] Kiddie marketing often strives for the
"nag factor," an actual measurement by the advertising industry of the
extent to which an ad drives a child to pester the folks about a purchase.
"How often do you see adults in children's ads?" asked Diane Levin,
professor of education and media culture at Wheelock College and author of *Remote Control Childhood?* "It's very rare. But when you do, the
adults either don't know anything or they try to stop you from getting
what you want."[49]

Children have been encouraged to nag their parents for products of all kinds, not just toys. That's the only explanation for Ford Motor Company advertising in *Sports Illustrated for Children* since no one in the magazine's pre-teen market yet has a driver's license.[50]

While corporations have increasingly defined childhood today, they can only do so because of the demolition of societal barriers that separated corporate commerce and childhood development. "When children's television was deregulated by the Federal Communications Commission in 1984, it became possible to market toys and other products with TV programs for the first time," Professor Levin told Congress. "Whole lines of very popular toys that were direct replicas of the violence children saw on the screen quickly became a dominant force in the toy market. The link-up between the TV and toy industries soon added movies and videogames. Parents and teachers quickly began reporting concerns. They were seeing more boys who seemed obsessed with war play that looked like exact replicas of TV shows. They also reported seeing increasing levels of aggressive behavior."[51] Norway, Belgium, Sweden, and Denmark have outlawed electronic advertising aimed at children. "The American Academy of Pediatricians recently recommended that children under two watch no television while older children be limited to one or two hours a day of quality TV or video games," Professor Kanner noted. "The American Dental Association has taken a stand against schools signing exclusive contracts with cola companies."[52] Kanner reported that the American Psychological Association began debating the ethical issues of psychologists consulting with child marketers. Kiddie marketing themes identified by Coco included exploiting the need for "peer acceptance," by sanctioning "cool" attitudes that are not always the most socially responsible, and "aging up," exploiting the desire of children to be older by populating commercials with children who are older than the ones a company is trying to reach, thereby encouraging children to grow up quicker than a family might like. The psychological impact on children of such tactics is very likely to be a loss of self-esteem and a predisposition for at-risk behavior.

With medical experts on one side and corporations on the other, the battle lines between culture and commerce are perhaps nowhere as clear as in the debate over the commercialization of childhood. However, the lines between culture and commerce have become so blurry throughout society that limiting children's exposure to corporate marketing only in school or in the home may not be enough, or may even seem hypocritical. For instance, the General Accounting Office could not finger in-school marketing for the impacts on children it noted "because advertising is ubiquitous in America, it is difficult—if not impossible—to distinguish between the effects of advertisement to which students are exposed inside and outside of school."[53] As communities begin to look more like corporations, it's increasingly difficult to distinguish one commercial sphere or commercial message from another, as well as to draw selective barriers to corporate intrusions.

The Corporation Is the Community

Corporations have altered the community's place as the driving force of American culture by replacing the community's values with corporate ones. This is a natural extension of the corporateer logic. If corporations are people, why can't they be free to form their own communities that transmit their own values?

- Why participate in an activist community group when you can drive a Volvo and be a vehicle of social change through RE-VOLVOLUTION?

- Why volunteer for Amnesty International when you can watch MTV, which, as the CEO of its owner, Viacom, Sumner Redstone, said, "is associated with the forces of freedom and democracy around the world"? (After the fall of the Berlin wall, Redstone claimed, "We put MTV in East Germany, and the next day the Berlin Wall fell.")[54]

- Who needs libraries when you can go to Barnes & Noble?

- Why play sports when you can wear Nike?

- Forget the reading group, head to Starbucks.

- Be an environmentalist; drive an SUV that guzzles gas but lets you truly enjoy nature.

- Freedom is not volunteering for the ACLU, but driving alone on the country roads in your luxury automobile.

The subtext of these brand messages is a call to individuals to join the values in the corporate community, to live one's life in the community of the corporate brand, what it stands for, and its synergies. For instance, Disney moved from theme parks to towns (Celebration, Florida), cruises, and branded holidays on its own private island in the Bahamas based on the power of its branded lifestyle. In the same way, Starbucks moved from selling coffee to furniture and books. This is also the lesson in the legions of corporate club cards, savings programs and gold/platinum/silver status membership reward levels. To become a part of the corporation's community is to save and to define yourself.

While the invisible hand's mantras cajoled, the corporation surrounded the individual by enlarging its presence and eclipsing the community's. During the last ten years, corporations have paid significant sums for the "naming rights" to civic institutions such as stadiums, theaters, hospitals, museums, and schools. The trend began in the 1990s with a handful of sport stadiums and spread to approximately sixty major league stadiums by 2001, and the idea is also growing in other civic institutions.[55]

- In 1995, TWA paid more than $1 million per year for twenty years to paint its name on the roof of the new football stadium in downtown St. Louis, which was built with mostly taxpayer dollars.

- In 2000, the mutual fund company Invesco offered $120 million for the naming rights to Invesco Field at Mile High Stadium in Denver.[56]

- By 2001, an individual could visit Los Angeles's Staples Center, the Hasbro Children's Hospital in Rhode Island, the Mattel Children's Hospital at UCLA, the Please Touch Museum Presented by McDonald's in Philadelphia, the PNC Bank Arts Center in New Jersey, and the General Motors Center for African American Art in Detroit.[57]

- In July 2001, the Smithsonian Institution offered General Motors the right to name its new transportation hall for $10 million. Ralph Nader said, "To let GM pay for, be associated with and be influential over a transportation exhibit, given its decades-long record of criminal convictions, buying up and displacing mass transit systems, producing unsafe and polluting cars, is to confess to a complete abdication of any standards of museum integrity and independence."[58]

- The Massachusetts Bay Transit Authority even tried to sell the naming rights for four Boston subway "T" stops until angry citizens derailed the sale.

During the last ten years, corporations have purchased the rights to replace in communities the once-honored role of individuals for whom civic institutions were named, increasing the visibility and value of their brand as "role model." David Cope, director of Business Development at Gilco Sports & Entertainment Marketing, said of the future opportunities for his industry in naming rights, "We are starting to see interest and are starting to move in kind of a different direction—less into professional sports, more into collegiate sports, into the performing arts and into specialized retail projects, things such as shopping malls and strip shopping centers, potentially even airports and convention centers."[59]

Corporate sponsorships of community events, music, art, and film has become ubiquitous as well. Critics have claimed that such sponsorship diminishes the value of that which is being sponsored. "It is not

Art for Art's Sake as much as Art for Ad's Sake," wrote Matthew McAllister in *The Commercialization of American Culture.* "In the public's
eye, art is yanked from its own separate and theoretically autonomous
domain and squarely placed in the commercial."[60] In the book world,
the quintessential example was Fay Weldon's 2001 novel, *The Bulgari
Connection,* which takes place in the London jewelry store and for which
Bulgari paid Weldon an undisclosed amount.[61] With regard to community events, children's musician Raffi Cavoukian performed at the
Vancouver International Children's Festival every year since 1979 until
the festival took on a corporate sponsor in June 2001. The musician explained that he voiced his concerns about commercialization of the festival, "in recent years, when corporate logos crept onto the grounds," but
that "this year, on the first day of the week-long event, I was stunned to
discover that, for the very first time, there was a 'presenting sponsor'—
an automobile company—that was allowed to turn a portion of the
festival site into an outdoor car lot with over a dozen vehicles and several large banners. I felt sick at seeing this and knew that I could not be
a part of this blatant display of corporate sponsorship." Raffi added,
"Pervasive, bottom-line marketing demeans public spaces and diminishes community."[62]

In October 2002, New York City officials faced a corporate graffiti
wave that dramatized Raffi's point. During the same week, Nike glued
decals to Central Park West sidewalks and Microsoft let loose in the
Manhattan skyline what *The New York Times* described as "a swarm of
large adhesive butterflies. They settled yesterday morning on sidewalks
and doorways; traffic signals, stop signs and planters. They alighted on
the blue paving around Grand Army Plaza and the granite corners
around Grand Central Terminal. Their blue, green, red and yellow wings
accompanied by a caption—'It's better with the Butterfly'—advertising
Microsoft's new MSN 6 Internet Service."[63]

Given the power of the corporation as an institution and its tendency to expand in any space it occupies, the shift from corporations

sponsoring community events to community events sponsoring the corporation will be inevitable. For instance, tennis fans who tuned in to watch play at the 2000 U.S. Open could hardly separate the action on center court from the quintessential corporate drop shot, the Mercedes logos carefully embroidered into both ends of the net. In all kinds of communities, such corporate symbols have increasingly moved off the sidelines to become a focus of the main event. This has reinforced with the individual that the corporation makes the community and that individuals should sponsor corporate communities.

The individual's growing commercial relationship with the corporation has coincided with the individual's shrinking social relationship to the civic community and to other individuals. In his book *Bowling Alone,* Harvard Professor Robert Putnam traced America's vanishing volunteerism and disconnection to family, friends, neighbors, and social structures of all kinds, be it the PTA, church, civic groups, political parties, or bowling leagues. Putnam's exploration in 2000 of all available research during the last century found that "[b]etween 1973 and 1994 the number of men and women who took any leadership role in any organization—from 'old fashioned' fraternal organizations to new age encounter groups—was sliced by more than 50 percent. This dismaying trend began to accelerate after 1985; in the ten short years between 1985 and 1994, active involvement in community organizations in this country fell by 45 percent. By this measure, at least, nearly half of America's civic infrastructure was obliterated in barely a decade."[64] During the age of the corporateer, the same decade that corporations began aggressively marketing their brands and communities, rather than their products, the civic volunteer sector literally lost half of its capacity.

Putnam does not examine the role of corporations or their marketing, but he does attribute the decline in civic engagement, and what he calls "social capital," more to certain direct factors than others.[65] These correspond, in many ways, to attitudes and behavior the corporateer has encouraged.

- While the time investment of individuals in civic organizations fell measurably, the time available for such activities did not. Americans seem simply not to have prioritized civic participation. (In other words, cultural commitment shrank as commercial commitment increased.) For this reason, Putnam believes pressure of time and money on individuals contributed no more than ten percent to the decline in civic volunteerism.

- By contrast, Putnam concluded, "The effect of electronic entertainment—above all television—in privatizing our leisure time has been substantial. My rough estimate is that this factor might account for perhaps 25 percent of the decline." (Commercial channels occupied more of the individual's time than social vehicles.)

- By far the greatest factor for Putnam was "generational change— the slow, steady and ineluctable replacement of the long civic generation by their less involved children and grandchildren. . . . The effects of generational succession vary significantly across different measures of civic engagement—greater for more public forms, less for private schmoozing—but as a rough rule of thumb we concluded in chapter 14 that this factor might account for perhaps half of the overall decline."[66]

Can American communities flourish under such circumstances, with commercial values of atomization dominating communities? "Social capital turns out to have forceful, even quantifiable effects on many different aspects of our lives," Putnam noted. "What is at stake is not merely warm, cuddly feelings or frissons of community pride. . . . [There is] hard evidence that our schools and neighborhoods don't work so well when community bonds slacken, that our economy, our democracy and even our health and happiness depend on adequate stocks of social capital."[67]

Most important, Americans do not appear ready to accept such cultural losses. Corporations have essentially been able to purchase individuals' legal rights, their kids' attention, and their communities. A purchase is a transaction that implies willing consent, yet Americans have been largely forced to accept such changes by the inequities of corporate power dynamics, and have been consistently offended by them after the fact. For example, individuals often do not recognize that they have waived their right to trial in the fine print of a commercial contract until a dispute arises with a corporation and their lawyer tells them. Similarly, most Americans disapprove of commercializing education. Putnam also reported that individuals were not happy about the breakdown of civic community. "In several surveys in 1999, two-thirds of Americans said that America's civic life had weakened in recent years, that social and moral values were higher when they were growing up, and that our society was focused more on the individual than the community," Putnam wrote. "More than 80 percent said there should be more emphasis on community, even if that put more demands on individuals."[68]

How have individuals incurred such unintended cultural losses? The lesson that the corporation comes first has had so much power because it is taught in the one place adults spend most of their time learning—the workplace. The next chapter shows how the corporate workplace has become a laboratory for incubating key tenets of corporateering in society.

WORKERS OF THE WORLD INCORPORATE

Labor is prior to, and independent of, capital. Capital is only the fruit of labor, and could never have existed if labor had not first existed. Labor is the superior of capital, and deserves much the higher consideration. Capital has its rights, which are as worthy of protection as any other rights. Nor is it denied that there is, and probably always will be, a relation between labor and capital, producing mutual benefits. The error is in assuming that the whole labor of community exists within that relation.

ABRAHAM LINCOLN
DECEMBER 3, 1861, ANNUAL MESSAGE TO CONGRESS

key part of the corporation's control over culture during the last two decades has been the persuasive force the corporation has exerted over the individual at work. The lessons individuals learn in the workplace have profound ramifications for how individuals deal with others in society. When individuals sacrifice for the corporation at work, they are more likely to do so outside of the job. When corporations force workers to accept new commercial priorities, the individual is likely to make these priorities into cultural mantras.

Corporate workplaces differ greatly, but certain trends since the

1980s have diminished the freedom of corporate workers in ways that reflect new restraints on the individual in society. New insecurities have replaced old freedoms.

Old Freedom	New Insecurity	Societal Reflection
To have long-term, in many cases lifetime, employment, based on merit.	To be downsized in even profitable times, regardless of merit.	To be minimized as a consumer, voter, citizen, and shareholder, regardless of merit.
To be a permanent worker with health-care and retirement benefits.	To work in a job (sometimes more than one) as a contract or temporary worker who receives no benefits but has the status of "free agent," so that many corporations can compete for your services.	To be subject to continual changes in relationships to corporations so that they can have more flexibility, such as changing networks of HMO doctors and more restrictive contractual clauses.
To be a professional who works hard for the corporation and, in turn, receives the latitude to have some personal privileges at work.	To be watched by cameras in the workplace, have your e-mail read, and have your telephone calls and voice mail monitored.	To suffer a loss of privacy in personal life.
To be a worker who can join a union that vigorously represents your interests.	To be a business person who always puts the corporation first and has no adversarial relationship to it.	To be part of a corporate community, rather than a civic community.
To not have future employment options limited due to an association with one corporation.	To have your future thoughts become the corporation's property by signing "non-compete" agreements that prevent workers from taking a job in the same industry or for com- (continues on next page)	To be restricted in your future choices through a commercial exchange with a corporation through, for example, pre-payment penalties for paying off loans too soon; relinquish- (continues on next page)

Old Freedom	New Insecurity	Societal Reflection
	peting companies for years after they leave their job.	ing the right to trial in an event a dispute arises; or having your "credit score"—which determines your purchasing power— lowered if you shop around too much and have too many credit checks run on you.
To take vacations and have a private life.	To be one with the corporation and constantly connected to the corporate hive electronically, even during vacations.	To have increasing personal time, energy, and space occupied by the corporations without recompense from it.
To have job security.	To be free from a dress code, a bureaucracy, habit, and a pension.	To have the illusion of commercial gain without the substance.

These changes were grounded in assumptions that became culturally accepted excuses for the corporation to be relieved of many duties
to workers. Greater technology made human labor in some cases super-
fluous. Cheaper global labor markets required that Americans diminish
their labor standards. To compete globally, corporations needed more
flexibility in how they treated their workers. In other words, the need
for economic growth outweighed the worth of societal standards. In
the 1990s, Fortune 500 corporations even used contract prison labor to
cut costs. Filmmaker Michael Moore reported that prisoners in Ven-
tura, California, served as TWA's flight reservation specialists, Colorado
inmates telemarketed for AT&T, an IBM subcontractor paid incarcer-
ates to build circuit boards, and a Microsoft contractor hired Washington State prisoners to package software.[1] "When I wrote the first
edition of *Downsize This!* there were weekly announcements of massive

corporate downsizings throughout the country," Moore noted in the 1997 preface to the paperback edition. "Then the backlash began, an anti-corporate mood started sweeping the country (remember *Newsweek* running the mug shots of certain CEOs on the cover with the headline 'Corporate Killers'?). Well, the Fortune 500 quickly wised up. They stopped issuing those big firing proclamations . . . [still] the number of people downsized actually increased by 8 percent over the past year [1996–1997]." Theoretically, increased stock value from such downsizing in the 1990s created more wealth. Mostly, however, the wealth rose to the one-tenth of Americans who owned nine-tenths of all stock.[2] The CEOs who made the decisions to downsize were chief among the wealth holders since their compensation was often tied to rising stock value. Downsizing that could hurt the corporation's value in the long term, by diminishing its capacity, helped CEOs get richer in the short term. By the turn of the millennium, the jury was out on whether downsizing resulted in more actual wealth. *Harper's Magazine* reported that only half the companies that downsized in the 1990s saw an increase in profits.[3] However, CEOs' personal stakes in curbing the number of and cost of workers provided a strong motive to change the nature of job security as well as the individual's freedoms at work.

To boost productivity, for instance, the most successful CEOs of the new millennium engaged in "behavior modification" of workers to an unprecedented degree in order to urge workers to "live the values" of the corporation. The problem for society, though, is that the overriding value of the corporation has been the commercial need to maximize profit and disregard social costs. G. William Dauphinais and Colin Price of Price Waterhouse interviewed the world's most successful CEOs for their collection *Straight from the CEO*. They found behavior modification of workers a key component of the new CEO ethos in the 2000s. "Why has this great opportunity emerged only now? Why not ten, twenty, thirty years ago?" the authors ask. "Because of the rhetoric of class war in the air [in the decades after World War II], it was not the time for management to make demands of its workforce for commitment and a greater share of mental energy."[4] Dauphinais and Price noted that while in the past "the prevalent 'stakeholder' view of corporate responsibilities made profit-seeking a coequal value with community, labor and national interests," the times have changed and "old constraints on profit-seeking have fallen away."[5] They point out, "Today's CEOs have, sometimes consciously and sometimes not, invaded the field of human relations and imposed their own stamp on it."[6] In other words, while the corporation once saw social institutions—such as labor unions, nation, and community—as significant priorities, in the post–Cold War world the corporation was freer to forget them. "By implication, the CEOs in our book are saying that workers will be happiest jettisoning the dialectics of labor-management conflict and making the fitness and health of their corporations their primary mission," the authors noted.[7] Changing how the worker thought about their relationship to the corporation entailed changing how individuals thought about themselves.

You Are The Corporation, The Corporation Is You

In the same way that the invisible hand sold the illusion of the corporation's human meaning to the public, it did so internally with its own workers. The rationale that the management gurus created for a "flexible workforce," one that could be erased and rebuilt based on the corporation's needs, was communicated in the language of the working person's liberation. Cast members, team members, associates were part of something larger. "Free agents," the contract workers, were free of a rigid management hierarchy that stifled human creativity and expression. The new corporation allowed telecommuting, casual days, and beards, as well as open-air offices and living room–style meeting areas. The new regime wanted to make sure there were no more lowly workers, only business people. This corporate "innovation" was defined by one of its prophets, Tom Peters, a consultant who shaped corporate custom in the mid-1990s through 200 seminars in 47 states and 22 countries. Peters had co-authored the best-seller *In Search of Excellence* in 1982. His 1997 book *The Circle of Innovation,* an encapsulation of Peters's slide-show seminars, offered up the new norms for the business people of the world to unite around. The following are among Peters's ideals for CEOs to embrace in order to destroy the corporation's social compact with workers and the individual worker's view of herself and her rights.

> DESTRUCTION IS COOL! CDO . . . Chief Destruction Officer. Easier to KILL an organization—and repot it—than change it substantially. Learn to swallow it: DESTRUCTION IS JOB NO.1 (before the competition does it to you).

> WELCOME TO THE WHITE-COLLAR REVOLUTION. IF YOU CAN'T SAY (SPECIFICALLY) WHY YOU MAKE YOUR COMPANY A BETTER PLACE . . . YOU'RE OUT! As of Now: ME, INC!/TAKE IMMEDIATE RESPONSBILITY FOR CHANGE!/ YOU(ME) ARE A BRAND. (Perform a PER-SONAL BRAND EQUITY EVALUATION . . . NOW!) There are no guarantees . . . and that can be liberating (i.e., stomp out indentured servitude to BigCorp).

> WE ARE ALL MICHELANGELOS. Convert every "jobholder" into a BUSINESS-PERSON. Convert every job into a BUSINESS.[8]

There were no workers in Peters's world. That's why "there are no guarantees . . . and that can be liberating." Peters's notion was, "Every person a businessperson. Every job a business/Business Units of 1"[9] so "Down with empowerment! Up with the b-u-s-i-n-e-s-s-p-e-r-s-o-n! Up with the Unit of One!"[10] Each person as a corporation. As CEOs of themselves, the individuals would presumably apply to themselves the same cool and cruel values that Peters recommended for top-dog CEOs, among the mantras, "destroy . . . cannibalize . . . forget."[11] The magic was in asking individuals to transcend the notion that a corporation as a powerful institution had a social duty to the worker. By the hocus-focus of sublimating one's self to the ultimate truth "the corporation > the individual," the individual can only assert himself by becoming the corporation. With the attainment came C-H-O-I-C-E to move from corporation to corporation ("free agency") and power to be as rich as you can without limit (albeit with odds about as promising as playing the lottery). Peters failed to mention the fine print of the "noncompete" agreements that proliferated during the 1990s, which literally gave the corporation an ownership right in the individual's future mind share by preventing workers from moving freely to competitors. Hairdressers, customer service agents, and doctors were among the employees required to waive their right to work for competitors at least in the immediate geographic area through such agreements.[12] Moreover, the social structures that protected workers in hard times, formal and informal, vanished with the other cultural architecture built into the corporation over the last century. When recession hit in the fall of 2001, for instance, the contract workers for auto makers were the first to feel the pain through forced wage cuts.[13] Without labor unions to represent them, the contract workers were free only to tighten their belts.

Every worker as a corporation unto herself internalized the values of the brand and the market, subverting the individual to the will of the corporate revolution. "What the hell is an organization now? It's me," Peters preached. "Why a white-collar revolution?" Because "Brand is (almost) all there is!"[14] "We" was reduced to "me," and it's every sailor for himself on the open seas of the market. Labor unions do not fit into this scheme any more than job security or protections. Cameras watch just to make sure LittleCorp (Me, Inc.) = BigCorp.[15] The real innovation of Peters and his brethren was reorienting the individual to an illusion that rapid economic growth was the only value there was. Profitability was no longer the goal. Extreme growth in profits was. "Brainware" (read "executive") mattered more than anything else because only it had the power to invent rapid growth. Workers that contributed to the profitability of a company still had no protections because the market said that profitability was not enough, that rapid growth was everything.

It's not hard to hear the inflation of the hi-tech bubble in Peters's exuberant riffs about the irrelevance of workers still on the other side of the digital divide and of Silicon Valley. "When I began working as a management consultant at McKinsey & Co. in 1974, 'we' (the professional service people—accountants, lawyers, consultants, ad agency denizens) were considered the PARASITES . . . living off the sweat of real people's brows. Times have changed. And how! The nerds have won! Bill Gates is the richest man in the world! It is the Age of Brainware. Now . . . the people who lift 'things' (the . . . RAPIDLY . . . declining fraction) are new parasites living off the carpal-tunnel syndrome of the computer programmers' perpetually stained keyboard hands. Overstatement? I think not . . . (or barely)."[16] It's just such a lack of proportion that led to the hyperinflation of technology stocks based on the grand illusion that brainware and mind share were all that counted, even if dot-coms captured only the mental share and not profits.

Peters showed the power of his logic in 1997 by pointing to the success of brainware stocks and pooh-poohing the companies built with labor, such as General Motors and Ford. His equation: "Stock market value of Microsoft + Intel > General Motors + Ford + Boeing + Kodak + Sears + J. P. Morgan + Caterpillar + Kellogg."[17] When the brainware stock bubble burst at the end of 2000, however, the correction for such excesses fell hardest on the working class that invested in the stock market with their retirement savings and pension funds. The hi-tech titans who grew rich off the hyperbole of Peters et al. offered their apologies for their exuberance for a never-ending growth economy. That was hardly a comfort to the hundreds of thousands of workers who lost their jobs in the recession of 2001, even if it did prove who the real parasites were. The roller-coaster ride of the stock market in the 1990s had not strengthened society in the cultural ways that would have prepared it for the recession to come. The market made a few rich but cost the many not just their college funds and retirement savings but also cultural freedoms in their workplace and society. BigCorp still existed, only it was disguised in new lasting illusions. The quintessential example was energy trader Enron, a nimble example of the new corporation. Enron sought to open new markets in public resources of energy, water, and bandwidth, as well as other "virtual assets," but it crumbled on Thanksgiving Day 2001 due to previously unreported losses.

Enron CEO Kenneth Lay would walk away with more than $180 million after exercising options over the previous three years, but the Enron workers' pension fund was the first casualty of his mismanagement. The retirement funds were frozen in Enron stock by executives at precisely the moment the stock plummeted below one dollar per share. Some long-time workers lost hundreds of thousands of dollars from their retirement plans.

While the duties of the corporation to its workers were vanishing, the duties of the worker to the corporation were increasing. The corporation's stock capitalization was more important than the worker's retirement security. The ethos of the corporateer's age required that workers' retirement savings be invested almost entirely in their own corporation's stock, in contrast to the diversified pensions of previous times. LittleCorp, in myriad ways, became physical and intellectual property of BigCorp. A key duty of the individual was curbing his dissent within the workplace, not only by "jettisoning the dialectics of labor-management conflict" but also by keeping secrets within the family tree. The change in the way individuals related to the parent corporation and to one another, absent societal concern and boundaries, diminished the power of workers to challenge corporate abuses and to make the invisible hand visible.

Silence of the Workers

The duty of workers to other individuals and society has often been replaced with a duty to the corporation, in much the same way that in the media the public interest has at times been erased by the commercial interest that sponsored it (as Chapter 7 discusses). This logic has created moral dilemmas for individuals with special knowledge within the corporation, such as the General Motors engineer you read about in Chapter 1, Edward Ivey, who knew of defective gasoline systems in GM automobiles but did not make that knowledge public. The societal invisibility of many corporate abuses, particularly those that threaten the individual's health and safety, have often been protected by a code of conduct in the corporation that censors moral expression of the individual and promotes the good of "the team." Dissent is all there is to reaffirm the mores and laws of society within the corporation and beyond it. Respect for dissent begins with respect for dissenters, and the modern corporation has made sure that insiders that tell of corporate abuse pay steep penalties. Corporate whistle-blowers become pariahs.

Pseudonymous postings on the Yahoo! Enron message board dating back to 1998 show that many insiders long understood the company's financial shell games, but they could not reveal themselves. "Dig deep behind the Enron financials and you'll see a growing mountain of off-the-balance-sheet debt which will eventually swallow this company," read one posting when the Enron stock was at $69. "There's a reason they layer so many subsidiaries and affiliates. Be careful." With the Enron share price at $57.30, another posting prophesied, "Enron will soon collapse. Enron has been cooking the books with smoke and mirrors. . . . Criminal charges will be brought against ENE executives for their misdeeds. Class action lawsuits will complete the demise of ENE." That Enron employees offered these cloaked warnings was clear enough to Enron management, which offered its own posting in 1998, threatening: "Enron International's computing equipment and services (this includes E-mail and Internet usage) are to be used for Enron business purposes. . . . Enron can, and does, electronically monitor the use of its equipment. . . . Failure to abide by these restrictions may subject the individuals to disciplinary action as well as civil and/or criminal prosecution."

Corporations have a very legitimate need to protect their trade secrets and integrity of information. Often, however, the health of society and the health of corporate profits confront each other, and protecting society demands that individuals of conscience be allowed a hearing. When commercial and cultural values clash, there needs to be an environment in which individuals feel safe to assert the long-standing assumptions of their culture—for instance, that human life is priceless. To assuage concerns about the unrestrained power of large corporations, CEOs often refer to the corporation as a "human organization." In the age of the corporateer, however, human values of individuality and moral conscience within the corporation have been diminished.

Much of the information my colleagues and I have obtained about corporations that have led to reform were provided to us by whistle-blowers. Many of them have managed to remain faceless, but others have been forced to come forward. Those that do typically face harassment from their employers—including threats of lawsuits endangering their financial stability—and they must resign themselves to likely never working again in their trade. While federal law offers important financial incentives for whistle-blowers who provide information about fraud committed against the federal government,[18] inadequate protections exist for workers who go public with evidence of other types of corporate threats to the public. The evidence these whistle-blowers have provided, however, has warned society about major dangers to its health and safety.

The 1999 motion picture *The Insider* portrayed the travails of tobacco industry whistle-blower Jeffrey Wigand. He lost his family, home, and financial security when he informed society that the companies knew of tobacco's addictive effects and tried to make their products more addictive. Fewer Americans have heard of Allstate Insurance staff claims analyst Jo Ann Lowe, a twenty-five-year employee of the company, who resigned because she was troubled by fraud at the company in the wake of the Northridge, California, earthquake. Many policyholders from all major insurance companies had difficulty collecting the full value of their claims in the wake of the January 1994 earthquake that shook homes off their very foundations. I worked with some of these earthquake homeowners just afterward, and the most common complaint was that insurers simply wanted to "paint and patch" when foundations of homes needed to be repaired. The breadth of the industry's bad faith was not fully clear until after the new century, when buried state reports became public in conjunction with the corruption scandal involving the state insurance commissioner, who was forced to resign by the dogged vigilance of my colleagues Harvey Rosenfield and Doug Heller. By that time, however, the statute of limitations on filing claims had passed.[19] In 1997, however, Lowe helped Allstate policy-holders by revealing that the good hands of Allstate routinely rewrote reports submitted by engineers who inspected homes, in order to low-ball the value of claims. In her 1997 legal declaration in a case brought by Allstate homeowners, a document Allstate sought to keep secret, Lowe stated:

> I became aware that many adjusters employed by Allstate were engaging in conduct which I believed was improper, unlawful, fraudulent, and in bad faith. I became aware of cases in which the adjuster retained an engineer and requested that the engineer provide a report determining and detailing the cause and extent of the damage caused by the earthquake. Allstate's adjusters were requiring engineers to provide a draft or preliminary report for the adjuster's review. Where an engineer's draft report attributed any amount of damage, in the adjuster's opinion, that could possibly have been exacerbated by the earthquake and/or damage which may not be covered under the policy according to the adjusters, the adjuster would instruct the engineer to alter the report to reflect the adjuster's changes. Engineers were repeatedly instructed to alter draft reports in order to minimize the damage attributable to covered losses in order to reduce any potential payments to the insured and in order to benefit Allstate's financial interests. In some cases, the draft report would be returned to the engineer by the adjuster and no copy of the draft report would be maintained in the

claim file and no record or notation would be made in the claim file that a draft report had been received. [20]

Lowe told the court that she complained to her Allstate manager but was led to believe the cases were isolated. "As I became more involved in the evaluation of the earthquake claims filed, I learned that the alterations of draft engineering reports were not isolated occurrences."[21] When she complained again, Lowe was warned, "Don't stand in front of a runaway train," and was told that managers were upset with her for speaking out.[22] As she continued to raise the issue in meetings, "I suffered an on-going and gradual erosion of my job responsibilities through the imposition of 'special job requirements.' . . . As a result of these mandates, my ability to carry out my job duties . . . was curtailed by the constraints and scrutiny that Allstate Home Office and Allstate local managers imposed on me. It was apparent that I was being punished for speaking out against certain of Allstate's claims practices, including the practice of requesting alteration of draft engineering reports which I believed to be unethical, fraudulent and in bad faith."[23]

When Lowe attended the trial of a homeowner suing Allstate for bad faith, she was instructed not to do so again by her employers because of "security" issues. Lowe hired an attorney to offer legal advice and obtain the trial transcript for her. In the trial testimony, the Allstate manager she complained to about the alterations of the engineer reports said that he believed the practice was wrong and would not condone it, though Lowe said she knew that he allowed it. A second manager testified that he did not have meetings with engineers to request revisions, but, according to Lowe, the same manager told her that the draft reports and revisions were "standard practice."[24] Lowe said she then resigned because she "refused to be a party to Allstate's continuing fraud."[25] Her testimony, however, forced Allstate to agree to review as many as 9,000 claims by policyholders to settle two lawsuits, and to set aside $60 million to pay for repair and restitution. Attorneys from our consumer group served as co-counsel in the case.

Lowe lost her job and received no financial reward. The system has been designed to make Lowe's public expression the exception, not the rule. Security expert David Grant, who has protected both corporations and individual whistle-blowers, told me, "Anyone who deals with whistle-blowers is familiar with the patterns of behavior exhibited by some corporations threatened with insider disclosures. There are some corporations that you have to assume that when somebody blows the whistle, almost immediately they're ostracized by management. In many instances, they are relegated to tasks that are far below them. You might have a top-flight manager who suddenly finds himself counting the number of stationery they have in a closet someplace. Because the whistle-blower is talking about something that could cause loss to the corporation, he could also cause a loss of jobs. For that reason, almost immediately the whistle-blower loses any support group that he had. So you see a whistle-blower becoming increasingly isolated."[26]

To Grant, it's natural that whistle-blowers receive negative reactions at corporations, but some corporate responses cross the line. Of the whistle-blowers Grant has protected, "A number have had threats. A number of them have been followed. A number of them suspected that their telephones had been tapped. A number of them had their garbage stolen." Why take someone's garbage? "Taking someone's garbage is known as 'garbage cover' in the jargon. You get a lot of personal information out of garbage. If they're on medication, you get pill bottles. So if you're going to make an allegation that someone is a little bit off, maybe it's because of the medication they're taking. You get credit card slips, so you know what they're doing, and the services and products they are procuring. You get telephone bills. If you've got someone who is consistently dialing 1-900-I'm Hot for You . . . that's the sort of thing you get. If they're having interpersonal relationships, if the wife is carrying on an affair and the husband is the whistle-blower, maybe that gives them some sort of control.

"There is a current, ongoing threat against American technology from foreign governments and corporations overseas," Grant said. "Foreign and domestic intelligence collection, both legal and illegal, is a fact of corporate life, and a corporation would be failing its fiduciary responsibilities if it failed to address these threats. Internal theft, fraud, and espionage all cost American taxpayers billions of dollars in increased prices, and these are all illegal acts perpetrated primarily by insiders. So from that standpoint, I can see a certain amount of investigation of whistle-blowers as being legitimate. Having said that, an awful lot of investigations that are conducted against whistle-blowers can only be construed as intent to cause the whistle-blower discomfort—to shut them up, to isolate them from their peer groups inside the company, to make the whistle-blower himself the cause célèbre instead of the issue that he's trying to talk about with the media or government." In other words, to place the interests of the corporation over the interests of the society.

Grant guarded a friend of mine, Dr. Linda Peeno, who, as a former HMO official, heroically, and at great personal cost, testified before Congress to inform the American public and lawmakers what really happened inside an HMO. Both Grant and Peeno identified for me the emphasis within the corporation on sacrificing for the team as a key to corporate control over information the public has a right to know. "Corporations cannot afford to be self-critical," said Peeno. "The number-one management problem is mid-level management not telling senior management problems. So you have this insulated senior management that have their rosy glasses on because no one wants to be realistic."[27] Peeno says that there should be a person within every corporation whose job it is to dissent about the corporation's problems so that those problems are solved. "We have probably never needed something more than a culture in which there is some sort of reflection, critical inquiry into what has happened." Linda also asked and answered this important question:

> Why do people become whistle-blowers to begin with? What is
> the motivating factor? I think the strongest factor is the knowl-
> edge that you are a witness to something and you don't want to

be a participant. You're so outraged by the system. Corresponding is a naïve belief that people will respect you for standing up for what is right. I honestly thought that people would admire me and respect me for standing my ground, only to find out that most people did not give a damn one way or the other. And that if anyone cared at all, it was usually in a negative way. I was jeopardizing the status quo. I was jeopardizing someone's job. Or I was forcing someone to think about something they did not want to think about. . . . I was a child of a particular era in time. I grew up in a rural community where self-reliance was valued. My father was a die-hard individualist. It was always the corollary of you have this independence but with the independence come these responsibilities. I had the dual sense of speaking out and this great sense of responsibility to speak out, even when I did not want to . . . One of the things that I think has enabled me to do what I have done is that literally from my earliest childhood I have never been a team player in the way it has been defined. The sense of being willing to make a decision and stand by it even when it ran up against prevailing opinion and having enough confidence that you could stick to it is the only thing that helped me through the past twelve years. Because it has only been in the last two or three years that I have gotten affirmation. For many, many years the medical community alienated me. I was alienated from the health-care community. The only affirmation I got was through my books, reading and sort of thinking through things, and just feeling absolutely confident about what I believed, at least I was moving in that direction. That's hard. You think about someone else in a position to take action—Where would their supports come from? What would sustain them when they have to fly in the face of their work environment, their social community, their professional community, their financial security, a whole cultural identity that

is associated with being the good team player? That's a powerful force.

Linda went to medical school to help people, not hurt them. She
found herself, however, in the role of medical reviewer for Humana,
one of the nation's largest HMOs. This led to the biggest regret of her
life. "In the spring of 1987, as a physician, I caused the death of a man,"
Linda testified before Congress in 1996. "Not only did I demonstrate
that I could indeed do what was expected of me, I exemplified the
'good' company doctor: I saved a half-million dollars."[28] Peeno explained that she was rewarded for this act with advancement in her career. She added details later in testimony in the California statehouse
on behalf of legislation, sponsored by our consumer group, to end bureaucratic control over medicine. "The decision about the California
patient [in need of a heart transplant] was made from the twenty-third
floor of a marble building in Louisville, Kentucky." Though Linda did
not mention the name of the company at the time, this was Humana's
headquarters. "The patient was a piece of computer paper, less than
half full. The 'clinical goal' was to figure out a way to avoid payment.
The 'diagnosis' was to 'DENY.' Once I stamped 'DENY' across his au-
thorization form, his life's end was as certain as if I had pulled the plug
on a ventilator."[29]

Linda was among the very first voices to stand against corporate
medicine, and she ultimately drew the entire medical establishment
into her battle. Her crisis of conscience did not come all at once, but
came like a "series of small, little gnats." The "first little gnat" was the
first interview at Humana where Linda said she was told to keep a minimum 10 percent denial rate. "On what basis could you possibly determine that a 10 percent denial rate was appropriate? Then he asked me
the question of whether I could be tough as a girl because I would be
dealing with physicians who were hostile." Linda could not imagine
why there were hostile physicians, since she came from a pro-physician
hospital environment. "There were other little things along the way. In

reality, the heart transplant was disturbing. But it was one of those things where when you are in this new terrain you cannot see the ethical quandaries because it is new. So here I was, sitting in this environment where I was expected to do something, and I did do it. So it took a long time for the ethical implications of that to seep in."

Linda said she made a point of keeping detailed notes of every review form. She had codes for why the case was denied. She then had staff make a copy of the reviews, and she brought them home. Then she made up her mind that she would quit when she was "asked to do something specifically unethical." Linda said that point came when Humana had to balance its books because it was losing money in some markets and profiting in others. In order to get the overall numbers in line, Humana increased the denial rates for those markets not doing well. "So two people with the same condition depending upon where they lived could get two different determinations." That's when Linda walked away. She was recruited by another HMO that needed a new medical director. "I spent a month talking to everyone, making sure they knew how I felt, and about my experiences and that I did not want to duplicate them. That I wanted a different philosophy." She was assured things would be different. Unfortunately, just months later, that HMO also began losing money, and "they resorted to all the standard simplistic measures; tighten down hospital days, deny referrals, deny emergency room requests." She left the industry after stints in other places, realizing that she could not do what was expected of her.

In 1996, she testified before Congress but did not mention Humana by name. Still, Linda recalled that Humana hand delivered a packet of information to the committee members about her, which included the fact that her husband, also a doctor, was still a contract doctor with Humana. "From the very beginning, I did not want the focus to be on a specific insurance company, I wanted to focus on the system." *Dateline NBC* filmed Linda's Congressional testimony for use in a segment about a child who lost the use of his hands and feet because of another HMO's obstruction to care. When the segment aired with footage of Linda, it did not identify Humana as her employer. Nonetheless, the morning after, Linda received an anonymous call. "Some gravelly voice, it actually sounded like an old man, who said, 'Dr. Peeno, you've gone too far this time,' and hung up the phone," Linda remembered. "I just chalked it up to a crank call. At about eleven o'clock in the morning, there was a phone message from the producer, saying, 'Call me right away, it's an emergency.' My heart just stopped. I called him, and he said that he already, first thing that morning, had a call from Humana, and they said, 'We want you to do a retraction piece. Dr. Peeno has lied and misrepresented herself,' and went on and on. The producer said, 'First of all, we verified everything she said. Second, we didn't mention Humana, so why are you calling?' I literally at that point was just terrified because I thought this could be just the beginning. . . . I always envisioned getting a knock on the door and being served with some lawsuit. God knows what they could conjure up. They could financially devastate us." Linda received no more calls until just before a case against Humana proceeded in which she was an expert witness.

"I was set to do my deposition, and that was the first case ever against Humana." Ultimately, the case led to a $13.1 million verdict against the company. Plaintiff Karen Johnson, a young wife and mother of two children, had cancer of the cervix, and her gynecologist recommended a hysterectomy. The family had argued that Humana denied approval even though without the hysterectomy Karen would have to undergo repeated surgical procedures, which would leave her at a significant risk that the cancer would become invasive. The jury heard testimony that reviewers were paid financial incentives to deny hysterectomies. "I was getting ready to leave to go to Midway College to do a talk to nursing students when the phone rang," Linda said. "When I picked it up, this guy—very nice, kind of educated-sounding, mid-thirtyish type of voice—said, 'If you don't stop making media appearances and testifying in cases, information about your husband's past affairs will be made public.' That was Tuesday. I get in my car. I am just sick. That was like a stake in my heart because Doug had had affairs in '85 and in '92. There are fewer than five people, if that many, including the two women, who knew about those two affairs. I was like the classic enabler. I perpetuated this myth of this perfect exemplary doctor, and no one knew about it. So that told me . . . that was like a neon sign that said, *We know everything about you down to the skeletons in your closet.*"

Next, Linda called her husband on the way to the lecture. He told her that he wanted her to stop speaking out. She gave her lecture to the nurses and heard their war stories of battling an uncaring system. "Something just snapped when I was there. I heard all this stuff that was happening. I got back out to the truck, and I called Doug and said, 'I don't give a damn if they publish it on the front page of the paper. That's your problem. I'm not going to let that stop me from doing something that's important to me.'

"At eight o'clock the next morning, Wednesday, the phone rang at Doug's downtown office." Linda said that his receptionist answered twice, but both times, the caller hung up. Then the phone rang again. "Doug answers it, and this time it is a female's voice who says that if I didn't stop doing the things I was doing, some harm is going to come to me and the kids. Well, he is just bananas at this point. That day, we got an alarm in the house and had a security expert come over. Nothing happened after that. I didn't hear a peep. That summer, I had one call when I was working in Indiana. When I picked up the phone, they said something about making pictures of Doug's affairs available. I crumbled. I got in the car and drove all the way home" to Louisville.

Linda received no more calls until two weeks before her husband left their home for good. "The first call said that if I would stop testifying in cases, somebody was prepared to exchange information about Doug's current affair. I didn't know there was a current affair." Linda did not say anything to Doug about the call. "Then I got a call about a week later. It was essentially the same thing. At that point, I just said, 'Are you threatening me?' And they hung up. It was at that point I talked to Doug. I certainly wasn't naïve enough to think Doug wasn't doing something. I was just busy and traveling. And my big fear was that somebody would mail me a picture the day before a deposition. Or do something in a deposition where they could just plop the question out and totally unnerve me. If they had done any kind of background, it was clear at this point that they knew this was my open wound." What did Linda do? "As a result of that call, Doug finally told me that there was somebody, and that he thought it was only fair to me that he admit it so that something like that would not happen. To some extent, he did me the biggest favor because, by leaving, he took away that ability, the hold of that, the threat of that, although it introduced all kinds of different things."

Linda still does not know who made those telephone calls, and cannot link the callers to Humana. It is remarkable, though, how whistleblowers like Linda report such similar torments. The lesson of the modern corporate workplace, typically far more subtle, has been that the corporation watches the individual, but the individual should not witness the corporation nor have expectations of it.

911 for Corporations, Not Workers

Often cultural assumptions become most visible during a societal crisis. Cultural acceptance of the diminishing obligations of the corporation to the worker, and of the increasing duty of individuals and society to the corporation, was striking in the aftermath of the September 11th attacks. One of the first official acts of Congress was to approve a $15 billion taxpayer-paid bailout of the airline industry—$5 billion in cash and $10 billion in loans—which was ten times the amount of its ground stop losses from the attack (estimated at $1.5 billion). The billions flowing from taxpayer treasuries included no aid to or safeguards for the airline workers who lost their jobs as a result of the disasters in lower Manhattan, in Pennsylvania, and at the Pentagon. In fact, airlines' announcements of the layoff of 100,000 workers[30] helped create the conditions for the bailout package, but industry executives claimed that the bailout would not restore lost jobs, and there were no govern-

mental strings to go with the taxpayer cash that would have prevented
further layoffs. The fired workers faced far greater financial hurdles
than airlines with fleets of assets that would be ready collateral for
credit to mitigate against short-term losses. The week after the industry
received $15 billion in taxpayer money, not only did the layoffs con-
tinue, but some airlines announced that they would invoke an emergency clause in contracts, called a "force majeure" provision, that allowed
them to give no notice, not offer standard severance pay, and not provide early retirement options usually required. The government, the
public, had bailed out Fortune 500 companies, and the industry returned the favor not only through firings but also by announcing it
would use the fine print of its contracts to avoid its responsibilities to
employees. [31]

American society hardly winced when the corporations laid off
100,000 workers in the midst of a national tragedy or when some of the
same companies then described themselves as patriots in television advertising. The market had no loyalty to any individual. The cultural assumption had become that the individual was a commodity, with worth
only at a given point in time, only in that "here and now," as the market
demanded or allowed, not the past or future. If the immediate needs of
the corporation in the market were not satisfied, then of course massive
firings would ensue.

Senator Ron Wyden (D-Oregon) described the $15 billion airline
bailout as a "leap of faith" during the Senate's floor debate because it
was based entirely on the airline industry's own assessment of its future
financial fate, not a single independent evaluation. The taxpayer assumption of shareholder burdens was but one manifestation of a new
societal duty to the corporation. Taxpayers also relieved the airline industry of its potential legal duty to the families of the victims of the
tragedy in lower Manhattan. The government set up a process by which
victims and their families who chose not to sue the airlines could collect economic and non-economic losses from taxpayers, but only if
they agreed to drop any claims against the airlines. A fund adminis-

trator to be selected by the Attorney General would decide who was entitled to recover what damages. Taxpayers would pay for security mistakes that very well could prove to be a product of airline industry cost-cutting that turned over passenger safety to minimum-wage security guards[32] and for which the airline's insurers should have been on the hook.

Corporations Go Socialist

Other big industries lined up at the federal trough in the wake of the September 11th attack like movie stars waiting at Spago. The hotel, restaurant, and insurance industries all sought direct taxpayer aid. The insurance industry was perhaps the most brazen in exploiting the crisis for its own ends. "Unlike airlines, which are reeling as travelers hesitate to fly, insurers have seen improved financial prospects since September 11," *The Wall Street Journal* reported just before Thanksgiving 2001. "Insurers expect to have to pay out $40 billion to $70 billion in claims related to the attacks. That sounds daunting, but in fact, it is manageable for an industry that collectively has $300 billion in capital. . . . Moreover, in response to September 11, insurers are already raising prices by 100% or more on some lines . . ."[33] This did not stop the industry from seeking a bailout of its responsibility for terrorist claims in the future, which it was careful to label a "back stop" rather than a bailout. The bailout was signed by President Bush on November 26, 2002, after his party captured control of the federal government in the election earlier that month with the insurance industry's help. Lloyd's of London explained on its website that the terrorist attacks on the United States presented "The Opportunity. Names [investors in the Lloyd's of London syndicates] may now have an historic opportunity for profitable underwriting. In the past, the ALM [Association of Lloyd's Members] has been cautious and in 1996 suggested that members should 'gear down' as rates plummeted. However, Lloyd's is now in a very different situation. The market was hardening strongly before the attacks, but since September 11th rates have shot up to a level where very large profits are possible." The advice harkened back to an embarrassing memo from Jeffrey Greenberg at American International Companies (owned by Jeffrey's father Maurice Greenberg) after Hurricane Andrew in 1992 that stated, "This is an opportunity to get price increases now." As *The Wall Street Journal* reported in the fall of 2001, "This embarrassment didn't stop Jeffrey Greenberg, now 50 years old, and his subordinates at March [his new company] from swiftly scouring the post–Sept. 11 business landscape for new opportunities."[34] Another insurance industry newsletter candidly stated: "Insurance companies will cite this terrorist attack and the catastrophes from the second quarter as evidence that their losses are growing [and] increase their rates. . . . This will bode well for the future of these companies. Bad news is good news in the insurance industry."[35]

In the wake of September 11th, Fortune 500 corporations also sought to have taxes they have paid since 1986 returned retroactively. Eliminating the alternative minimum tax, put in place in 1986 to make sure corporations paid some taxes after all their deductions, would have returned, in time of crisis, around $25 billion to America's largest corporations, erasing their tax payments from the last fifteen years. The change would have delivered a $1.4 billion refund for IBM, $832 million for General Motors and $671 for General Electric.[36] Passing this "stimulus" provision in the House of Representatives, some politicians claimed that this was the price necessary to keep corporations from laying off workers. "The bill's sponsors claim that the money would be invested and used to create jobs, but it's hard to see why: a potential investment that Texas Utilities or ChevronTexaco wouldn't have made a week ago, because the project won't yield a sufficiently high return, will seem no more profitable after each company gets its $600 million thank-you gift," wrote Princeton economist and *New York Times* columnist Paul Krugman. "And there are no strings attached to those gifts: if the companies want to, say, pay huge bonuses to top executives, they can."[37] To fathom the reach of the logic "the corporation > the individual" in

modern culture, one need only try to imagine a legislative proposal passing the House of Representatives that returned all the taxes paid by any
individual during the last fifteen years. No one even contemplated ex-
tending such largess to individuals who lost loved ones at the World
Trade Center. For the corporation to aspire to a taxpayer handout in
time of war showed that corporations were not capitalists, but pragma-
tists. Corporate welfare was no less socialism that any other public assistance program. When it was to its advantage, the corporation would
advocate socialism.

Americans have seen such contradictions less because they have
more illusions, many of which have originated in the workplace. Boundaries and borders between the individual worker and the corporation
were to disappear because the individual was to be the little corporation.
The strategy was to animate the part of the worker, mind and body, that
was the corporation and to inanimate the part that was an individual
and had loyalty to society. For instance, corporations contended that
demanding more of workers as well as outsourcing, downsizing, perm-
temping, and laying off long-time, expensive employees were changes
necessitated by the need to be competitive globally. This seems to have
resonated with a public that had tremendous anxiety about their job
security in the 1990s but blamed global competitiveness, not the corporations making the changes during a time of unprecedented prosperity. [38] Such empathy with the corporation made it easier for the
corporation to dominate individuals in their other roles as taxpayers,
citizens, voters, and shareholders.

The individual's mind and body can become corporate property
only when what the corporation takes from the individual is blurred
and what it gives becomes the focus. With regard to workers, the corporation focused on a partnership of equals where successful employees took a cut of increased stock values. Such success—defined as
sacrificing completely for the corporation—was often elusive. Precari-
ous stock wealth had replaced real wages as a source of pay, but the
promise of wealth was potent, even if, like a lottery, it only struck a few.

For example, United Airlines was widely portrayed as the worker-owned airline, one of the partnerships with workers making corporations and individuals "co-equals" because of employee ownership of stock. Blurred from view was the reality that United executives, not its workers, decided to lay off 20,000 employees in the aftermath of 9/11. United terminated more workers than any other airline, and a higher percentage of its workforce than major rival American, because—as with most corporations—corporate managers, not workers, were in control.

In the long run, it is probably more cost-effective for corporations to nurture and respect long-term employees so that institutional knowledge can be maintained and talent retained. In the same way, if corporations retained employees in hard times, those individuals would have money to revive the economy, since consumer spending is two-thirds of it. Similarly, allowing workers to dissent based on social mores would forewarn the corporation about problems that the corporation might one day have to deal with in court, such as the multimillion-dollar lawsuits against Humana based on conduct Linda Peeno objected to. Unfortunately, the horizon of many corporate leaders is months, not years. Executives have claimed that pressure from mutual fund owners to turn significant profits quickly by pumping up share value has been the reason they focus so much on short-term growth in stock price and profit. Such short-term growth also happens to be financially beneficial for the executives themselves when their bonuses are tied to spikes in stock. Easy fixes such as trimming costs and squeezing workers become the easy default, and market conditions the ready excuses.

Some corporate leaders have even faced industry pressure to cap employee benefits. For instance, John Hughes co-owns a Hollywood animation company, Rhythm & Hues, that in 2001 employed 300 permanent employees and up to 500 employees when large projects arose. Hughes spent about $10,000 per employee per year in 2001 to give his workers the best health-care benefits available. He "self-funds" the plan, bypassing insurers to simply pay all claims, and adds benefits whenever an employee's needs arise, such as dental, vision, or a special surgery.

For Hughes, it is a matter of principle. Even though Hollywood tends to be generous with its workers, it reacted poorly to a newspaper article about Rhythm & Hues' benefits policy. "We received a phone call from a high-level executive with one of our clients, complaining about our health-care package, that we were spending too much on our employees, and that's why our prices were high," Hughes told me, noting that he received the project because he was the lowest bidder. "We didn't lose the business, but you know there's still fallout from that article. There are still clients complaining about our benefits package. And you know, what's hypocritical is that these clients typically have million-dollar houses and drive Mercedeses and BMWs and Jaguars. . . . I live in a small town house, and I drive a Honda Civic. So, instead of living in a million-dollar house, I've decided to give the money back to the employees and their health care. . . . They consider that a bad business practice, and they're angry at me for doing that. And if I took exactly the same amount of money and bought a huge mansion and drove expensive cars, they would think that's okay. They would love that. They would think that would be wonderful. But if I give that same amount of money to the employees in terms of benefits, now they're angry."[39]

Hughes had broken a taboo in the modern workplace where the worker was to sacrifice for the corporation. Such values internalized in the corporation during the age of the corporateer were also externalized to the American financial system. The next chapter shows the strategies by which a critical part of the corporateer's success in controlling American culture has been the individual's growing debt to the corporation.

INDEBTED TO THE
CORPORATION

*The real price of everything, what everything really costs to the
man who wants to acquire it, is the toil and trouble of acquiring it.*

ADAM SMITH, *THE WEALTH OF NATIONS*, 1776

If one person wanted to control another, he would put her in his
debt. Similarly, the corporation's growing control over culture has
depended on the individual's growing financial indebtedness to the
corporation. If the individual owed the market and the corporation,
then the individual could more easily see sacrificing herself and her
freedom for it.

Standards of living for Americans rose during the last two decades.
But wealth for the individual became speculative and illusory in many
of the same ways it had for the corporation. In 1999, a time of unprecedented economic prosperity, the national savings rate declined to
below zero.[1] The federal government, fueled by the tax surplus of the
booming economy, balanced its books in the summer of 1999. But the
Commerce Department reported in June 1999 that Americans, for the
first time in sixty years, were spending more money than they earned.
With the economy roaring, the savings rate declined to −1.2 percent in
May 1999 from −1.0 percent in April, the lowest since the Depression.

Many individuals' deficit spending extended to credit cards. The average credit card balance for national households was $8,100 in September 2001, compared to $3,000 in 1990.[2] The threat of such debt to the individual's financial security became more apparent in harder economic times. In the weak economy before September 11th, credit card delinquencies reached a 29-year high. After the attack, as corporations showed their national pride through massive layoffs of workers, the situation significantly worsened for low- and middle-income workers. Credit card companies did not show any more loyalty for consumers in the recession than employers did. While the Federal Reserve's short-term interest rate stood at 2.5 percent, a 39-year low, in October 2001, the average annual percentage rate on credit card debt was 14 percent. Overall household debt service, which is the payments of interest and principal on all debt as a percentage of take-home pay, was also near its highest mark, established in 1986.[3] Our consumer group even received reports about some gamblers on the stock boom taking cash advances on their credit cards to bet on Internet stock that they believed would yield a higher rate of return.

For the average American family, the debt-building period of the 1980s and 1990s extended to their most important and valuable asset, their home. Following the attack on the World Trade Center towers, mortgage refinancing was seen as the bright spot of the economy. The Federal Reserve repeatedly cut interest rates, and mortgage interest rates dropped to a 30-year low by November 2001. The economic and societal expectation was that even consumers who had recently refinanced would take advantage of the low rates to refinance again and use the extra dollars taken out of their equity in their home to pay off credit card debt and to spend, thereby improving the economy. The government even announced the end to its long-term Treasury Bond, which the mortgage rate is based on, in order to drive mortgage rates down further and to encourage individuals to refinance their homes as an economic stimulus. Borrowing against the individual's home had been a standard practice during the previous two decades. While families built up equity in their homes during the 1960s and 1970s, the Federal Reserve Board reported that the average household's share of home ownership declined to a record low during the 1980s and 1990s. During the booms in the 1990s, Americans borrowed even more against their homes.[4] The use of the funds withdrawn from one's homes to gamble on corporations in the stock market became a common enough problem during the 1990s for financial planning experts to warn against it.[5] Such spending shows how the individual's attitude toward home ownership and the financial system had fundamentally changed. The home had been sacrosanct in the 1950s, 1960s, and 1970s. Paying down or off a mortgage was a rite of passage for the average American family. During the 1980s and 1990s, Americans' attitude toward spending had come more to reflect the corporation's view of seeking short-term economic gain, maximizing profit by pumping up the portfolio, rather than seeking long-term protection of one's home and social standing in a community. "When you make borrowing dependent on your home, then you erode the fire wall that protects your standard of living," said Nicolas Retsinas, director of the Joint Center for Housing Studies at Harvard. "The home is not just a financial transaction, it defines what you are and what kind of community you live in. When all of a sudden you get into trouble, you can't just rip it up like a credit card."[6] Sucking equity out of a home to gamble on markets or pay down other debt has had an impact in economic downturns, placing families at greater risk and putting society on the hook for caring for those who cannot take care of themselves. For instance, the Federal Housing Administration reported in the second fiscal quarter of 2001 that its mortgages had a record 10.79 percent delinquency rate.[7] By the summer of 2002, the *Los Angeles Times* noted a growing trend of average home buyers entering into "interest-only" loans, where borrowers paid off interest, but no principal, in order to have lower monthly payments.[8] At the end of the typical five- to ten-year interest-only period, the borrower has paid off none of the loan amount and may owe more than the house is worth. That such risks became routine in a recession showed that buying a home was no longer about owning a home, but gambling with one.

Americans' decision to leverage their homes was not made in a vacuum. Corporations created many products that treated the home—and by extension the community—exclusively as a financial product. The government, of course, sanctioned them. Home equity lines of credit allowed individuals to utilize the equity in their home as security to buy on credit. No-cost refinancing encouraged borrowing against one's home. Zero-down loans at higher interest rates put first-time home buyers into properties without a down payment, but so-called "sub prime" lending had a sinister side as well. Major banks developed "sub prime" arms with different names that approached seniors and minorities with practices that came to be termed "predatory lending." For instance, seniors were solicited, often at their doors, to refinance homes that they already owned, in order to get quick cash but at extraordinarily high rates with mortgage payments they sometimes could not afford. This became known as "equity skimming," and predator lenders would then foreclose to secure valuable property or collect double-digit interest rates. The home became commodified for its financial value and taken for granted in its social worth by a financial system that encouraged extraordinary social risk for the promise of rapid financial gain. To many, not trading away equity in one's home for equity in a growing corporation's stock seemed foolhardy when the stock market gained 15 percent per year during the high-tech boom. In recession, of course, the debts from busted dot-coms and eroded corporate equities came due. The positive side of the higher risk mortgage products was mostly for first-time home buyers who could purchase a house with no down payment or a significantly reduced one, even though their equity was nonexistent. This is one reason that more Americans own homes in the new millennium than ever before—more than two thirds of all households—even though their equity may be tiny. The negative side was not limited to double-digit interest rates that come with the higher risk products, steep penalties for prepayment so one

cannot find a better rate, bogus mandatory insurance, or other predatory lending tactics. There was also the illusory nature of the individual's heightened standard of living, which could crumble quickly in
bad times, and with it the family's place in a community.

From Caveat Emptor to Amat Emptor

If "the corporation > the individual," then the only way for the individual to be a co-equal was to become a corporation, to merge with it, into
its network, brand, and values. Within the workplace, this reasoning
fed the logic that "the worker = the corporation," where workers were
willing to forgo labor protections and security to be contract business
persons with the power of the market on their side. The same reasoning
also undergirded the corporate seduction of the consumer. With that
marriage of the consumer and the corporation (the consumer = the
corporation), the individual had the most hope for satisfaction. One
reason corporations approached individuals as "people," with the human persona, soul, and meaning, was to seduce them. The corporation
wanted to be "intimate" with the individual. Courting the individual in
an "intimate" affair became the new buzz of management theories of the
new millennium that utilized new technologies to achieve "customer
intimacy" and "customer relations management" (CRM). Customer intimacy was more than a term of art, but a prevalent corporate perspective that integrating the individual into the corporation brought the
greatest profit over time. If an individual fell in love with a brand, they
would love it for life. The evolving corporate science of CRM depended
on procuring intensive data collection about individuals' personal
spending habits, but also spoke in remarkably intimate terms for a science. Stanley A. Brown, the head of PricewaterhouseCoopers's International Center of Excellence in Customer Care, wrote the bible on CRM.
He explained that "Creating Loyalty" was about the phases of "The
Courtship," "The Relationship," "The Marriage," and then, "From Customer Loyalty to Customer Dependency." The commercial goals esca-

lated at each stage, from "product" to "share of wallet" to "share of life."[9] Successful CRM was based on sorting out the best customers and treating others with less care (segmenting), intensively tracking customers' behavior (profiling customers, researching customers), and seducing them through personalized offers (managing customers) that may not be the most competitive but were based on customer loyalty and dependency.[10] "Competitiveness" became a strategy to capture not just the individual's consciousness but also her affection; to deal with the consumer as an "intimate," not to offer the lowest price or best quality. In fact, CRM practitioners recognized that the apparatus to be intimate added costs to the product, but sellers would have to go through corporations that effectively practiced CRM because they had control of the buyers. The more effective the CRM, the less free the seller was to see the buyer, the less free the classical market.

Publicly, however, the corporation ubiquitously promoted the illusion that the individual was happiest and freest when giving herself over fully to the corporation, when fully submitting, trusting, and sublimating exclusively to her corporation's commerce. When "the consumer = the corporation," individuals could achieve their ultimate fantasies and greatest freedoms simply by giving all their money to the corporation that is their intimate. Corporations wanted you to enter their cars and go out of your way to drive with them alone on deserted highways for miles on end. They wanted their financial products to fulfill your every desire and morph your life into the greatest pleasures, smiles, and satisfactions known on earth.

To trust is to spend, and individuals in the era of the corporateer trust corporations far more than any such large institution with the goal of maximizing profit deserves to be trusted. The corporation has effectively replaced "Caveat Emptor," or "Buyer Beware" with "Amat Emptor," or "Buyer Beloved." Corporations may court individuals like lovers, but they often treat them more like one-night stands. Consumers are often not prepared for the fact that a corporation will give them a loan, credit card limit, or installment plan even if they really cannot afford it. This is one reason an American in 1997 had as much chance of declaring bankruptcy as an American during the Depression era.[11] Financial institutions that have seduced Americans to spend were so concerned that in 2001 and 2002 they proposed a federal overhaul of bankruptcy laws to force the bankrupt to treat paying off their credit card bills with the same priority as paying their child support.[12]

Spending Is Saving

In the wake of the September 11th attacks, Americans were told to show their national pride by spending—going out to dinner, making a major purchase, refinancing their home. Consumer spending was elevated to a patriotic act, not as much to demonstrate that Americans were still free to live their lives as normal (which did not take a refinancing) but to drive the economy. For instance, San Francisco Mayor Willie Brown distributed 15,000 posters in storefronts that read "America: Open for Business" and showed an American flag with shopping-bag handles.

By contrast, the corporation did not have to spend. The mighty consumer would be the engine of the economic renaissance. The oft-repeated mantra has been that consumer spending accounts for two-thirds of the economy. The type of pressure on workers to grow corporate profits within a corporation has had a corollary during the last few decades in societal pressure on the consumer to grow the market. The social cost of such policies, a people in debt to corporations whose social fabric would be more fragile, was outweighed by a commercial benefit—corporations freer to give consumers any product or service even if they could not afford it, and to return their lost retirement savings through greater stock value.

During the last decades, widespread financial products reflecting the irrational premise that spending was saving showed the degree to which consumerism had become an article of cultural faith, a national religion, rather than a rational economic choice. Customers that gave their loyalty to a store by spending over a certain amount, likely at a higher level than they would have spent otherwise, received a free video rental, airline miles, or cash back. These illusory perks made little sense financially. Casinos had used the same techniques for decades to keep marks spending at their tables. Credit card companies, for instance, gave cash back when balances subject to high interest rates were carried over from one month to the next. One solicitation from American Express and Costco for a "special Platinum Cash Rebate Credit Card" offered, in addition to cash back on purchases, "an additional .5% on purchases during months in which a balance is carried over." The APR, however, was 17.99 percent. So, as with most of these products, spending did not save as much as not spending or as saving in the first place.

The marketing genius that ran American Express's Membership Rewards Program, where one must spend $10,000 to receive a $100 gift certificate at Coach, devised a market solution to the dearth in savings. His new company, Upromise, offered a network of companies that would give consumers a rebate for buying that would be applied to a tax-sheltered college savings account for their kids. A prospective saver would register with Upromise and receive 1 to 5 percent cash back for a 401(k)-like fund managed by Fidelity Investments, Salomon Smith Barney, Merrill Lynch, and TIAA-CREF. "Right now, we have the lowest rate of savings in sixty years," Michael Bronner, the executive, acknowledged. "It's a huge problem, a train wreck, but you can't preach. What drives this economy is consumerism, so you have to recognize that fact."[13] The program has commercial appeal for corporations, according to Bronner, because of the consumer intimacy it breeds—since some families will spend to save for nineteen years. "For a company, that's a two-decade relationship with a consumer. No program has ever offered that kind of customer relationship. That's the Holy Grail of American business."[14] The tuition payoff for the consumer, though, would require some intense spending. For instance, a family of four spending 15 percent of their income with Upromise companies would after fifteen years earn only $15,000, assuming an 8 percent annual return in the stock market.[15] Mechanisms that help Americans spend under the guise of saving have fed a financial system that has offered up the illusion of gain.

Many Americans have paid the savings of tomorrow for the lifestyles and corporate gambles of today. Equity in corporations even took on social worth for young adults coming of age in the stock boom. "Your investment in the market reflects your status," 24-year-old law student Bruce Gibney told *The New York Times Magazine* in October 2000. "It's not about being invited to one of Mr. and Mrs. Astor's parties anymore; it's how many people you know in really good start-ups. Or you mention 'Series A'—that's a great way to get somebody's attention: 'I was in Series A, I was in the seed round, I got in for pennies a share.'"[16]

Columnist Jeff Turrentine reported, "That's the dream: stocks now, the world at 40. Retirement at 40. Dinner parties and families and novels at 40. I heard it again and again as I talked to these prudent 20 and 30-somethings. But I worry how possible it will be to achieve."[17] Many in the generation bankrupted their present by selling their youth to the market for equity in a future that never materialized. They epitomize the extent to which the casino of the market has moved individuals toward becoming shareholders in an America where everything should be sold and traded, lost and gained on the market's whims, rather than citizens with inalienable societal rights, protections, and choices.

Gambling in the National Interest

The logic that the market is greater than society has been reflected in national monetary policy of the last two decades designed to encourage the consumer to let it all ride. The Federal Reserve all but eliminated interest rates in the economic valleys of recent years, so it did not pay to save. Seniors and others who relied on interest income from federally guaranteed certificates of deposits paid a price with their income, even though they were least able to. "It's basically [a transfer of money] from people who are thrifty and save to people who are spendthrift," retiree

William Buchman told the *Los Angeles Times*.[18] Once again, the best consumers win, the least consumptive lose. Few in the mainstream considered the Fed's move the wrong thing to do from the point of view of a
culture built on the promise that the individual's highest and best role
was as a consumer.

In the same vein, Congress in 1999 felled Depression-era financial
barriers that required insurers, stock brokerages, and banks to be separated. With these corporations integrated, dominoes would fall much
quicker once there was a significant jolt to any one of the markets, and
society would have to bear the burden. However, corporations claimed
that the deregulation of the industries would allow their profitability to
increase through innovative services, and with it, in the short term at
least, the values of their shares. The argument that shareholders would
win (along with the potential for consumers to) weighed heavily on
Congress to make such changes. In retrospect, shareholders lost, because the changes created even more conflicts of interest for Wall Street
brokerage and bank analysts who could not speak honestly about companies integral to their firm's other interests.

For example, a ten-month investigation by New York Attorney
General Elliot Spitzer found internal Merrill Lynch e-mail in which,
during the dot-com boom, analysts privately disparaged stocks that
they publicly recommended, calling them "a powder keg" or "piece of
junk." Merrill's research department never once recommended that investors "sell" or "reduce," the lowest ratings available.[19] Spitzer said,
"This correspondence shows that the people writing stock reports at
times functioned essentially as sales representatives for the firm's investment bankers."[20] Even with these smoking guns, the logic "market
> society" won out in the end. Spitzer settled his case against Merrill
Lynch with no admission of wrongdoing by the brokerage. Conventional wisdom was that, with consolidation among the major stock
brokerages in recent years, if Merrill went under, the whole market
would, so Spitzer could not afford to be too punitive.

The Federal Reserve policies of the last two decades have also reflected a strong preference for helping those who invest heavily in the stock market, as opposed to those simply making a wage, who need the most help. Journalist William Greider, who wrote the book *Secrets of the Temple* about the Fed, explained that the successful attempts by the Fed to restrain inflation during the 1980s and 1990s decreased the relative value of wages paid but increased the value of dollars invested in the stocks and bonds.

> With the inflation rate steadily subsiding, moving downward in most years, the dollar's value was growing, particularly if it was invested in the future through stocks or bonds. Thus, monetary policy effectively delivered a discreet dividend, year after year, to the wealth-holders. . . . Their stocks and bonds or other financial assets would automatically be worth a bit more when they sold them because they would be paid in harder dollars—currency that had more purchasing power than the dollars they had originally spent to purchase the stocks or bonds. . . . Industrial workers, on the other hand, felt lousy, as did a majority or more of all wage earners, because their wages were being discreetly depressed, in real terms, by the same process. . . . [F]or most of Greenspan's tenure, average wages did not keep up with inflation. Many families experienced the paradox—*their* purchasing power seemed to be shrinking, even though inflation rates had fallen. Confused people sometimes blamed this squeeze on rising prices when the real problem was stagnant or falling incomes.[21]

That the market, any market, was more important than society could hardly be contested by witnesses to the markets of the 1980s and 1990s. In the 1980s, Americans' societal sensibilities were tested by the rise of corporate raiders who made billions by taking over and strip-mining manufacturing and production companies, as well as the jobs within them. The logic was that shareholders would receive more value for their shares if raiders dismantled these companies and sold their assets rather than kept them running. Speculation on destruction paid, even if it was not in the national societal interest of keeping Americans working and companies alive. The liquidations of the companies and jobs reflected a societal shift to the permitting of dismantling even productive economic structures for higher short-term yields and narrower pecuniary gain. From their rise in the 1970s, transnational corporations threatened the environment, the worker, and the consumer, but the destruction of not-unhealthy companies for cash—because growth was not rapid enough—marked a regression in which markets forgot key societal priorities.

Similarly, the nation's financial system bet against itself (and sometimes society) through increasing speculation on the fall of stock. Derivative portfolios, short sales, and hedge funds were all built speculating on destruction. Hedge funds, for instance, made billions by betting against companies, as did those engaged in short sales. In a short sale, borrowed stock is sold betting that the price will drop and the borrower will make money by buying the stock at the lower price to repay the debt. Ralph Nader said of hedge funds, which borrow money to bet against markets, "The non-regulated world of hedge funds contains all the warning signs of eventual crisis and demand for bailouts."[22] In 1998, the Federal Reserve inspired a $3.6 billion Wall Street bailout of Long Term Capital Management, the speculative hedge fund that made bets with borrowed money and almost brought the banking system to its knees.[23] The short sale, not unique in history, was exploited just days before the attacks of September 11th, where some investors made huge bets against the airline industry and reaped huge rewards off the death of thousands. The short sales were so conspicuous that some even believed that the terrorists responsible for the hijackings had placed the bets. Similarly, in the first few days of trading that followed the attacks, investors bet against the system, sending the market plunging. "The realm of bulls and bears turned out to be a field of sheep," *Los Angeles Times* columnist John Balzar wrote. "Yes, there were some who stood firm. But they were dragged down by the overpaid mutual fund managers who led the retreat, by the brokers who churned orders as they spread fear, by the hedge fund players who could see no further than the closing bell. . . . These same investors who were glued to their TVs and who scooped up newspapers in a frantic effort to keep informed promptly drove down the value of these same media companies—Wall Street's twisted rewards for American enterprise."[24]

Arbitraging, betting the price in one market against another, was similarly an unproductive enterprise for society that yielded huge commercial rewards during the last two decades based on disparities in markets, not economic creation or production. At the core of the corporate monetary system prevalent since the 1980s has been an emphasis on unproductive, short-term speculation and exploitation of illusion, rather than long-term economic creation and production. (Enron epitomized this.[25]) In this way, the volatile corporate financial system has become dominated by the mentality of a gambler that divorced itself from the social fortunes of the masses of people whose money and lives it bet with.

What the Market Does Not Disclose Can Hurt You

Americans' illusions about how corporations actually behave in markets has been a critical reason corporations have often come first in society and markets. Commentators and economists who participate in markets typically refer to financial markets as organic entities, uncontrollable living things. The dynamic portrait has a mystical and spiritual quality that suggests one cannot dare to question workings of the market any more than one can the ways of a god. Markets have often been cloaked in such mystiques. It's an element of why consumerism has become a national religion and economists such as Alan Greenspan have been regarded as the national equivalent of high priests. (Greenspan condemned "infectious greed" in 2002 for skewing the market's natural workings, yet he earned his collar through a 1963 essay that argued, "[I]t is precisely the 'greed' of the businessman or, more appropriately, his profit-seeking, which is the unexcelled protector of the consumer."[26]) The market being perceived as incomprehensible, except through ideological rules by which one can get close to but never predict, abets corporate control over culture. If markets move based on supply and demand, just as oceans by winds and weather, but they have an essence that is organic and mysterious, corporations become the only significant point of reference. Such reasoning has been a key source of the corporations' cultural power. It's become accepted lore that corporations are interpreters of omens in the market but that they cannot control markets. In fact, in many ways corporations can and do.

The public would look at corporations differently if they were not simply riders on a storm but were the makers of the weather. Competition, it is said, keeps corporations honest in organic markets. However, due to consolidation, much of what happens in new-millennium markets has been artificially manipulated by handfuls of corporations that control them. Collusion is the legal term that defines federal anti-trust violations by companies that have literally sat down together to set prices or restrain supply. The classic case in modern times was agricultural producer Archer Daniels Midland (ADM), which made secret deals with its competitors to keep the prices of products artificially high. The meetings were secretly taped by an FBI informant. At a meeting in Irvine, California, for instance, "FBI hidden cameras captured scenes reminiscent of drug lords or mob bosses cutting up turf," *Dateline NBC* reported. "But these guys were top executives in the biggest Lysine [an essential animal and human nutrient] companies in the world. . . . With representatives of all five Lysine makers present, FBI hidden cameras rolled again [in Hawaii]. Watch as one of the executives passes out a phony agenda. It's a cover in case anyone asks why they were all at the same place at the same time, and everyone has a good laugh as he passes it out. All this to make it look like an illegal price-fixing scheme was nothing more than an innocent trade association meeting."[27] On tape, however, the FBI actually secured this definitive statement by one of the participants, "So five companies agree to total quantity. That's the first time."

Dateline interviewed the FBI informant within ADM about the 'company motto,' "The customer is our enemy. The competitor is our friend." The informer stated, "I heard that hundreds of times, because they felt that the competitors could make you money."[28] ADM ultimately paid a $100 million fine and claimed to have implemented internal controls to prevent such a scandal from occurring again. However, ADM is still functioning today and controls more than half the nation's supply of ethanol, which is an additive to make gasoline cleaner. This says much about the cultural place of the corporation in society. It can be caught fixing markets and still not be liquidated.

When there is no videotape of a smoky back room, however, there generally can be no legal collusion. This has created a gray area for the handful of corporations that have dominated many industries and can simply "follow the leader" to make markets more amenable to all. This is a remarkably common practice in corporate America today, and while it does not necessarily defy a narrow legal standard, it does betray a cultural trust placed in the corporation by the public that expects competition, not coordination, to run markets.

Consider these few prominent examples of the artificiality of markets maintained by corporations that work together against the consumer rather than competing to serve him better:

- The high price of diamonds is based on supply and demand, but a diamond cartel very strictly limits the release of diamonds to drive up the price by limiting supply.

- The American drug industry has priced drugs so that 74 percent of the cost is something other than manufacturing and distribution.[29] (Consumer Reports found Research and Development was only 16 percent of the cost while profit, administration, and marketing accounted for 49 percent. Taxes were 9 percent.) Competition has never undercut this unwritten, mutually beneficial arrangement. In fact, costs have been escalating in recent years.

- Insurance companies often raise premiums based not on claims filed with the company (product cost), but on their investment opportunities. The focus of the modern insurance company has been not to insure a market but to draw income from investing premiums. When interest rates increase (so investment yields are higher), insurance companies reduce price to attract greater capital for investment, underwriting greater risk. When interest rates are low, premiums increase to maintain profit levels. This well-documented "insurance cycle" produces premium increases based not on the costs of the insurance product (claims made), as an efficient market would, but based on the investment climate and profitability levels insurers seek to maintain. When investments fail, as well, policyholders pay more. For such reasons, insurers might also stonewall or lowball claims payments to make greater interest on their capital by investing it in capital markets longer.[30]

- The small group of companies controlling global media have so many overlapping agreements that, according to TCI chairman and media magnate John Malone, "Nobody can really afford to get mad at their competitors because they are partners in one area and competitors in another."[31] News Corporation's Rupert Murdoch said more bluntly, "We can join forces now, or we can kill each other and then join forces."[32]

- Wall Street brokerages have been so riddled with conflicts of interest that consumer dollars directed to stocks were not necessarily based on real market strength but the fact that analysts held shares of the stock they recommended. After the new-millenniun plunge in stock value, some companies moved away from the practice. The even larger problem was that lucrative investment banking fees paid to the brokerages came from corporations that wanted high ratings from analysts regardless of whether their market standing merited it. The dot-com bubble was inflated by such conflicts of interest, where bankers who took companies public that had no profits received kickbacks from some mutual and hedge-fund investors for retroactive allocations of stock that had shot up hundreds of percentage points in a day from the opening price. The investors then "flipped" it, that is, they sold the artificially inflated stock almost immediately.[33] Similarly, conflicts have riddled auditing firms whose numbers Wall Street analysts and investors rely upon.

- The public quarrel between Firestone and Ford over the safety of tires on the Explorer was so noticeable because of the din of criticism between corporations in general. In particular, car makers know better than anyone else about the defects in their competitors' brands, but they never disclose them. Such industries know that they don't win by competing too aggressively.

The notion of a self-regulating and self-balancing market, as organic in self-maintenance as the human body or an ecosystem, has become the prevalent cultural ideology and article of faith during the Corporateer Age. It has moved government and regulation out of markets and privatization into public realms. Even after the September 11th attacks proved private airport security forces had an incentive to keep costs low and not security high, Republicans in Congress refused for two months to break with the logic that the market and private enterprise could do it better alone. They resisted creating a government airport security force, apparently not appreciating the difference a public fire-fighting force has made. The legislation ultimately passed only because of an overwhelming public outcry. Ironically, on one of the days that Congress debated the matter of federal security, three American economists won the 2001 Nobel Memorial Prize in Economic Sciences for pointing to the imperfections of market systems that required external corrections and, as such, warranted less blind faith and more scrutiny. One of the winners, Joseph E. Stiglitz, a Columbia University professor, was honored for research that showed government needed a strong role in a market system to ward against damage from imperfect systems. "One part of the market knows more than another and in a sense imperfect or asymmetric information is at the heart of our work," Stiglitz said.[34] For instance, as co-winner George A. Akerlof of the University of California, Berkeley, showed, the problem with the used-car market was that dealers know the status of cars but buyers can only guess. Hence, the need for lemon laws to make the market work. Many, including the winners, speculated that the Nobel's choice showed hope for transition out of an era when the market ruled all spheres and public oversight was eliminated. "There's a pendulum that swings back and forth, and I think it's swinging back," said the third recipient, A. Michael Spence of Stanford.[35] Stiglitz noted, "The choice reflects where much of mainstream economics is today, which is that competitive equilibrium is not a useful model."[36]

If these theories represent the modern state of economics, they do not seem to reflect the individual's or public's cultural perception of markets. The priorities of the last two decades have rested on the presumption that unrestrained markets gave the consumers a surfeit of knowledge, not a deficit, by connecting more buyers to more sellers. If markets were restrained, consumers were restrained. Much of this illusion has been accomplished by the drumbeat invocation of Adam Smith, who in 1776 first coined the term "invisible hand" of the market in urging acceptance of certain economic rules for a free market. In fact, Adam Smith's theories would condemn the type of markets that modern corporations control. Smith saw corporations of his time as impediments to the free market because they represented monopolistic power that restrained free trade. The monopoly power that governments and kings once sanctioned by charter have in modern times been simulated through massive consolidation. Smith would no doubt agree that modern consumers are at a disadvantage when they are uninformed of how a few large corporations work together to keep them in the dark or in the red. Smith wrote the following of corporations in 1776, whose privileges he viewed as enlarged monopolies:

> A monopoly granted either to an individual or a trading company has the same effect as a secret in trade or manufactures. The monopolists, by keeping the market constantly understocked, by never fully supplying the effectual demand, sell their commodities much above the natural price, and raise their emoluments, whether they consist in wages or profit, greatly above their natural rate. The price of monopoly is upon every occasion the highest which can be got. The natural price, or the price of free competition, on the contrary, is the lowest which can be taken, not upon every occasion indeed, but for any considerable time altogether. The one is upon every occasion the highest which can be squeezed out of the buyer, or which, it is supposed, they will consent to give: The other is the lowest which the sellers can commonly afford to take, and at the same time continue their business.
>
> The exclusive privileges of corporations, statutes of apprenticeship, and all those laws which restrain, in particular employments, the competition to a small number than might otherwise go into them, have the same tendency, though in a lesser degree. . . .[37]
>
> It is to prevent this reduction of price, and consequently of wages and profit, by restraining free competition which would most certainly occasion it, that all corporations, and the greater part of corporation laws, have been established.[38]

Far from being interpreters of markets, the corporations of Adam Smith's day ruined them. Before turning attention to how large modern corporations sometimes do the same today, another word about Adam Smith. Smith's voluminous economic treatise *An Inquiry into the Nature and Causes of the Wealth of Nations* was, in 1776, the harbinger of an economic revolution as surely as the American Declaration of Independence harkened a political one. Both revolutions were compatible with each other. Smith respected individuals and society and argued not for the preeminence of markets over societies but for competitive economic markets organizing themselves around individuals who pursue their own self-interests. The individual, not the corporation, was the centerpiece of Smith's work, because the book relied on understanding human, not organizational, conduct.

In fact, Smith mentions the term "invisible hand" only once in his gargantuan treatise, though the expression has taken on a life of its own that bears little resemblance to its first use. Smith wrote of individuals who own businesses that "[b]y preferring the support of domestic to that of foreign industry, he intends only his own security; and by directing that industry in such manner as its produce may be for the greatest value, he intends only his own gain, and he is in this, as in many cases, led by an invisible hand to promote an end which was no part of his intention."[39] In Smith's world, societal identification of the individual was key to properly functioning markets. Self-interest was broad enough to include national identity. (Of course, transnational corporations have no such identity.) Smith's other great work, *The Theory of Moral Sentiments,* which he rewrote before his death, showed that he believed not only in the pursuit of economic self-interest by the individual in order to satisfy basic needs. Beyond markets, Smith was fascinated by the capacity and proclivity of individuals for moral virtue, which he saw as essential to living a full existence. Within markets, Smith and his followers also recognized, as international development specialist David Korten wrote, that "[b]uyers and sellers must be too small to influence the market price. Complete information must be available to participants and there can be no trade secrets. . . . Investment capital must remain within national borders and trade between countries must be balanced."[40]

Cheating Rather Than Competing

Did you ever wonder what really accounts for the cost of gasoline? Like many other American markets, gasoline prices have been a blind trust that a few corporations hold for us. I knew little more about the gasoline market than any other motorist until after the new century began. California's gasoline prices were shooting up above the two-dollar-per-gallon mark, the highest in the nation, when I received a phone call from the speaker of the California State Assembly. He asked that I represent the Assembly on the state Attorney General's task-force investigating the price spikes. Until sitting through the task-force meetings, I was under many of the same illusions about the gasoline market that most Americans shared. The main illusion was that power over price was based in OPEC and that only changes in the cartel's output sent gasoline prices up or down. The oil companies blamed the price spikes on crude oil production cuts by OPEC, shortages of fuel due to refinery outages, and California's special clean-burning fuel standards. But the two-dollar gasoline in California defied those assumptions because, at the same time, gasoline was far cheaper across the rest of the nation. If crude oil from OPEC was the problem, gas prices across the country would have risen in unison. Instead, a simple fact proved to be the root cause of the gas price spikes, one most Californians never heard. Six refiners controlled more than 90 percent of the state's refining capacity and also owned the majority of retail gasoline stations. (Since then, the number has been reduced to five.) The power exerted by these gasoline companies allowed them to corner the market, artificially reducing supply at key times to send the speculative price of gas soaring. The key indication for me was that every price spike represented almost pure profit to these corporations, not actual costs of production or even a reflection of actual motorist demand.

When the market has appeared to move, it is often just the corporations within them moving simultaneously, without the actual impetus of a real change in demand or supply. The gasoline market, like

many, had become increasingly dominated by speculative shifts resulting from artificial maneuvers by corporations. For instance, when
refinery fires flared in California, the six refiners had so reduced inventory levels prior to the event that a speculative shortage was perceived
to exist when no real one did. There were never lines at California's gas
pumps, as there had been during the gasoline crisis of the 1970s. Instead, there were only paper shortages that sent the speculative price in
the market above two dollars per gallon even though the cost of production for the companies remained the same and demand could easily be met. The system was rigged for a speculative price hike at the first
sign of trouble. This is why the refiners' profits skyrocketed.

Refiners have long maintained that environmental standards for
cleaner gas have been a cause of inflated prices and a barrier to new refineries opening. In fact, California's greener gas formulation adds only
pennies to the gallon, but because the formulation was so different
from the rest of the nation's, the regional refiners had a lock on gas in
the West. The state could not import the special blend from anywhere
else when the Big Six pushed up their prices. The major gasoline refiners in California had already reduced the number of refineries to nearly
half of the number in 1982, when the gasoline market was deregulated
federally, despite a burgeoning population. After deregulation, the big
refiners used their power to drive out or buy up smaller independent
refineries. Evidence made available by Senator Ron Wyden of Oregon
during an investigation of the gasoline industry showed how. Internal
1996 memorandums from Mobil laid out the strategies that would successfully keep smaller refiner Powerine from reopening its California
refinery. The document makes it clear that much of the hardships created by California's environmental regulations governing refineries
came at the urging of the major oil companies and not the environmental organizations blamed by the industry. An alternative plan discussed in the event Powerine did open the refinery, "was buying out
their production and marketing ourselves" to insure that the lower
price fuel didn't get into the market. In the memo, Mobil acknowledged

that the strategy of buying its competitors' gas to keep it off the market was utilized in the previous year and resulted in significantly increased prices. Not surprisingly, the West has had significantly higher prices than the rest of the nation for longer periods of time, and West Coast refiners have posted higher profit margins than in the rest of the nation.

Adam Smith would have winced at the oligopoly created by removing government regulation over gasoline prices in the early 1980s. This amounted to a monopoly, since the corporations behaved very similarly. The corporateer logic encouraging consolidation had allowed the oil companies to maintain these profits to an astonishing degree of control from the refineries to the local service station. The six companies moved refined product through jointly owned pipelines to shared truck-loading terminals to branded stations. Un-ringing that bell proved impossible for our task force, which did, however, conclude that the anti-competitive behavior of refiners led to the price spikes. The way these corporations established their hold over product delivery helps explain how corporations can make markets instead of having markets make them.

Gas pricing once relied on competition for the motorist's business among major oil companies through their "branded" operations, on one side, and "unbranded" independent operations, on the other. Unbranded independents were retailers who bought unbranded gasoline for resale to the public at non-company stations, so they were free to buy from any source, including an importer, that offered the best price on any given day. Tension between "the majors" and the unbranded independents kept the major companies honest on price and supply.

Causes of the new-millennium price crisis can be partly traced to the demise of the unbranded independent operations, whose eventual extinction was hatched in a confidential 1982 memo from the "Strategic Pricing Unit" of ARCO, a major oil company. In the secret memo, only made public after ARCO was subpoenaed and threatened with contempt charges by the Nevada Legislature, top company managers declared the "traditional two-tier, major-independent market system no longer able to co-exist."[41] The ARCO executives' outline foresaw "market control eroding as consumer goes to lowest price mode of delivery (independent stations)," and they hatched a plan for one-tier "market control" that included taking over the business of unbranded independent operations (eliminating competition), as well as reducing surplus supply at refineries. ARCO has claimed that the memo has been misunderstood and that it simply wanted to make itself the most competitive company, but in my view, the document spoke to the type of pressure the majors put on the most competitive independent sector of the market.

The memo's date, 1982, has particular significance because federal price controls of gasoline had just ended. After that, some major oil companies began refusing to supply stations unless they signed an exclusive "branded" contract—where the company could control the price of the gas. Petroleum industry expert Tim Hamilton, instrumental in making public the ARCO memo, told me, "Chevron held the largest refinery capacities in the West and announced it would no longer sell any gasoline to unbranded independents. Following the announcement, the company branded hundreds of existing stations under its trademark." Another tactic major companies used in driving out unbranded independent operations was creating artificial "zone pricing," where gas prices at the branded pump in some areas were fifteen cents below the price paid by the unbranded station to the refiner for its fuel. Independents were forced to fly the company flag or go out of business. Zone pricing is why some motorists today can see differences at the pump of up to twenty cents at stations of the same brand only a few miles from each other.

The *National Petroleum News* reported that the number of unbranded independent stations in California declined from 892 in 1980 to 167 by 1995.[42] "By 1998," Hamilton pointed out, "the unbranded independent sector had declined to the point of near nonexistence in most markets." Oil companies achieved what ARCO executives hoped for in 1982: "a lasting period of quite acceptable profitability,"[43] and motorists continued to pay more than they should.

Hamilton's presentations to the gas pricing task force so impressed me that, after gasoline prices spiked up to $2.50 per gallon in the Midwest during the spring of 2000, I hired him to study the similarities to the California situation. Once a gas-station owner, Hamilton represented independent gas stations from his outpost in rural Washington state and has become one of the few sources of knowledge willing to criticize the powerful gasoline industry. For instance, Hamilton has found manifests showing that ships of gasoline bound for areas with low inventories of gasoline were turned away on the open seas, which helped drive up the price of gasoline. The report that Hamilton wrote for The Foundation for Taxpayer and Consumer Rights, which was released in Chicago in the fall of 2000, found oil refiners' manipulation of supply and inventories to blame for the Midwest price spikes as well. The study concluded about the Midwest price spikes in the spring of 2000:

- just prior to the price spikes, hundreds of millions of gallons of gasoline were shipped by Midwest refiners to other parts of the country and exported to foreign destinations—inventory manipulations that precipitated the shortages which led to the price spikes;

- despite repeated oral and written assurances to the Environmental Protection Agency (EPA) that inventories were at adequate levels, the oil companies drew the inventories down to critically low levels and chose not to restore the inventories;

- OPEC production cut-backs and new, greener gas reformulation had no significant impact on the price spikes;

- an estimated $374.4 million was artificially tacked on to pump prices during a ninety-day period in the state of Illinois alone.

After the 2000 election, the Federal Trade Commission released its findings on the cause of the Midwest price spikes. The FTC found there was no illegal "collusion" between the refiners, but did fault them for knowingly letting inventories run down and not refilling them promptly when a crisis was emerging. One company told the FTC that the reason it did not respond quickly was because it was more profitable not to.[44] As Hamilton pointed out, there was no need for a meeting in a smoky back room among companies to decide not to fill inventories. The companies had shared storage facilities and knew well what the other company was doing. All they had to do was follow the leader.

The perception among Americans has been that OPEC is largely to blame for high gasoline prices. In fact, in 2000 only 46 percent of the nation's imported crude oil came from OPEC countries, and America imported only 60 percent of all its oil.[45] (Canada, Mexico, and Venezuela, of which only Venezuela is an OPEC nation, were the biggest sources.) In the unregulated market system, though, when a large American oil corporation ships crude from its fields in Canada to its refineries in the Midwest, one unit of the company will charge the other the OPEC price. This is the market price, though it bears no relationship to the cost of production. It does not cost the company more to extract the crude from Canadian fields when the OPEC price is high. In a competitive market, the corporation with non-OPEC sources of crude would greatly undercut its competitors' prices and win greater market share. However, the reason all major domestic oil companies' profits spike upward in unison when speculative prices rise is that the corporations have figured out that in a large market supplied by a small number of corporations, it is easier to cheat than compete. It's easier to profit every time the speculative market shoots up than to profit only when you have the right goods to make it in the right market. Such cheating defies a cultural trust that has allowed extraordinarily high legal standards for bringing corporations to justice for collusion. Would the public support the "free market" of a few very large corporations if it believed that this meant the freedom to make as much money as possible by rooting out competition rather than by pricing through competition? Illusions can be costly for individuals in many markets, and the level of collusion among corporations, as in the gasoline market, can be highly sophisticated, subtle, and, often, legal.

What Consumers Don't See Robs Them Blind

There are many competitive markets in which cheating has become acceptable. Though there may be many corporations, if they use the same tactics, real competition withers.

For instance, the highly competitive credit card industry, scramblling to get individuals hooked on their credit lines, very often does not grant the advertised rates for which consumers are supposedly "pre-approved," but much higher ones. "Approval rates are lower than actual interest rates," said Robert McKinley, president of the credit research group CardWeb.[46] Other widespread scams among companies include:

- charging late fees for on-time payments, which was so common that in 1996 Congress debated legislating the postmark as the date of payment;

- deceptively low interest rates for balance transfers that become extravagant when fees in the fine print are added;

- bogus credit card insurance that is far more expensive than life insurance;

- requiring payment of lower interest balances first;

- "fixed rates" that are good for no more than fifteen days because 80 percent of credit cards are variable by nature;

- vastly different (and increasingly steep) fees for purchases, balance transfers, and cash advances.

Then there are the highly competitive, flat-rate telephone calling-card plans that rarely result in the flat rates promised. Companies offering the cards sometimes have to use another corporation's line to carry the call, and consumers must pay that second company handsomely. Most consumers do not read the fine print that permits such excessive charges, or realize that this is common practice rather than the exception because of bold corporate claims of "one simple flat rate." That is, until they read their bills. They also find that while residential long-distance calling rates have been below ten cents per minute, long-distance carriers have marked up their calling-card rates extravagantly in many cases. Those who are not careful about their bills can pay rates that amount to one dollar or more per minute.[47]

Even in the supermarket, a place where competition often does work well, cheating and exaggeration have created the illusion of better buys. When production costs escalated during the last decade, manu-facturers turned to what is known as "the weight-out." This is when a manufacturer such as Frito-Lay puts fewer chips in bags of its brands but charges the exact same price as the old size. The packages also shrink slightly so that consumers do not know the difference. Makers of items such as snacks, coffee, tuna fish, candy, diapers, and water have all used the weight-out. The weight-out allows for effectively raising prices without angering consumers. "The key is to do it without the average consumer ever noticing," said John McMillin, a Prudential analyst who watches the food industry. "Some consumers will be able to tell, but you'd be hurt a lot more if you changed the price. Then every consumer would notice."[48]

"What individuals do not see will not hurt them" has become a key element of many markets. Adam Smith's free market relied on informed buyers and sellers. Inuring the American to the corporation has relied on exaggeration, hyperbole, and, at its worst, outright lies.

If "the market = the society" as well, then the lessons corporations teach in markets about hyperbole can be followed by society, too. Americans might ask themselves if they have an exaggerated view of not only the freedom of their markets but also the wealth of their society. In my experience, middle-income Americans, saddled with more debt than ever before, identify more with the wealthy than with other middle-incomers who are in similar financial circumstances. This seems to me to account not only for their spending—the competitive race to climb a ladder—but also for their lack of class consciousness that could be a force for social change. Cornell University professor Robert H. Frank, author of *Luxury Fever*, noted that modern consumers in the media age are very aware of their relative economic standing, and this measure most determines how they spend.

Consider a choice between these two worlds.

World A: You earn $110,000 per year, others earn $200,000.

World B: You earn $100,000 per year, others earn $85,000.

The figures represent real purchasing power. Your income in World A would command a house 10 percent larger than the one you could afford in World B, 10 percent more restaurant dinners and so on. By choosing World B, you'd give up a small amount of absolute income in return for a large increase in relative income.

So which would you pick? A majority of Americans, it turns out, choose World B.[49]

In other words, one's worth relative to others appears to be more important to the individual than their absolute worth. The cultural standard for being "well off" has thus become greater today than ever. The race to live up, beyond one's needs and means, has become a national obsession. The societal perspective encouraged by the corporation is for the individual to look up, not down. In this way, many individuals fail to see the actual distribution of wealth in society. Frank pointed out in 2000 that there were more than 590,000 American households worth $5 million or more.[50] In 1997, *Forbes Magazine* stopped even trying to count all the world's billionaires.[51] At the same time, real wealth for most others was eroded and erased from the national consciousness. How aware are most Americans of these year-2000 statistics on poverty from the *Harper's Magazine*'s Index?[52]

> Rank of the U.S. among the seventeen leading industrial nations with the largest percentage of their populations in poverty: 1
> Percentage of the poverty level for a family of three earned by a full-time minimum-wage worker in 1998: 82
> Percentage of the 1968 poverty level earned by a full-time minimum-wage worker that year: 111
> Percentage change since 1989 in the number of children living in poverty who have at least one working parent: +30
> Chance that a U.S. adult does not have a checking account: 1 in 5
> Estimated number of people [worldwide] today who live on less than $31 per month: 1,300,000,000

Out of sight, out of mind, perhaps. The corporation's visible hand shows us the rich not the poor; the desired, not the undesirable. However, the lack of perspective and proportion among the public about their real financial condition, the failure to acknowledge the gap between the economic condition they have and the one they wish for, and the inability to see the world as it is versus the world as they would like it to be, has given corporations a great means of cultural control. In the age of the corporateer, getting rich quick was a value for both the corporation and the individual, but it led to an exaggeration and an inflation both of the potential of markets and of the individual to exist only through commercial pursuits, as well as to be upwardly mobile in society. Commercial values, such as greed, could overtake societal institutions, such as the family. Just ask America's children, for whom their parent's money meant more to them than their mom and dad's time. Twenty-three percent of U.S. children said their greatest wish was for their parents to make more money, while only eleven percent said their greatest wish was for parents to "spend more time with me."[53]

So many Americans speculated about being the less than 2 percent of households that were millionaires that they forgot not only their actual economic condition but also the social glue necessary to make the standard of living for the many rise to meet that of the few. The tone of marketing took on the feel of a lottery. Not many win statistically, but it could be you. Even if the middle class family was not better off than thirty years ago, the lottery mentality could make them feel like they could be. This illusion made many forget the odds against winning. The commercial value of speculation was externalized to a culture where Americans spent nearly $95 million daily on lottery tickets during the last five years of the 1990s.[54] The lack of proportion and perspective about the average individual's economic condition made many Americans forget their class connection to others in the same economic straits and made it less of a priority to fight back against those elements of the financial system that kept them down. The resulting atomization created conditions by which corporateers could act far more boldly on their own interests.

SELLING THE FREE PRESS
AND THE PUBLIC INTEREST

The writer of this remembers a remark made to him by Mr. Jefferson concerning the English Newspapers which at that time, 1787, while Mr. Jefferson was Minister at Paris, were most vulgarly abusive. . . . The remark was that "the licentiousness of the press produces the same effect as the restraint of the press was intended to do. The restraint, said he, was to prevent things being told, and the licentiousness of the press prevents things being believed when they are told."

THOMAS PAINE, 1806

F reedom of the press is guaranteed only to those who own one," media critic A. J. Liebling said.[1] The half dozen corporations that controlled the American mass media at the beginning of the twenty-first century operated under such a logic, which presupposes that corporate owners of the media have the ultimate say about how free the press is. Such a proprietary notion of the free press may not even offend many individuals today who could accept the commercial truth that possession is nine-tenths of the law. The American founding fathers shared a different view. To these men, the free press belonged to a sprawling public sphere from which the individual's public societal entitlement flowered, such as public safety, public debate, the public trial.

Of course, the public sphere's breadth was often troubling for individuals' private lives. "There were numerous laws that intervened in private life—laws against blasphemy, Sunday recreations, the Comstock laws," noted Columbia University professor of history Eric Foner. "The notion of a private realm insulated against public interference was much less powerful then than it is now. . . . At that time people's rights and freedoms were public entitlements; they did not extend into private life."[2] This arrangement created serious problems for the freedom of the individual. Yet it also entrusted the free press as a protector of the public interest rather than merely as a private servant of corporate commerce.[3] Regardless of their predilection in favor of the Constitution or against it, in favor of the Bill of Rights or against it, the founders who participated in the debate about the Constitution unanimously revered the liberty of the press, which was "the sacred palladium of public liberty," wrote Arthur Lee, a Continental Congress delegate from Virginia, using the pen name Cincinnatus.[4]

"As long as the liberty of the press continues unviolated, and the people have the right of expressing and publishing their sentiments upon every public measure, it is next to impossible to enslave a free nation," wrote Samuel Bryan, pen-named Centinel, a Philadelphian who opposed ratification of the Constitution in the *Freeman's Journal* during October 1787.[5] James Madison, a champion of the Constitution, agreed: "A popular government without popular information, or the means of acquiring it, is but a prologue to a farce or a tragedy, or perhaps both."[6] Modern tension in the media has been over whether it serves the public interest or the commercial interest first, and to what degree service of one compromises the other. This push and pull will determine whether the media becomes a tool primarily of public enlightment or of commercial interests, and whether most of the public will be able to see any difference between the two.

As a public interest advocate, I have found that the "free media" can be the greatest tool of the citizen to combat abuse by the government, the corporation, or the individual. Some public interest advocates have come to call free press "earned media," because of the increasing difficulty of focusing media attention on matters of public interest.[7] Few of my colleagues, however, would disagree that media remains the reformer's biggest megaphone, particularly when corporate abuses are involved. Corporations often deny our charges, but, when caught red-handed over a discrete matter, the company can be embarrassed and reformed.

My colleagues and I at the Foundation for Taxpayer and Consumer Rights (FTCR) have effected substantial changes in corporate practices simply by focusing public attention through the media. The same day we issued a press release denouncing Kaiser, the nation's largest HMO, for investing $5 million in tobacco maker Philip Morris while asking patients to quit smoking, Kaiser divested. In 1988, my colleagues Harvey Rosenfield and Ralph Nader beat an $80 million paid-media campaign against Harvey's California insurance reform initiative, Proposition 103, entirely through a free-media effort that focused on auto insurers' abuses and misrepresentations. The national HMO patients' rights movement was fueled by focusing free-media attention on the plight of patients who had had medically necessary care delayed or denied. For five months in 1998, our group faxed daily a different picture and story of another HMO "Casualty of the Day" to every member of both houses of Congress and to four hundred members of the media—more than one thousand faxes daily. The drumbeat of the campaign was so successful in drawing media attention to patients' problems that the industry launched a counter campaign, the so-called "Medical Miracles," which highlighted HMO success stories. The industry campaign backfired, however, because it was the equivalent of Ford issuing a press release about every Pinto that did not explode. CNN's Brooks Jackson reported at the time, "Far more effective [than industry advertising] is this shoestring California consumer group; no ads, just a fax a day to keep the HMOs at bay."[8] In countless ways, the free media can advance the public interest.

The commercial emphasis in the media can also make the public interest disappear. Freedom of speech depends upon the ability to be heard. Speech reflecting commercial and corporateer priorities has greatly expanded during the last two decades. Expression in the public interest and speech critical of corporateer logic has shrunk. Increasingly, commercial speech has taken priority in the media over societal speech. Public interest groups and citizen reformers make no political contributions. They have, in addition to media exposure, two other main tools in their arsenal—grassroots organizing and litigation. Shifts in the media's focus and purpose from the public interest to the commercial interest impact not just the reformer's access to the free press but also the state of mind of citizens who volunteer and can be organized, and of juries and judges. How "free" the media is, how broad its debate of "public" matters, has ramifications for how free all of society is—for how narrowly or broadly individuals and the public view their self-interest.

Robert Putnam's research in *Bowling Alone* correlated the highest volunteerism rates in civic life with those individuals who watch television the least. In part, this suggests what our grassroots organizers, who have increasingly struggled to move citizens away from their television sets, have come to know. "Private" commercial values centered in the corporation and transmitted through the media are often incompatible with acknowledging the needs of the public interest and the community.

The growing commercial emphasis in entertainment, news, and information during the last few decades has shifted the content and flow of information and debate in American society from "what is" to "what sells." Commercial values have replaced public interest values, at least in part, because of the media corporation's impact on the public's consciousness. For instance, coverage has been decidedly skewed toward the buying and investing classes—the best consumers—not the majority of society ("the individual = the consumer"). This, in turn, makes more of society into a buying and investing class. In recent years, the "free press" has consolidated into the hands of a few large corporations who want to maximize profit through what sells and to keep the customer's attention focused on their advertiser's products—often through sex, status, and violence. Lacking has been concern about the public impact of what is aired or told, and also lengthy debate about in-depth issues that are necessary to make a society flourish through open and honest exchange. Society certainly benefits from the companionship the media provides to some individuals who are stressed, alone, or alienated. To entertain and to inform is neither mutually exclusive nor mutually compatible. However, the media's exclusive focus on the commercial interest has beggared analysis of the public interest and the individual's ability to decipher crucial forces at work in society and to debate them publicly. Some matters are not in the commercial interest of the corporation to point out to the public—because they undermine key tenets of the commercial logic and culture—and these can be erased from the public mind. Other stories simply do not sell advertisers' products—even though the public deserves to be told.

The notion that information and viewpoints are restricted in America may be hard to swallow for individuals with access to a thousand satellite channels and a half-dozen all-news networks, not to mention the Internet. When there are so many choices overall, then the shrinkage of vital information, public debate, and dissenting voices about critical societal changes is hard to fathom. After all, there should be a big enough market for a "free press" to keep the individual sufficiently informed. The greatest evidence that the corporate media says too little to the public about stories that are not in the commercial interest of the media corporation is the lack of public understanding of media consolidation. Despite all the additional hours of television watching and Internet surfing that Americans have added in their lives, few know how small the number is of corporations that control the flow of information and entertainment in their society.

The Six Fingers of the Media

"As the United States enters the twenty-first century, power over the American mass media is flowing to the top with such devouring speed that it exceeds even the accelerated consolidation of the last twenty years," the Pulitzer Prize–winning journalist Ben Bagdikian reported in 2000 to update his 1983 book *The Media Monopoly.* Bagdikian is America's foremost chronicler of media consolidation and was the associate managing editor of *The Washington Post* who secured the Pentagon Papers for publication. "For the first time in U.S. history, the country's most widespread news, commentary, and daily entertainment are controlled by six firms that are among the world's largest corporations, two of them foreign."[9] The public sees the myriad expressions and faces of these companies all the time, but few people know their identity or the concentration of their holdings. Even with the rise, and fall, of proliferating Internet firms, "the controlling handful of American and foreign corporations now exceed in their size and communications power anything the world has ever seen before," Bagdikian noted.[10] His research showed that the Big Six—General Electric, Disney, Bertelsmann, Viacom, Time Warner (before joining with AOL), and Rupert Murdoch's News Corp—had more annual revenue than the next twenty media companies combined.[11] These six controlled the content, the distribution channels, and the technology necessary to receive and send information worldwide. Across the marketplace of ideas and information, competition is narrowing.

- Half of America's daily newspapers are owned by eleven corporations, compared to forty-six in 1983.[12]

- Five corporations control more than half of book publishing.[13]

- Eighty percent of daily newspapers in the new millennium are owned by corporate chains, while in 1946 80 percent were independently owned.[14]

- The combined number of all AOL Time Warner subscribers (55 million) is more people than vote in presidential primaries.[15]

Americans have been deeply concerned about the impact of the OPEC cartel on the price of their gasoline, but they have not similarly despaired of a media cartel with the power to control information and consciousness in society. The speech of six corporations has achieved unprecedented reach without Americans' awareness not simply through marketplace consolidation and a diminution of serious coverage but also through new societal rules lobbied for by the media corporations. These radically changed rules have eliminated many of the public interest duties of the commercial media, and have been the product not of public debate but of the potent corporateer logic promoted during the last two decades, which has undermined the public entitlement to the free press. Legal decisions and government rulings have increasingly adopted the logic that "the corporation > the individual," hence "the corporation's free-speech rights > the individual's free-speech rights." Competition no longer seems to be required if the corporation declares that a competitive market is not necessary to sustain its sponsorship of free speech. The free-speech rights of corporations to consolidate, control, and co-own an increasing share of media markets has trumped the government's right on behalf of the public to enforce rules that demand diversity of opinions. These are among the rule changes:

- As a condition of license, the Fairness Doctrine required that television stations and broadcasters provide coverage of controversial community issues and balanced views about them. The rule, in effect since 1949, was eliminated by the FCC in the late 1980s. "Free" airtime for public interest advocates to educate the public on issues simply no longer exists. The corporations that lobbied to invalidate the Fairness Doctrine wanted to reclaim that valuable airtime for paying customers. Often forgotten is that television broadcasters use the airwaves on which they broadcast from the taxpayer at no cost, even though the FCC valued the analog spectrum at as much as $132 billion.[16] Each broadcaster was granted a free monopoly on a publicly owned frequency with the provision that they operate in "the public interest," which is no longer enforceable.[17]

- In 2001, the FCC relaxed rules that prohibited one television network from owning another and undid a 26-year-old ban on the same company owning a television station and newspaper in the same market.[18]

- Also in 2001, the U.S. Court of Appeals for the District of Columbia invalidated government rules that limited the size of cable companies and warned about a similar fate for rules limiting the nationwide reach of broadcasters.[19] In 2002, the same court ordered the FCC to reconsider a rule preventing a company from owning more than one television station in a small or mid-sized market. In response, a former chief of staff for the FCC, Blair Levin, told *The New York Times*, "To a very significant extent, the rules are going to go away."[20]

- George W. Bush–appointed FCC chairman Michael Powell, Colin Powell's son, has led the push to deregulate further, including deregulating the cable industry despite widespread consumer dissatisfaction with service and price. Powell has declared dead on arrival the "public interest" standard that has governed approval of media actions in the past, claiming it "is about as empty a vessel as you can accord a regulatory agency and ask it to make meaningful judgments."[21]

Their FCC license requires broadcasters to operate in the public interest because the public technically owns the airwaves. The public interest has not been erased from the broadcaster's vocabulary, just redefined (the public interest = the private interest). In July 2001 testimony before the U.S. Senate Commerce Committee, Mel Karmazin, chief of Viacom (which owns CBS), argued that removing limits on his networks' acquiring of more media outlets would encourage better quality media, communications, and journalism. "We need to see that thirty-five percent arbitrary cap [on network acquisition of stations] removed so that we can make money on our TV stations, so we can bid for programming on free, over-the-air broadcasting."[22] A few months later, a federal court ultimately permitted such expanded network ownership, acknowledging the corporation's First Amendment right to association and the corporateer's logic. At the same Senate hearing, Jack Fuller of the Tribune Company echoed Karmazin's sentiment. This was a convenient policy stand for his corporation, which had acquired newspapers in three markets where the Tribune already owned television stations, including the *Los Angeles Times* in what was essentially a one-paper town. "We're not in a period of concentration," Fuller insisted. "We're in a period of radical fragmentation. And what you're seeing is serious journalistic organizations trying to find ways to deal with that so they can continue to support serious journalism for their communities."[23] In other words, without unfettered corporate commerce, broadcasters cannot afford high-quality, community journalism. Without a free market, there will be no free press. Without a free market, where corporations are free to consolidate their power, there can be no free society.

You've Got Public Interest

Echoing Fuller and Karmazin, Gerald Levin lobbied government regulators for approval of the proposed AOL Time Warner consolidation, of which he would become CEO, by proclaiming that his new empire would not only operate in the public interest, but would define and embody it.

> We'd like to state very clearly, which we have, that this company, put aside its financial size, is going to operate in the public interest. We're going to try and make a better world. Now,

you would ask, well, you're in business to make money. Government is in the business of the public interest; educational institutions are . . . non-profit organizations. And our intention is to try and establish like-minded individuals with a committed workforce and a group that really feel we can do that. And that's one of the messages that we're delivering.[24]

Forget maximizing profit and pleasing shareholders, trust the corporation that is the product of the largest corporate merger in history to protect the public interest. Levin probably realized that given the unprecedented power of the AOL Time Warner proposition, such a declaration had to be made (even if only Pollyannas could believe it). Ten days before that statement and the public consolidation announcement, Levin floated an even more candid view of the coming power of the global media corporation on a talk show on his company's flagship news network, CNN. CNN's Jeff Greenfield hosted the fortuitously timed "CNN Live Event," "Millennium 2000: Media in the New Century." The announcer's first words setting up the roundtable "debate" echoed Time Warner's best argument for approval of the yet-to-be-announced consolidation: that the Internet explosion created so much competition that the merger posed no danger. "The media: What were once three are now more than fifty. And with the Internet growing at a phenomenal pace, what will our media be like?"[25] In retrospect, the show, which actually allotted far more time to a debate of the media than was standard for commercial television, proved an omen of how the yet-to-be-married AOL and Time Warner would uphold their vows to protect the public interest through broadcasting diverse voices. Of the seven participants, three were current employees of Time Warner: CEO and chairman Levin, managing editor of *Time* magazine Walter Issacson, and CNN's Greenfield. A fourth was a past employee, former *Time* writer Kurt Andersen, whose novel *Turn of the Century* was at least critical of the media culture. The critique of the only public interest advocate in the group, communications professor Bob McChesney of the University of Illinois at Urbana-Champaign, that the news was skewed toward the upper quarter of society, had no reverberation in such a crowd. Still, Levin may have said more than he would later like people to remember when he predicted that the global media company would supplant government, education, and non-profits:

> So then where are we? It's my view even philosophically, so you can take this as being a danger or an opportunity, that global media, if you define media, in all its formats and not just digital but traditional storytelling, will be and is fast becoming the predominant business of the twenty-first century, and we're in a new economic age, and what may happen, assuming that's true, is it's more important than government. It's more important than educational institutions and non-profits. So what's going to be necessary is that we're going to need to have these corporations redefined as instruments of public service because they have the resources, they have the reach, they have the skill base, and maybe there's a new generation coming up that wants to achieve meaning in that context and have an impact, and that may be a more efficient way to deal with society's problems than bureaucratic governments. It's going to be forced anyhow because when you have a system that is instantly available everywhere in the world immediately, then the old-fashioned regulatory system has to give way.[26]

There would be no public interest checks and balances on AOL Time Warner as there had been on government, educational institutions, and non-profits. For AOL Time Warner, power would not corrupt. The pledge to be "instruments of the public interest" need not be broken because a media corporation like AOL Time Warner had the power to redefine the public interest as its own interest by promoting corporateer logic. For instance, the $106 billion AOL purchase of Time Warner was approved on January 12, 2001, and by the end of August,

AOL Time Warner had cut 3,100 jobs from its "committed workforce," including more than 10 percent of the 16,000-member AOL staff. [27] This did not appear to be in the public interest of AOL's 26 million subscribers, who were promised greater service after the consolidation. Nonetheless, it met with little media criticism because, applying the corporateer logic, only by destroying jobs could AOL Time Warner later create them. The same logic of "the public interest = the corporation's interest," had resulted in the deal's approval. Government's ascent had been contingent on the "public interest" standard that had been redefined to incorporate the logic that "the market = the society," so "product innovation = societal innovation." As William Kennard, the FCC chairman who approved the merger, made clear in this exchange with PBS reporter Ray Suarez, a free market does not necessarily mean free competition, but a corporation free to innovate because of greater capital.

RAY SUAREZ: Are you really creating competition, though, when the largest Internet service provider, which is looking forward to the future of streaming video and broadband, real-time communications, hooks up with the second-largest cable company in the country, allowing them access to those fat wires rather than the skinny they're using to enter homes now?

WILLIAM KENNARD: Well, remember, it's a careful balance here. There are some pro-competitive aspects of this merger as well; for example, putting these two companies together hopefully will spur the deployment of lots of new products and services to consumers. When you can marry a company like Time Warner that has lots of content and libraries with a company like AOL, we don't want to deprive consumers of these new products. . . .[28]

The conditions the FCC placed on the merger were that AOL allow instant messaging with subscribers of other service providers and that AOL Time Warner broadband cables could not deny access to people

who chose other service providers. These reasonable conditions, however, could not counter the force of the new corporation's power to
sway, if not control, consumer choices. While AOL had 26 million
members at the time, its next nearest competitor, Earthlink, had 4.6
million. Boosters of the deal liked to point out that AOL subscribers
freely chose the company and future subscribers would have the same
free choice. "Well, freedom of choice is to choose from choices that are
handed down on high through marketing," commented Norman Solomon, author of *The Habits of Highly Deceptive Media.* "I'm afraid a nice
theory, but a ludicrous claim that somehow people have all these different choices irrespective of the concentration of capital. The reality is
there is enormous capital vested in these two companies, and they have
the capability now to shift the entire terrain to tilt it in a certain direction
so that when people go on-line, they're pointed in a certain direction in
that process."[29]

Individual choices are made based on the power to influence them,
and the consolidation gave AOL Time Warner the power to use old media to influence choices in the new media, and visa versa. The first evidence of this in the months after government approval was the deluge
of advertisements for AOL subscribership in Time Warner's old media
outlets such as CNN. In its news format, CNN enhanced its morning
report with a giant Internet screen and Internet reporting that looked
at different sites to stimulate greater appetites for access to the new media, which AOL largely controlled. (By April 2002, CNN broadcast in its
newscast a web cam shot with banner advertising at the top of the web
page for AOL's latest version.) Time Warner's old media also promoted
the company's old media network. For instance, CNN dedicated much
coverage to the first printed interview with Gary Condit in *People,* another Time Warner property. In turn, the interview drove *People* readers to view CNN's 24-hour coverage of Condit's movements, the very
type of event—like the O. J. Simpson trial—that CNN made a killing
on but that steers societal attention away from pressing matters, such as
campaign finance reform, patients' rights, and terrorist threats. As for

the new media, corporate ownership of key Internet portals such as AOL or Disney's "GoTo" have increasingly steered people to certain choices, typically corporate synergies. "I'm afraid that we may look back on January 2000 [when the AOL Time Warner acquisition was announced] as the time when de facto, the World Wide Web became essentially the World Narrow Web, which is counterintuitive because there's all this talk today, all this smoke being blown about how AOL and Time Warner will create these multiplicity of choices through the new media," Solomon observed. "The reality is, however, that these new media are being used to herd and goad and leverage the consumers, the media consumers, into essentially cul-de-sacs where the links in these various new media are self-referential, not often labeled as such. People are going to be directed to and encouraged to go to various media products on the Internet and elsewhere under the guise of giving them a great deal of choice."[30]

In 2001, the first year of AOL Time Warner's joint operation, if AOL Time Warner was really bigger and more important than government, the company's coverage of its own operations and commercial interests in outlets such as CNN was anemic. For instance, given the momentous nature of the relaxing of legal rules about media ownership to allow "cross ownership" in television and print media in the same market (rating front-page coverage in *The New York Times*) the amount of mention on CNN was an aside.[31] The yet-to-be merged AOL had fought for "open access" to cable monopolies' Internet hookups, but suddenly dropped that position when it joined with the nation's second largest cable operator.[32] Coverage in the AOL Time Warner empire of the open access/forced access issue was similarly neglected.[33]

Then shortly after the merger, eighteen CNN journalists wrote a letter to Walter Isaacson, CNN's new chairman, protesting the departure of the network's chief counsel, Eve Burton, a First Amendment champion. Among the signatories were anchor Judy Woodruff, foreign correspondent Christiane Amanpour, and legal analyst Greta Van Susteren. "Eve is an unabashed champion of journalism and CNN should expect no less," the letter read. "She is a key resource in helping CNN to maintain its high level of credibility." Burton, the consummate attorney, refused to comment publicly on the dispute, but inside sources told *The New York Times* it reflected a change in the network's position on the First Amendment.[34] Burton had previously filed a brief with other news organizations, citing the First Amendment to support publication of *The Wind Done Gone,* which had angered the heirs of Margaret Mitchell, author of *Gone with the Wind.* Warner Books (an AOL Time Warner enterprise) owned the copyright on *Scarlet,* an authorized sequel, and argued against Burton's position. On a later brief, CNN's name disappeared. "Four people interviewed . . . said that disagreements on the role of CNN's legal department were a reason for Ms. Burton's departure," *The New York Times* reported.[35] Isaacson claimed Burton's departure was for personal reasons and that AOL Time Warner was committed to the First Amendment.

Most visibly, the changes in format and focus at CNN were rapid after the union and the tensions between reporting and marketing were more apparent. Coverage degraded. The revamping of CNN's Headline News channel on August 6, 2001, dramatized the conflict between selling and telling. Television news had steadily evaporated as a source of serious information. For many years, to me, CNN's Headline News had largely been a holdout that relayed the top stories half-hour by half-hour with a relatively informative regurgitation of the best of the daily newspapers and CNN's harder news. For such coverage, it had won a reliable viewership with an average age of 54 years. To the new company, with its commercial emphasis on ripe markets, cross-promotion, and corporate synergy, this posed a marketing dilemma. The advertisers' and entertainers' target age for a consumer was 14 to 34.[36] Giving advertisers what they wanted, not the public, Levin's company revamped Headline News with large half-screen graphics, soft news, and more telegenic faces reporting, such as Andrea Thompson, former *NYPD Blue* actress, who became co-anchor.[37] Long-time anchors such as Lynne Russell, who actually asked intelligent questions during live interviews with advocates such as myself, disappeared. Additionally, the cross-promotion on the network with other products of AOL Time Warner, such as movie releases and magazine cover stories, turned the network into a commercial portal to other AOL Time Warner outlets. Media reporter Elizabeth Jensen relayed this account in the *Los Angeles Times:*

> Since its launch two weeks ago, CNN's new Headline News has made the evening TV lineup at some of its sister networks a regular part of its news headlines. Last week, the rotating "Headlines" part of the crowded screen, in between carrying sports scores, celebrity birthdays and breaking news, plugged upcoming movies at sister networks TNT, Turner Classic Movies and the WB. On Tuesday, the headlines promoted the Walter Matthau–Jack Lemmon movie "The Odd Couple" on TCM, while Wednesday's tune-in headline was devoted to the WB's airing of "Beetlejuice" and TNT's "American Graffiti." TCM's "Gigi" and "An American in Paris" were plugged Friday, along with TNT's "Lethal Weapon." . . . One headline last week even seemed to make a sly play to boost AOL Time Warner's chance to lure NBC's Katie Couric: "Come With Us, Katie," read the headline, followed by news about the courting of the "Today" show anchor, whose contract is up next year. . . . There has also been extensive promotion of upcoming programs on sister network CNN, a policy that Headline News announced when it launched.[38]

"Cross-promoting" products in news goes beyond mere annoyance. It drives at the heart of the question of whether those who report the events around us in our society can be trusted to do so honestly whenever their financial interests and those of their advertisers are at stake. When CNN interviews Tom Cruise the week his new film is due out from another AOL Time Warner subsidiary, can we trust that the movie is as good as CNN says? When the mass media becomes a commercial trustee rather than a public trustee, information becomes suspect.

The biggest boons for CNN in recent years have been in covering scandals that have riveted the nation—Clinton/Lewinsky/impeachment; Princess Diana's death; O. J. Simpson; and Condit/Levy. During the impeachment scandal, CNN's viewership grew by 40 percent, which meant that its advertising revenue grew too.[39] (Without CNN's nonstop coverage, could there have been an impeachment?[40]) CNN constantly tries to reinvent its next bull media market. But how significant are these issues really for the American people? To what degree does a commercial media manufacture an interest by the public in scandals that sell? Media companies like AOL Time Warner claim they simply give the public what it wants. If the individual's appetite really drives the news media, though, why has the news media consistently disregarded overwhelming public disapproval of violent marketing, sexually suggestive children's programming, and the overabundance of advertising? Appetites that sell have been nourished, but the public's social hungers are often ignored. For example, the number of households listening to stations funded by the nonprofit Corporation for Public Broadcasting doubled during the last five years of the 1990s, likely because of the steady diet of commercialization and trivialization in the for-profit media.[41] Yet the commercial sector does not seek to satisfy this appetite.

Violence and sex not only sell to the young audience most likely to buy but they also come cheap. Investigative reporting requires more resources. For the same reason, media organizations severely cut back on foreign bureau reporting by the turn of the twenty-first century, even though it compromised the American public's understanding of a hostile world. The handful of media corporations know that even if there is a limited menu, viewers still have to eat. The same rule has applied for those issues where it simply is not in the commercial interest of the media to inform—issues such as media consolidation, telecommunications deregulation, and political giving by corporations (since the telecommunications industry is the fourth largest political giver). These are societal topics largely relegated to non-commercial reporting on public radio and television. A citizenry more informed on such matters as the failure of the 1996 telecommunications deregulation law, most dramatically demonstrated by the rise in cable prices, might be opposed to policy changes that accelerate consolidation and deregulation in broadcast, voice, cable, data, and video markets that companies like AOL Time Warner want to control. Violence is a far better product for the continuation of the media corporations' profits. It makes commercial sense for a commercial media industry, even if it fails to feed the public interest and, sometimes, begets societal imitation of the vices it exhorts. It also begs the question, How far will corporate behemoths like AOL Time Warner go to limit the supply of investigative news in order to meet the demands of corporate advertisers and owners?

Tearing Down the Wall

Journalistic integrity in modern times had been predicated on the notion of a firewall separating news and business operations. With increasing frequency, this wall has fallen. Walter Cronkite, who set the modern standard for television news reporting, stated in the late 1990s that the impact of commercial pressures turned the format he pioneered into "a stew of trivia, soft features, and similar tripe."[42] Journalists like Cronkite were reared on the inviolate notion of the hard wall between business operations and journalists—in industry lingo called "separation of church and state." AOL's Steve Case, Levin's partner in running AOL Time Warner, when seeking approval for the acquisition, stated, "I completely respect the journalistic traditions of *Time* magazine, as Gerry [Levin] said, of Henry Luce and many others and recognize it's important to have a separation of church and state and recognize it's important to really empower journalists to do their job and the whole thing unravels if there is any question about that."[43] Executives like Levin and Case no doubt see a difference between, on the one hand, altering the news format for the corporation's commercial needs by devoting time to plugging its own product lines or reducing news to sound bites and, on the other hand, altering content. They might also agree that you could make the same loaf of bread by using half the flour. (By February 2003, both Levin and Case had left AOL Time Warner, when the promised synergies never materialized enough to inflate the company's stock price.) When commercial priorities become the only ones in broadcast programming, shows that both tell and sell can be replaced with others that simply sell more. For example, ABC sought to replace Ted Koppel's *Nightline* newscast with *Late Show with David Letterman* in March 2002, not because *Nightline* was unprofitable but to attract a younger demographic more sought after by Madison Avenue.[44] "Executives involved in the situation pointed to the older audience makeup of the program [*Nightline*], viewers who are less attractive to many advertisers, as well as to generally declining ratings for the program over the last several years," *The New York Times* reported. "The decline, one executive said, was because of the expansion of all-news cable channels, which now cover exhaustively the big news story of the day, formerly the special province of 'Nightline.' 'The relevancy of "Nightline" just is not there anymore,' the executive said."[45] Koppel and others argued that in the post-9/11 world, *Nightline* was more relevant than ever. Of course, they were arguing for a societal relevancy, while the unnamed executives talked from a purely commercial logic— freer commerce makes a freer society, a growing market grows society.

"*Nightline*'s viewership remains, to this day, four or five times that of the highest-rated programs on cable; and broadcasts like our five-part series on Congo have no outlet anywhere else on television," Koppel stated. "The program continues to be profitable to this day. . . . I would argue that in these times, when homeland security is an ongoing concern, when another terrorist attack may, at any time, shatter our sense of normalcy, when American troops are engaged in Afghanistan, the Philippines, Yemen, and Georgia, when the likelihood of military action against Iraq is growing—when, in short, the regular and thought-

ful analysis of national and foreign policy is more essential than ever—
it is, at best, inappropriate and, at worst, malicious to describe what my
colleagues and I are doing as lacking relevance."[46]

Journalism had been a cultural vehicle that, as a canon of the
modern profession, was designed to be independent of commercial
forces. It's true that newspaper owners had sometimes intervened in the
affairs of their publications in order to serve their own political agendas.
Henry Luce promoted his anti-communist beliefs by focusing his empire on the "red scare." The Chandler family that owned the *Los Angeles
Times* worked with other founding families of the city to keep L.A. a
non-union city for much of the twentieth century.[47] For routine reporting, however, advertising had been a separate enterprise from journalism. But since the 1980s, journalists have begun to confront the new
consolidated owners routinely exerting their ownership rights in ways
that precluded scrutiny of their other attenuated enterprises and advertising customers. As the following examples show, the struggle of doctors
against corporate medicine in fact mirrored the travails of journalists
against corporate journalism—fighting for the integrity of the profession as well as the quality of the product.

CEO of Disney Mike Eisner said not long after his company purchased the ABC television network, "I would prefer ABC not to cover
Disney. . . . I think it's inappropriate. . . . ABC News knows that I
would prefer them not to cover [Disney]."[48] Such statements have a
way of becoming self-fulfilling prophecies. Just days after Eisner made
the comment on National Public Radio's *Fresh Air* program, ABC executives killed a story by *20/20* investigative reporter Brian Ross about
safety issues at Disney World in Florida.[49] A failure to run criminal
background checks on Disney World employees permitted convicted
pedophiles to work in the park. Disney officials claimed that the decision to shelve Ross's report was ABC executives' independent call, not
Eisner's. *Brill's Content*, a media watchdog magazine, said that its investigation found "a well-sourced story, one that, by all available evidence, met the standards of fairness and reportorial backup commonly

found in investigative television newsmagazine pieces." It labeled the
ABC decision "mousekefear."[50] Conflicts of interest from corporate consolidation can create pressure, whether real or perceived, to put selling
the brand above telling about problems with it. Such consolidation can
also foster self-censorship among journalists. For instance, *Brill's Content* asked twenty-one ABC News employees if they would be comfort-
able working at ABC if Disney short-circuited Ross's story. Two-thirds
would not comment, including some of the network's most loquacious
commentators—Sam Donaldson, Peter Jennings, Ted Koppel, Diane
Sawyer, and Barbara Walters.[51] (Unfortunately, *Brill's Content* closed its
doors in October 2001.)

Even well-intentioned corporate executives can foment scrutiny of
stories about their companies that, in effect, chill reporting about
them. Time Inc.'s editor-in-chief Norman Pearlstein stated that he
specifically informed his journalists that he wanted AOL Time Warner
covered like any other company and that editors should alert him to
every story about the company so that he can make sure it receives fair
treatment.[52] Such exceptional scrutiny of company coverage could no
doubt weigh heavily in the minds of reporters who would have to deal
with Mr. Pearlstein on everything they write about their employer.
Pearlstein told the *Columbia Journalism Review,* after the Time Warner
merger but before the AOL compact, that he thought he covered the
negative aspects of the company critically but the real problem was
with positive stories: "Will we have the self-confidence to write it . . .
knowing that the *Columbia Journalism Review* will be jumping all over
us for touting our corporate parent? My hope is that the answer to that
is yes."[53] The *Review* noted of Pearlstein's healthy self-confidence, "*Time*
recently published a cover on the Pokemon phenomenon while Warner
Bros. was releasing *Pokemon: The First Movie.* Pearlstein claims that
not to have put Pokemon on the cover 'would have been strange, given
how ubiquitous the stuff is,' even though the article was one more example, among several, of Time Inc. bestowing cover stories on Time
Warner products such as Stanley Kubrick's film *Eyes Wide Shut.*"[54] In

such an environment, it's not hard to see that pitching a story with a perspective critical of the corporateer's commercialization of childhood, for example, might not fit in with the prevailing values of the newsroom.

Do reporters restrict themselves from delving into certain areas of public interest because they compromise the commercial interest of their owners? A 2000 poll by the Pew Research Center for the People and the Press found that one-quarter of editors and reporters, from both print and electronic media, themselves avoided reporting on legitimate stories, and an even greater number thought other fellow journalists did so more often. "Investigative journalists—drawn from the membership list of Investigative Reporters and Editors and separately polled—were the most likely to cite the impact of corporate pressure as a cause of self-censorship," reported the *Columbia Journalism Review,* which requested the poll. "But many other journalists also cited the factor as well."[55]

In my experience, good reporters are always looking for "gotcha" stories about corporate abuse. Nonetheless, corporate consolidation can change the values in newsrooms, and many reporters internalize this, which affects their reporting. Stories challenging corporate abuses are never "easy stories," because corporations have the resources to fight back. Personally, I have found that many reporters shy away from muckraking stories of corporate abuses because they are often complex, not simply because they require the will to challenge a big corporation.Both factors together are quite daunting.

The increasing commercial pressure on reporters to churn out more stories, due to the downsizing of many newsrooms over the last decade,[56] allows less time for digging and sorting. In addition, selling to the 19-to-34 demographic means holding the attention of the average member, not necessarily advancing the public interest. Again, this is the tension between telling and selling, between the public interest and the commercial interest that, according to the Pew study, many reporters appear to internalize. *The Columbia Journalism Review* reported:

Pew found that by far the biggest reason journalists censor
themselves . . . is that a story is considered too dull or compli-
cated for the average reader. Seventy-seven percent of the journalists said their peers avoid stories that are "important but
dull," while 52 percent said their peers shy away from topics
they consider too complex for readers. . . . Yet "dull" and "com-
plicated" can be code words. Twenty-six percent of the local
journalists Pew surveyed indicated that, although editors had
told them to avoid certain stories that were dull or overly com-
plicated, those journalists suspected the real reason for resistance was potential harm to their organization's financial
interests. (In contrast, only 2 percent of national reporters believed that.)[57]

Such codes spread through newsrooms and filter out stories. Former FCC commissioner Nicholas Johnson explained the process of
self-censorship this way:

A young reporter writes an exposé, but the editor says, "I don't
think we're going to run that."

The second time the reporter goes to her editor, the editor
says, " I don't think that's a good idea." She doesn't research
and write the story.

The third time the reporter has an idea. But she doesn't go
to her editor.

The fourth time she doesn't get the idea.[58]

Okay, so NBC might not cover in-depth claims of problems at its
parent company GE—for instance the EPA's decision to force GE to
dredge New York's Hudson River to rid it of pollution. But ABC and
CBS certainly would. This reasoning could have made me feel better.
Then I read an August 2001 report that, to save money, CNN, CBS, and
ABC were in high-level talks about creating a joint newsgathering op-

eration that pooled resources.[59] By October 2002, ABC and CNN announced that the two networks were getting serious about joining forces, which fueled speculation by analysts in *The New York Times* about whether CBS would then have to team up with Fox News Channel.[60] CBS had rejected a similar offer from CNN because it was not ready to relinquish control over its news operations. "Part of the decision was, if you do this, you're deciding that you're out of the news business," stated media analyst Tom Wolzien, who had discussed the offer with Viacom executives. "If you do that, you lose a lot of intangibles that news brings you, like relations with news affiliates—it's an important part of holding that affiliate base together. And, it's an important status vehicle in Washington."[61] The national networks continue to flirt with such plans. In Los Angeles, the local CBS (KCBS) station and the independent station KCAL (channel 9) merged their operations, so news reports from one station are seen on the other. If such plans succeed nationally, will the public question putting the resources of the free press in essentially a few corporate baskets, in the same way it would a government-run media? Will the public have enough information to know to?

Wanted: Cereal Killers for Hire

The commercial lifeblood of the media, advertisers, began to exert new demands and controls over the content of news during the last decades. Media chronicler Ben Bagdikian noted that while local television broadcasters had long been susceptible to the interests of local advertisers, by the new millennium it had become acceptable in national newsrooms for business chiefs to dictate to editors about content.[62]

The man who brought the wall down nationally was Mark Willes, *Los Angeles Times* publisher and CEO from 1997 to 1999, who remained chairman, president, and CEO until April 2000. Willes was known in newsrooms as the "Cereal Killer" because his background was not in newspapers but as an executive at the cereal maker General Mills, and

Willes tried to translate the basics of the cereal business to journalism. Willes brought to the *Los Angeles Times* newsroom a new dictate, which I witnessed firsthand from my contacts with reporters. The wall that separated journalists and business managers would fall: Each editor would have a co-editor from the corporate office who understood "the market," and the two would decide together which news to cover and where to put it. For the first time, a major national newspaper's coverage would be jointly decided by those with commercial interests and editorial interests. The Cereal Killer was up front about his motives when he told the *American Journalism Review* of the wall: "Every time they point it out, I get a bazooka and tell them if they don't take it down, I'm going to blow it down."[63] Willes killed the wall, not only at the *Los Angeles Times,* which had become L. A.'s only major newspaper, but in dozens of other smaller newspapers that followed his lead. "Papers around the country—in Florida, Texas, Minnesota, Arizona, Kansas, Colorado, and Massachusetts—followed the Willes policy openly and proudly," Bagdikian reported. "In 1999, the *Fall River* (Mass.) *Herald News* told advertisers that for every inch of advertising, the advertiser would get an inch of staff-written 'news' items about the advertiser's business."[64] Willer's tactics eventually resulted in a scandal from which *Times* management was forced to distance itself. In the fall of 1999, a special Sunday *Los Angeles Times* magazine was dedicated to L.A.'s new Staples Center arena. Undisclosed was that the newspaper and Staples Center jointly shared the advertising revenue from the issue. An editorial rebellion, which included pressure from a member of the newspaper's founding Chandler family, forced the newspaper to air its dirty laundry publicly, which it did in a special investigative article. Willes's power diminished, and he ultimately left the paper after the Chandler family sold it to the Tribune company in 2000. The Tribune vowed to keep advertising pressures separate from editorial control. Nonetheless, the merger of reporting and advertising had been tested publicly and, while reporting ultimately won, the lengths that publications would go to please corporate sponsors were pushed to new limits.

The Mind Machine's Messages

The power of the corporation to degrade debate is rivaled by the power of the corporation as a public relations machine to steer it. The majority of press releases and news pitches received by newsrooms across America are from public relations firms working for corporations that pitch their news all the time.[65] The downsizing in newsrooms during the last two decades has created conditions by which reporters are more receptive to ready-made stories and satellite-fed video news releases (VNRs). VNRs are professionally produced video news stories that are scripted, filmed, and narrated by P.R.-agency employees and made available via satellite or Internet to sell the client's story. Since citizen groups rarely have the money to produce them, VNRs are typically the medium of corporations. "VNRs are used heavily by the pharmaceutical and food industries in particular, which provide a steady stream of stories touting new medical breakthroughs and previously unknown health benefits that researchers attribute to oat bran, garlic bread, walnuts, orange juice, or whatever product the sponsoring client happens to be selling," reported Sheldon Rampton and John Stauber, authors of *Trust Us, We're Experts!* "On the evening news every night you see—but probably don't recognize—VNR footage mixed in with stories that reporters have gone out and gathered themselves. Sometimes VNRs are used as story segments without editing whatsoever, let alone a disclaimer to inform audiences that what they are watching was produced by a PR firm on behalf of a specific client with a specific propaganda interest."[66]

One might expect print journalists to hew to a higher standard. The business sections of daily newspapers are often filled with uncritical reporting of corporate press releases, and these sections are rapidly expanding while community coverage shrinks. "A comparison of PR Newswire releases [which carry mostly corporate news releases] to actual newspaper stories shows that they are frequently repeated verbatim, usually with no disclosure to tell readers that what appears on the page as a journalist's independent report is actually a PR news release," Rampton and Stauber reported.[67]

The resources that corporations have dedicated to shaping the news since Lewis F. Powell's 1971 memo have given the corporation the very power that Powell sought: media deference to the corporation's priorities.

Political Power of the Media

By gaining power over what is and what is not told, media corporations can control what is sold both commercially and culturally. The power to control the individual's and the public's perspective is the ultimate political power. Freedom of the press was one of the fundamental liberties for which the United States fought global communism. Yet the spoils of the Cold War have allowed corporations to become far more aggressive in making demands of the media and attacking it for coverage that is too critical of corporate interests. With the discrediting of the socialist alternative in the 1980s, capitalist corporations found new bravado to consolidate and flex their power over the media by attacking it as too "liberal." The notion of the "liberal media," planted in the 1970s by Powell's strategy, gained new legitimacy despite the fact that the media's owners had much wealth to conserve through their protection of the status quo. These post–Cold War corporations promoted the new corporateer selection process—acceptance of equating commercial progress with cultural progress—in the free press through their power as owners, advertisers, political patrons, propagandists, and experts. By gaining control over the free press, corporations of all kinds expanded their political power.

- Private, not public, involvement became the acknowledged purpose of the free press. The overwhelming emphasis is on selling, not telling, which limits the public knowledge of the invisible hand's reach and how to stop it. Voices that have pointed out contradictions in the new corporateer logic of "free market = free society" have often been avoided or diluted in the mass media.

• Due to the pressures of the commercial format, substantive debate has given way to the eight-second sound bite—which is the "equal time" that citizen leaders have to counter corporate voices and the invisible hand's marketed drumbeat. Not much can be said in a sound bite other than what people already know. One reason corporations can control politics is that there are few public forums for a longer discussion of how corporate power works, which could turn into a societal drumbeat.

• Instead of the media looking deeper into the corporation, the media corporation looks more deeply into the individual and his morality. Reality programs such as "Big Brother," "Fear Factor," "Who Wants to Marry a Millionaire," and "Survivor" turned the public's attention on the individual's moral response when asked to starve, marry a stranger, or dine on buffalo testicles. The public's attention turned away from looking too deeply into dot-coms, Enrons, and the auditing profession—that is, until it was too late.

The awesome power of today's media is harnessed to focus on individuals and their morals, rather than the corporation and its values. Individuals become one another's problems, and the corporation in its commercial and cultural role is there to solve them.

Media power has recently become overtly political as well. Michael Bloomberg used the money and pulpit of his media company to become mayor of New York, spending $99 per vote.[68] Conservative Italian media baron Silvio Berlusconi won control of the Italian government in May 2001 largely based on the power of his media empire. In America, the 2000 presidential election showed the power of the media to control political fates. The decision by the networks to declare George W. Bush the winner was a self-fulfilling prophecy that defied the popular vote for Gore. "Once those [media] calls were announced, the nearly impossible burden of reversing the presumption shifted to Al Gore," stated Congressman Henry Waxman (D–Los Angeles). "His legal case was made all the harder by the label 'sore loser' instead of 'defending champion.' That's no small thing. In fact, it turned out to be nearly as important in deciding the 2000 election as the Supreme Court's 5–4 decision in favor of Bush."[69] Acting on information that GE chairman and CEO Jack Welch, a Bush partisan, was in subsidiary NBC's control room election night and helped Bush, Waxman asked NBC for a video-tape of activities in the control room from that night, which allegedly showed that Welch influenced the network's decision. Waxman said that Andrew Lack, then-president of NBC News, refuted the charge but promised to cooperate with Congress to find the truth. "Under oath, Lack denied the rumor but promised to supply the advertising video-tape if it existed," stated Waxman. "Neither he nor the NBC lawyers at the hearing raised 1st Amendment reservations. After the hearing, NBC confirmed that it had the footage. But the network is flatly refus-ing to release the video, and now Lack appears shocked and aggrieved that anyone expects him to honor the commitment he voluntarily made under oath."[70] Whether Welch was in the control room that night, and what he said, will likely never be disclosed, because NBC claimed protection under the First Amendment.

A free press is the journalist's right to speak, not the corporation's right to manipulate and conceal. In this case, the public's right to know how free their press was warranted release of the tape. The Tribune-owned *Los Angeles Times* did not see it that way and editorialized against Waxman in his hometown. "NBC, like any news organization, is protected by the 1st Amendment," the *Los Angeles Times* editorial read. "Lack's statement may have been incautious, but it does not fol-low that NBC surrendered its constitutional rights. . . . The notion that Welch could have had much effect on the election defies credibility. All of the networks were in a state of meltdown. Whether Welch might have urged NBC anchors to call it for Bush hardly merits a full-blown Congressional investigation."[71]

"NBC is a special entity," Waxman pointed out in rebuttal. "It exists because it has the use—without charge—of the public airwaves." In addition, "It is owned by General Electric, whose corporate interests range from toasters to promoting nuclear power to selling defense systems. All of those interests are significantly affected by who's elected president."[72] If Welch made the call that night, the public has a right to know, because a corporate chief will have used his ownership of the media to impose his political preferences—the election of a president who is far more favorable to his positions—on the American people. Yet one of America's largest daily newspapers and one of its four major television networks disregarded the public's right to know in order to protect the media's right to conceal.

If You Don't See It or Hear It on TV, It Doesn't Exist

Illusions have a great cost for the American people in terms of their cultural awareness and political preparation. While there is no justification for the brutal felling of the World Trade towers, there may be an explanation for why the American people and government were so unprepared for the heinous attacks. Seven months prior to the tragedy, the U.S. Commission on National Security, headed by former Senators Gary Hart and Warren Rudman, issued a report concluding that America had to prepare for a major terrorist attack in its homeland by creating a new cabinet level "homeland security agency" due to the scattered focus of and lack of coordination among federal agencies. The report garnered little media attention, and hence no government response, even though it would have been critical to averting the 9/11 disaster. Why did news of such great societal importance as the Hart-Rudman report not receive the attention it deserved?

A more honest public debate in the media about Osama bin Laden's motivations after the bombings of the U.S. embassies in Africa and the USS Cole might have helped at the very least prepare Ameri-

cans for the threat of terrorism and move their government to be more
prepared. "In the hours that followed the September 11 annihilation, I
began to remember those other extraordinary assaults upon the United
States and its allies, miniature now by comparison with yesterday's casualties," wrote Robert Fisk, the Middle East correspondent for *The Nation* and London's *Independent* who interviewed Bin Laden in 1998.
"Did not the suicide bombers who killed 239 American servicemen
and 58 French paratroopers in Beirut on October 23, 1983, time their
attacks with unthinkable precision? There were just seven seconds between the Marine bombing and the destruction of the French three
miles away. Then there were the attacks on US bases in Saudi Arabia,
and last year's attempt—almost successful, it turned out—to sink the
USS Cole in Aden. And then how easy was our failure to recognize the
new weapon of the Middle East, which neither Americans nor any
other Westerners could equal: the despair-driven, desperate suicide
bomber."[73] Fisk pointed out that the simplification in the media of
"mindless" terrorists failed to give the American public an understanding of Bin Laden's motives, which could have helped prepare Americans for the reality that, sooner or later, security in their homeland
would be breached. The violence was "unthinkable" not simply because
of its horror but also because Americans did not understand how their
enemy thought. Thinking of terrorists as "mindless" was one way of
erasing them from the consciousness of a public that had more to fear
than it knew. Before 9/11, having Americans forget such threats certainly seemed better for selling tourism, consumer confidence, and the
Dow. How this weighed on reporting of Bin Laden's and terrorism's
real threat has yet to be determined. The unthinkable springs, however,
not just from heinous acts, but from what is not thought about. The
corporate media's underlying assumption that globalization would
only create commercial (and hence cultural) progress prevented proper
attention to terrorism's real threat and risks. The most visceral example
of the ability of the media to blur what tells and focus on what sells may
be the February 1999 issue of *Esquire* magazine. The issue contained an

interview with Osama bin Laden, but the cover featured a shot of a smiling Pamela Anderson in her underwear pulling up a tight T-shirt that embodied the issue's headline theme, "The Triumph of Cleavage." John Miller's article, "Greetings, America. My Name is Osama bin Laden. A conversation with the most dangerous man in the world" (page 96) followed features such as "Breasts, Reassessed," "A Few Words About Her Breasts," and "Things a Man Should Know (About Women)." The warning from Thomas Jefferson that opens this chapter, that licentiousness in the media has the same impact as censorship, preventing that which is seen from being believed, had a perfect modern corollary.

Even in the aftermath of the tragedy, the American media failed to focus on the reality of the enemy and its potential for more damage. The most intelligent discussion of the issues I heard in the all-week, 24-hour news coverage following the Tuesday attack was ABC News' Saturday morning special, "Answering Kids' Questions," where Peter Jennings interviewed children about their perceptions. Two teenagers were the first to raise the issues of the role of American foreign policy as a motivation for the terrorists. A teenager named Nora entered into a colloquy about how the American military's violence in the Middle East had caused suffering that precipitated the terrorism. Joel, another teenager, who wore a Christian cross, questioned whether the United States was David or Goliath. Perhaps only children could be allowed to raise such issues for a raw, exhausted, and mourning nation that could comfort themselves if not in their own security then with the valor of firefighters and rescue workers. The exchange among these kids below highlights critical questions missed by a far less curious media in the months before and days after the attack.

NORA: Yeah. I think it's very important to get back to the question, Why? And these people, like Julie said, with their families, what has the United States done to instill such hatred into these people's hearts?

JENNINGS: What do you think?

Nora: Well, for one thing, putting sanctions into countries where you can't—with this—you can't—they don't have—the kids don't have enough food to eat and medicine, and putting bombs and killing them. I mean, are we only getting a taste of our own medicine? Are—we're doing this to the rest of the world, too?

Jennings: Well, that's pretty tough. Anybody agree with that? Any kids agree that we're—that the United States is getting a taste of its own medicine and that people in the other parts of the world are—what was the rest—part of that question? The statement?

Nora: Well, are there—the people, the terrorists, they're horrible and awful for doing what they did. But then again, were their families killed in any of these things? Because it takes a lot for a person to commit suicide, to commit suicide and take 10,000 people with them. That's a lot.

James: Well, I don't think we're getting a taste of our own medicine, but we're definitely doing something to make some people really mad, and one of the steps we have to take so we don't get in a war or anything is to figure out what that is and correct it, and try to make everyone— try to not make everyone really mad and everything.

Michael: I agree with her in some parts, like, because we have been helping other countries in, like, planting bombs in people's homes, and along the streets so when, like, kids would come out to play, they would step on a mine and then it would just blow up. And I think we kind of are getting a taste of our own medicine, but we—I don't think that it should have been—taking down two of the biggest things that resemble our country the most, and the Pentagon.

Connor: Well, I just want to say, Nora, I don't really think that what we're doing is getting a taste of our own medicine, because as—the things that we might do and the things that we might say, we do not intentionally—unless that country has committed an act of war upon us—kill thousands of innocent people. That's not what we do.

NORA: Well, are we always getting the whole story on the news? Do we . . .

JENNINGS: Don't grab. Don't grab. She'll . . .

NORA: Well, what I'm trying to say is, that people are dying in other countries. Are we using our power more to cause destruction across the world than help people? We have wealth and all of this, and maybe they're jealous, but don't you think maybe they have a good reason to be?

CONNOR: Well, they certainly have reason to be jealous. We have a lot, and our country is very lucky, but it's not our fault that they're not. I mean, you might think on some level, well, we should be helping them, and we should. We should be helping people who are less fortunate than us. But if people who are less fortunate than us, who we have not gotten around to yet, are going sail building—are going to sail planes into our office buildings, we're not going to let them do that.

NORA: Well, what are we doing to them? That's what I'm trying to say. We're doing—for how long have these people been suffering? Just a second. These people don't—you're saying they don't have enough to eat. How do they even have the power to come down here and do such horrible things to us?

JOEL: I want to thank you for what you said, Nora, I want to thank you a lot, because I have been wanting to say it through this whole time. I know I said a lot, but I wanted to say that, because what she was talking about, you know, David and Goliath—pastor, how David asked the Lord to give strength to he—to take down Goliath. Well, we've been bombing them, it's true, we've been bombing, and we don't mean to kill their families, but we do, and they don't care whether we mean to or not. So—I mean, so are they—are they like, 'Oh, they're the bad guys, and so let me pray to the Lord and let me be David and let me kill—let me make sure that these guys get a taste of what they're doing to us'? That's why I'm so confused.[74]

Such vigorous debate is difficult and upsetting, but out of such conflict often arises real societal resolutions. The lack of such genuine, broad-ranging national debate among adults on critical issues of American security, which like all real debates may lead to some taking offense, has left the public bewildered about critical issues in their lives. Prioritizing the commercial over the public interest has shrunk the range of debate and voices for fear of losing the attention of a demographic. In the days following the attack, for instance, some organs of the American media began sanitizing themselves so as not to upset consumers. Clear Channel, the nation's largest radio chain, distributed a list of inappropriate songs to its disk jockeys that included AC/DC's "Highway to Hell," Simon and Garfunkel's "Bridge Over Troubled Waters," Steve Miller's "Jet Airliner," Don McLean's "American Pie," James Taylor's "Fire and Rain," The Beatles' "A Day in the Life," Led Zeppelin's "Stairway to Heaven," Peter, Paul, and Mary's "Leavin' on a Jet Plane," and Frank Sinatra's "New York, New York."[75] No explanation was given, but the unarticulated fear had to be that such songs would upset listeners. The subtext was that feelings the songs could conjure would not put people in a happy enough mood to buy. Like difficult debates, difficult songs can help people heal. The presumption of the Clear Channel, and increasingly of other major corporations, is that the media is the public's parent, not its child. Until the roles are reversed, and the public reminds the corporation who owns what, the public interest in a broad debate will continue to be beggared in subtle and overt ways to the commercial interest.

GLOBAL CORPORATEERING

Just between you and me, shouldn't the World Bank be encouraging more migration of the dirty industries to the LDCs [less developed countries]? I can think of three reasons:

1) Measuring the costs of health-impairing pollution depends on the earnings lost due to increased morbidity and mortality. From this point of view, polluting should be done in the country with the lowest cost, which will be the country with the lowest wages. I think the economic logic behind dumping a load of toxic waste in the lowest-wage country is impeccable and we should face up to that.

2) I've always thought that underpopulated countries in Africa are vastly under-polluted compared with Los Angeles or Mexico City. Only the lamentable facts that so much pollution is generated by non-tradable industries (transport, electrical generation) and that the unit transport costs of solid waste are so high prevent world welfare-enhancing trade in air pollution and waste.

3) The concern over an agent that causes a one-per-million change in the odds of prostate cancer is obviously going to be much higher in a country where people live long enough to get prostate cancer than in a country where mortality is 200 per 1,000 under age five.[1]

1991 MEMO WRITTEN BY LAWRENCE H. SUMMERS,
WORLD BANK ECONOMIST, TO WORLD BANK COLLEAGUES.
SUMMERS LATER BECAME SECRETARY OF THE U.S TREASURY AND
PRESIDENT OF HARVARD UNIVERSITY[2]

During the last two decades, transnational corporations have created their own international commercial governance structure
based on the logic that "the market = the society." Commercial
value has become a standard of societal measurement. The instruments
of the market's rule have been an ever-growing alphabet soup of agreements, jurisdictional bodies, and terms with names such as AGOA,
AoA, CAB, GATT , GATS, GSP, IMF, ISO, MAI, NAFTA, OECD, TEP,
TRIMs, TRIPs, WTO.[3] To most individuals, the list would read like a
foreign code. In fact, it represents a corporate commercial code that can
trump national law and cultural consensus to have real consequences
in the daily lives of individuals around the world. For example, the
soup allows trade bureaucrats meeting in secret trade tribunals, such as
the World Trade Organization (WTO) in Geneva, to invalidate national
and state environmental protection, food safety, and public health laws
if they offend the commercial code of corporate trade.

My first experience with the threat that the commerce of transnational corporations posed to national and cultural sovereignty was
working with Ralph Nader in November 1994 to oppose U.S. ratification of the Uruguay Round Agreement of GATT, which established the
powerful WTO. The U.S. Congress signed off on the agreement, dis-
missing opponents' cautions as alarmist, but as I wrote in a *San Francisco Chronicle* column at the time, it was not American democracy's
finest hour. "The 98 lame duck Congressional incumbents ousted by the
people on November 8 will vote with impunity next week for the budget waiver needed to approve the General Agreement on Tariffs and
Trade, or GATT, a vote that was unattainable before the election." California had among the toughest environmental and worker safety laws in
the nation, and my concern was that the terms of the treaty threatened
those laws that impeded a corporation's ability to trade freely. As I
warned then, "If the WTO found a California safety standard illegal, the
U.S. government would be required to do everything in its power to

force the state to repeal it, including cutting off federal funds, or American citizens would be forced to pay the costs of international trade sanctions. This is the significance of the trade pact that the White House continues to obfuscate: Nations will be bound by WTO verdicts."[4] Few recognized the seriousness of the threat at the time, a moment when unrestrained markets seemed miracle cures. Since then, many of the fears of those of us who opposed the WTO have been realized.

- The WTO found that U.S. Clean Air Act rules limiting gasoline contaminants that cause pollution violated trade rules after a challenge from Venezuela. The U.S. government reverted to weaker rules that the U.S. Environmental Protection Agency had earlier rejected as unenforceable. As WTO director-general Renato Ruggiero noted, environmental standards in the WTO are "doomed to fail and could only damage the global trading system."[5]

- U.S. dolphin protections were undermined after Mexico threatened a WTO "enforcement" action of a global trade law and the Clinton administration responded with amendments to the dolphin–safe tuna provisions of the Marine Mammal Protection Act.[6]

- Sea turtles took to the streets of Seattle because of a WTO ruling against the Endangered Species Act protections for shrimpers to use nets with turtle excluder devices.[7]

- The WTO approved sanctions of $116.8 million against the European Union for not abiding by a WTO ruling against a ban on beef with artificial hormone residues.[8]

- Guatemala banned labels depicting healthy babies on infant formula in order to deter illiterate mothers from buying formula bottles, which are easily contaminated in poverty-stricken areas, rather than breast-feeding. Gerber threatened to challenge the ban at the WTO, and Guatemala was forced to back down rather than face sanctions.[9]

While countries challenge others' trade restrictions in the WTO, nations often represent the interests of corporations and industries that have essentially become the country's clients. The U.S. has frequently used the WTO to help its biggest industries. On behalf of the pharmaceutical industry, the U.S. threatened laws in Southern Africa, Israel, Brazil, and Thailand that make generic drugs more available and certain drugs, including AIDS medicine, cheaper. [10] The United States challenge to Brazil's right to discount anti-AIDS drugs seemed particularly hypocritical to Brazil after the U.S. government discounted anti-anthrax drugs in the fall of 2001. With public health becoming an international crisis, the freedom of sovereign soils to protect the public health will increasingly conflict with global trade law that protects the corporation's profit motive. For automakers, the U.S. threatened, under WTO rules, fuel-efficiency standards to implement Japan's Kyoto treaty on global warming. [11] To help the electronics industry, the United States threatened with a WTO challenge a European proposal to ban toxics and make corporations responsible for disposing of used electronic equipment. [12]

Like kings, corporations create their own authority as they go. The new world agreements, organizations, and tribunals allow for an institutional affirmation of such a right that can trump national law. Large corporations lobbied for these treaties as well as the terms that allow the corporations to create their own authority based on the desire to open new markets. Corporateers have created a new internal order that puts the free movement of corporations and markets above the common good of societies, that places things ahead of people. Like a sovereign's court, the commercial code's challenges to cultural tradition have been argued in forums where public process and representation have no part. In the case of the WTO, bureaucrats based in Geneva make decisions based on trade law without the necessity of hearing human testimony or looking into human eyes.

This system drove tens of thousands of protestors onto the streets of Seattle, Genoa, and Washington, D.C., in 2001 and 2002. For all their numbers and statements, however, a coherent message of the threat

posed by the global corporateer governance system still has not perme-
ated the American mind. The public saw turtles and masked maraud-
ers complaining vaguely of the threat to workers and the environment.
The populist mind has yet to understand that beyond the single issues,
the larger stakes are the same gripes at the heart of the founding of the
American nation—national and cultural sovereignty.

Wars have been fought in this common defense. The American War
for Independence was a battle over the cultural principle of no taxation
without representation, no taxes imposed without the rights of the
American people to be represented politically and therefore determine
for themselves the shape of their society. In 1812, Americans went to war
with Britain over sovereignty of the high seas—the imprisonment of
American sailors and freedom to sail. In 1861, the Union fought with the
Southern states not just over slavery, but over the cultural values and
composition of the frontier states. Would they be free or slave? In his pivotal book, *Free Soil, Free Labor, Free Men*, historian Eric Foner argues that
the social concept of "free labor" ingrained in the Republican party ideology of the time, and its future in the Western territory, was critical in
sparking the Civil War. Slavery was the quintessential example of the economic overtaking the cultural. The Civil War was not simply a battle over
economic systems—the plantation economy that depended on slavery
versus the manufacturing economy that encouraged free, not slave, labor.
It was the manifestation of a long-burning, irrepressible conflict between
cultures—Northern and Southern ways of life that simply could not co-
exist in Western territory—and over how the new nation would determine for itself what culture would exist there. The cultural question that
it answered was whether American society would accept economic domination of any individual's basic freedom. The same question lingers
about global corporateering, albeit to a less brutal degree—except in
those cases involving the modern equivalent of slave labor.

"Free Soil, Free Labor, Free Men and Women" could be the war cry
of twenty-first-century protestors against the global law that "the market = the society." "Free trade" has become the highly effective brand of

the global corporate governance system. (How many Americans are against "free trade"?) The protestors, however, have yet to effectively brand their movement. Even their "anti-globalization" banner sounds as if they are against global connectivity. Yet the protestors' concerns have essentially been about "free society." "Free Trade versus Free Society" might be a fairer fight than the one over free trade. One should, of course, be able to be for both free trade and free society. In my experience, many of the groups protesting against trade policies that erase national law are for both society and trade but have been mislabeled as anti–free trade. Their gripes have really been with corporations that want more freedom than national cultures will allow. Unfortunately, progressives who are the most vocal in these fights have often been too proud to seize upon the successful lessons learned by corporations that pioneered the power of proper branding. The tactic would be the modern equivalent of the American colonists refusing to use muskets because they were the weapons of the redcoats. The global issues bringing protestors to the streets offend deep-seated beliefs of the people in America and those in other democratic societies. The problems simply have not been marketed to demonstrate that core freedoms are at stake globally. The vast majority of people in democratic nations across the globe, who fought as hard as Americans for the rights of democratic self-determination, would be far more concerned if they recognized the true nature of the conflict, one reflective of the most defining moments in American history, the Civil War. How many individuals across the globe would approve of unaccountable corporations being able to create their own global authority to subvert free soil, free labor, and free people?

Free Soil vs. Free Corporations

Two major international trade agreements created rules whereby the priorities of corporate capital investment outweighed the rules and sovereignty of free soil and cultures. The North American Free Trade

Agreement (NAFTA) in 1993 and the Uruguay Round of the GATT in 1994 both received Congressional approval, but under rules very foreign to America's democratic system. The Fast Track procedure, which was enacted in 1974 and expired in 1994, gave the U.S. president unprecedented Congressional authority to negotiate trade treaties and, thus, transferred constitutional powers of the legislative branch to the executive. Under Fast Track, the executive branch negotiates the treaty and signs it, locking in the terms before Congress votes on the deal. Congress can only vote yes or no, not amend the treaty, forcing members to take or leave the voluminous treaty within ninety days. Only thirty hours of Congressional debate is allowed.[13] Presidents rarely use Fast Track because it is such a serious altering of constitutional authority. Fast Track was utilized only five times, including the Tokyo and Uruguay Rounds of GATT and NAFTA, prior to President George W. Bush's administration. In August 2002, President Bush won reauthorization of Fast Track for trade deals through 2007. Perhaps only such a constitutionally compromised process could have allowed for the creation of new tribunals for world commerce that defied democratic culture.

The WTO clearly stated, "Each member shall ensure the conformity of its laws, regulations, and administrative procedures with its obligations as provided in the annexed Agreements."[14] NAFTA overtly prevented the government from conditioning investments on non-commercial standards, such as labor or environmental protection.[15] The principles underlying both agreements sanction corporateer logic as a preeminent rule of global law. Under the treaties, cultural standards for the protection of health and safety, the environment, or other societal priorities must be accomplished in the "least trade restrictive" manner, and where international standards do so better than national ones, the tougher national criteria should be replaced. In addition, WTO and NAFTA require that health and safety laws pass a "risk assessment" test (a.k.a. cost-benefit analysis) where certain risk is always tolerated. A "zero-tolerance" policy, such as exists for certain environmental hazards in the United States, becomes unacceptable.[16] In other words, commercial benefits become greater than societal costs ("commercial benefits > societal costs"). The sovereignty of national soil and the environmental integrity of it must withstand the commercial litmus tests. Americans may have some of the most significant consumer, environmental, and worker protections in the world, but the new agreements can render many of them moot. NAFTA and WTO created a means for global standardization, or self-dubbed "harmonization," to make laws meld. In many cases, nations with stronger laws, like the United States, must give, while corporations that do not like them can take. National standards that are more generous than the tests applied by NAFTA and WTO can be challenged as unfair trade barriers. In the long run, the lowest common international denominators will tend to become the rule. Public Citizen's Global Trade Watch, which monitors both agreements, reported in 2001, "Currently the U.S. is involved in international harmonization in the areas of genetically modified foods, meat and poultry inspection, medical devices, pharmaceuticals, chemical classification and labeling, pesticide residue levels, veterinary drugs, and automobile and aviation safety regulations, just to name a few areas."[17] The "harmonization" outcomes can compromise U.S. law validly created through the process of public representation both by statute— laws enacted by Congress and state legislatures—and through regulation, by appointed officers of the executive branch. For instance, Global Trade Watch reported in February 2001 about a NAFTA ruling, issued by a secret tribunal, requiring the U.S. to allow Mexican trucks access to U.S. highways. The U.S. Department of Transportation under the Clinton Administration, which consistently documented the safety risks of Mexican trucks, had permitted only limited access to areas close to the border region. Mexican truck safety standards were significantly less rigorous than U.S. standards, but the NAFTA arbitration panel ruled that the U.S. had to allow free movement of Mexican trucks on its soil or pay stiff trade sanctions.[18]

Chapter 11 of NAFTA provides an excellent example of how these types of decisions are made, and that "harmonization" of commerce can amount to subversion of state sovereignty to commercial dictates. Californians discovered in the 1990s that the additive it used for gasoline to make the air cleaner sank into the ground from storage tanks and polluted the soil and the water. MTBE, methyl tertiary butyl ether, caused groundwater contamination and proved to be carcinogenic for rats and mice in a study by the University of California, Davis. The EPA classified MTBE a "possible" human carcinogen.[19] In 1999, California decided to end use of MTBE to protect its soil and its citizens. The right decision for thirty million at-risk Californians became a global trade problem for Methanex Corporation, which made MTBE. Under NAFTA's Chapter 11 "Expropriation and Compensation" section, which allows foreign corporations to directly sue governments in an international tribunal for actions that unnecessarily undermine their profitability under trade law, Methanex quietly challenged the sovereignty of the state of California. In an offshore, secret arbitration sanctioned by NAFTA, Methanex sought $970 million for losses it sustained when California pulled the plug on its possible carcinogen. The proceeding went unnoticed by most Californians, and many state officials had difficulty receiving information from the arbitration. NAFTA rules allow only the corporation and the federal government of the country being sued to be represented, not the state whose law is questioned.[20] The secret process, from which there can be no judicial appeal in U.S. courts or under U.S. law, could charge California a global tax for its environmental protection. For Californians like myself, this would amount to taxation without representation. NAFTA could not invalidate the California law, just make the public pay a steep price for protecting itself through a democratic process of self-determination. In August 2002, the NAFTA panel ruled that Methanex had not yet proved its case that the corporation was unnecessarily targeted for commercial injustice, but left the door open for the company to refile its claim. Nonetheless, the calculation applied by NAFTA, like corporateer logic, has the power to value the economic costs to Methanex above the social costs to Californians. The familiar assumption of the trade rules is "the corporation > the individual." Through NAFTA and WTO, such logic has become international law. Already, Chapter 11 of NAFTA has challenged these nationally determined boundaries to commercial incursion in the signatory nations.

- The Canadian government was forced to reverse a ban on the gasoline additive MMT.

- Foreign corporations that lost two lawsuits in U.S. courts challenging American jurisprudence have sought to have their case retried before a NAFTA tribunal.

- Investors successfully challenged Canada's agreement to two global environmental treaties, and Canada owes damages in these cases.[21]

The environmental, consumer-protection, and even constitutional rights, such as jurisprudence, have become a casualty of a global commerce that knows no boundaries. William Greider, senior correspondent of *The Nation* magazine, investigated Chapter 11's history and found that it originated with conservative corporate law firms trying to revive the essence of a 1905 U.S. Supreme Court ruling limiting government and allowing laissez-faire economics. "NAFTA's new investor protections mimic a radical revision of constitutional law that the American right has been aggressively pushing for years—redefining public regulation as a government 'taking' of private property that requires compensation to the owners, just as when government takes private land for a highway or park it has to pay a fair value," Greider reported. "Because any new regulation is bound to have some economic impact on private assets, this doctrine is a formula to shrink the reach of modern government and cripple the regulatory state—undermining long-established protections for social welfare and economic justice, environmental values and individual rights."[22] Greider reported on a March 2001 meeting of the Federalist Society about "Rolling Back the New Deal," where University of Chicago law professor Richard Epstein presided on the subject of "regulatory takings." Epstein wrote the book on the topic, *Takings: Private Property and the Power of Eminent Domain,* in which he acknowledged, "It will be said that my position invalidates much of the twentieth century legislation, and so it does. But does that make the position wrong in principle?"[23] He told Greider, "Most of economic regulation is stupid. . . . What possible reason is there for regulating wages and hours? If my takings doctrine prevails, you have no minimum-wage laws. That's fine. You'd have an OSHA (Office of Safety Health Administration) a tenth the size. That's fine too. You'd have no anti-discrimination laws for privileged employees, which would be a godsend." What of the democratic process that created the public laws and protections of the twentieth century? "We will allow the majority to have its way so long as it's willing to buy off its dissenters at a fair valuation," Epstein said.[24]

Such arguments have quickly become global law for corporations. Free soil can pay a tax when it limits the privilege of free trade. But free trade offers no representation. Labor also has become less free under the new global corporate governance structure.

Free Labor

Public Citizen's Global Trade Watch, the preeminent global trade watchdog, has estimated that more than 550,000 manufacturing jobs were lost in America in recent years due to the global accords. The U.S. government spent $153 million between 1994 and 1999 to help U.S. workers laid off as a result of NAFTA, though each of the 211,582 workers approved for the aid only received $718.40 each.[25] The math of why certain jobs have moved away from America has not been difficult to do. While the visible hand sold hundred-dollar sneakers in America as the emblems of the ultimate freedom, the largely invisible hand produced them in third-world sweatshops for a pittance. Nike, for instance, paid the Indonesian workers who made its shoes two dollars per day.[26] Disney gave its CEO Michael Eisner a ten-year pay package of up to $771 million in 1997, and offered former president Mike Ovitz a

$128 million platinum parachute for fourteen months of work. By contrast, Haitian workers who made Disney products were paid 28 cents per hour.[27] Even in El Monte, California, seventy Thai workers were found working in prison-like conditions in 1995 to make clothes for major Southern California retailers.[28] Activism on college campuses has made America more aware of the sweatshops behind the brands. The wage disparities offend many sensibilities, even in America where the lack of proportion and perspective about material wealth and its relativity has been as pervasive in twenty-first-century life as the Sharper Image's Razor scooter. A majority of responders to the *St. Petersburg Times* said they would think twice about buying another Disney movie or toy, based on disclosures about its sweatshop labor.[29]

The real threat to sweatshop workers has not been merely poverty, but conditions that hearken back to Charles Dickens's London. Corporateering, maximum pursuit of commercial profit without regard for cultural cost, has led to repeated, avoidable sweatshop tragedies that resulted from blocked exits, careless storage of flammable material, and locked doors to prevent theft. The worst industrial fire in modern history ignited not in Dickens's London but in 1993 at a toy factory outside of Bangkok that produced Sesame Street and Bart Simpson dolls. 188 workers died and 469 were seriously injured. Similar tragedies occurred throughout Asian toy factories in the 1990s, many with hundreds of casualties.[30] Many of the factories, designed for maximum profit, typically sleep workers on the top floor with the factory and warehouse on the bottom floors. Fires overtake and trap the workers on the top floors. These labors are not free by American standards. William Greider described the conditions for young women in China undertaking such factory labor, pointing out that China officially outlawed the three-tiered factory but that it is still a prevalent mode of production.

> Typically they are recruited from remote villages by a government agency that collects a fee from them for the job. They must pay for their own travel, then place a "deposit" with fac-

tory managers, who will withhold their wages for the first month or two and frequently also take away the workers' official ID cards. Hired under three-year contracts, they cannot leave or jump to better jobs without losing their money and perhaps identity papers too. Their factory dorms are fenced and guarded, the workers cannot come and go freely, the stories of brutality by security guards are commonplace. This is not slavery, to be sure, but it does resemble a sly form of indentured servitude, imposed on people who are powerless to resist its terms.[31]

The American public deplores such treatment. However, prodded by the media, Americans have blamed such "human rights" abuses on China, not on the corporation that places the order for and has no cultural standards for the labor that makes its goods. (Despite its human rights record, China was admitted into the WTO in 2001.) Since toy, clothing, and other sweatshop manufacturers typically have not directly owned these factories but have "outsourced" the jobs, they have attempted to insulate themselves from criticism, and responsibility. However, corporations of the free market have been uniquely responsible for the less-than-free labor in the world because they created the system of maximizing profit by minimizing people. Changing labor practices has been something uniquely within their control. In too many cases, large corporations have treated the global workers with less care than the things they make.

The enslaved labor of the world has made American labor less free also. The corporation has leveraged the global labor market as a threat to dismantle American workers' traditional rights and privileges. If the corporation does not win concessions, it will transplant itself to a cheaper labor market. Under such pressures, American labor unions and workers have relinquished social entitlements, protections, and status in deference to the corporation's global capacity to subjugate labor across the globe. In this way, the global labor market has gravitated toward the lowest common social denominator in order to yield the highest possible commercial profit percentage. "The less you do to protect people, the more money you make" has become a powerful global maxim for the corporation and those within its networks. Commercial progress demands social regression. In a borderless market, corporations do not seek just to capitalize on local cultures less hostile to enslaving workers but also to use their considerable power to make social regression, not equalization, the global norm. For instance, motor companies threatened to move more factories south of the border, where labor is cheaper and environmental rules less stringent, if American unions did not cut wages, benefits, and overtime. Local governments have also been compelled to offer American corporations huge tax subsidies to stay in their town. For example, Toledo, Ohio, handed DaimlerChrysler $300 million in subsidies for a Jeep factory expansion that was expected to reduce the number of workers from 5,600 to about 4,000.[32] Alabama gave Mercedes $253 million in subsidies to build an auto plant that cost taxpayers $169,000 for every job that Mercedes said it would create.[33] Of course, moderating executive compensation has been overlooked as a cost-saving alternative. For example, the year NAFTA took effect, AlliedSignal paid its CEO three dollars for every two dollars the company paid in total wages to its 3,810 Mexican maquiladora laborers.[34] Societal standards for protecting free labor have to be traded for a society or region's economic survival. Societies and regions have effectively been pitted against each other as though their only worth is how conducive their climate is for the corporation's commercial gain. The less free the labor, the better for the corporateer.

That corporations will flee an area or nation if the climate is not right has become an accepted rule of global politics. The forgotten fact, even before the rise of the WTO and NAFTA, was that governments could always punish businesses that fled or did not observe labor standards through its taxing power. Even if politicians had the will to offend corporateers all too ready to spend whatever it takes to unseat political enemies, they might no longer have a way to. The new global corporate governance structures created by WTO and NAFTA have the potential to invalidate such nationally imposed "trade barriers." In recent years, American attorneys have tried to hold corporations that violate labor standards accountable in U.S. courts. The outcomes will test the resiliency of the American justice system to export higher standards for workers to the world. If the lawsuits succeed, however, one very real possibility could be the threat of U.S. corporations to move abroad if politicians in Washington, D.C., don't provide greater insulation. Unless the business climate on the Potomac radically changes, many politicians will be all too likely to oblige. Rather than being called sweatshop protection, the measure would doubtless be dubbed the Domestic Economic Retention Act. In difficult times, politicians representing laid-off Americans would be hard pressed to resist the logic.

Corporateers have sought to purchase the freedoms of workers in America with the threat of a global marketplace of infinite possibilities, and many labor unions have been forced to capitulate. In the same vein, international support for freeing people politically and socially across the globe has become contingent on the nation's commercial priorities. Accepting the logic of the corporateer, not the principles of democracy, has become the sine qua non of receiving international monetary aid.

Free People?

In the wake of World War II, General George C. Marshall devised an ambitious plan to rebuild, restore, and improve the institutions of war-torn Europe in order to strengthen democracy. The terms of the international aid in the post–World War II and Cold War era was political, to build European democracy so that it would not be susceptible to fascism or communism. The Cold War era diverted American dollars to dictators and tyrants, but the purported goal was political and cultural—to stop the spread of fascism and communism in order to keep the world safe for democracy. Similarly, from political aims, the United

Nations was developed to prevent future world wars. During the last two decades, however, an international apparatus of commercial governance replaced the political goal of spreading democracy with the commercial goal of spreading unrestrained corporate commerce. The market, not democracy, had won the Cold War, and so international aid became contingent upon the priorities of the corporations that created the free-market brand.

International monetary organizations that bolster the WTO's goals have forced upon ailing societies the flawed corporateer logic. The World Bank, of which the United States Treasury holds a controlling interest, and the International Monetary Fund (IMF) act as the economic heavies for WTO priorities through "triggers" that mandate trade policy consistent with the WTO in exchange for societal reconstruction. For instance, nations that receive a World Bank loan to build a school must also accept myriad trade policies as a "conditionality." The terms average more than one hundred per nation and, according to the former chief economist of the World Bank, Nobel Prize winner Joseph Stiglitz, these policies have been harsher than official WTO rules.[35] Before winning the Nobel, Stiglitz criticized World Bank policy, and he ultimately left the Bank because of complaints that the organization's economic policies bled societies dry. Independent of Stiglitz, the London newspaper *The Observer* received confidential World Bank documents that it said confirmed Stiglitz's accounts. *The Observer*'s Gregory Palast reported on the four-step program routinely imposed by the World Bank and IMF on poorer nations from information he pieced together from the documents and interviews with Stiglitz.

- First, the world bodies forced privatization of state industries by what Stiglitz called "briberization." Local officials were anxious for "commissions paid to Swiss bank accounts [from private corporations and investors] for simply shaving a few billion off the sale price of national assets," which included electricity and water companies. Such privatization forever shaped Russian society because the kickbacks from the purchasers fueled the re-election campaign chest of Boris Yeltsin, whose continued leadership was a priority for the complicit U.S. government. "Most ill-making for Stiglitz is that the US-backed oligarchs stripped Russia's industrial assets, with the effect that the corruption scheme cut national output nearly in half, causing depression and starvation."[36] Ironically, Enron privatized the energy sectors in many such countries with billions in public financing from agencies like the World Bank and the Overseas Private Investment Corporation.[37] The results were not unlike deregulation of electricity in California, price spikes and blackouts.[38]

• The customarily imposed "capital market liberalization" caused Asian and Latin American financial crises. The goal of opening markets to foreign capital boomeranged when the investment capital fled the country. The IMF then forced the countries to greatly increase their interest rates, "to 30%, 50% and 80%," in order to bring money back in. The value of property, wealth, and national treasuries plummeted due to the inflation of interest rates.[39] Touring a mountain town in Jamaica in 2002, I talked to residents who complained of 30 percent interest rates that prevented them from buying land to farm. The rates stemmed from the same source.

• "Market-Based Pricing," the third step identified by Palast, called for raising prices on food, fuel, and water, without concern for social consequences. Indonesians rioted in 1998 after the IMF ended food and fuel subsidies, Bolivians similarly took to the streets over water prices in 2000, and Ecuadorans followed in 2001 over the prices of cooking gas imposed by the World Bank. Of one internal document, Palast reported, "The secret report notes that the plan to make the US dollar Ecuador's currency has pushed 51% of the population below the poverty line. The World Bank 'Assistance' plan simply calls for facing down civil strife and suffering with 'political resolve'—and still higher prices."[40]

- The last step, dubbed "poverty reduction" by the world bodies, made economic aid dependent on the "triggers" for conditions of free trade imposed by the IMF, World Bank, and WTO. Stiglitz expressed special outrage over WTO's intellectual-property-rights treaty, which forced an extraordinarily high price to be paid by poor nations to pharmaceutical companies for branded medicines, which poorer people simply could not afford. The corporations and banks loaners "don't care if people live or die," Stiglitz told Palast.[41]

Western Banks, the U.S. Treasury, and corporations have taken advantage of these conditions to profit from the pain, suffering, and, sometimes, death of the poorest people in the world. These people may be freer to smoke cigarettes (as the tobacco industry goes global to find less suspecting customers) but they are far less free to determine their own cultural fate and social future without the encumbrance of the corporateer's priorities and rules. Economically advanced nations have been told that such developing world pain from unrestrained corporate capital is often necessary to create a rising worldwide market tide. It's a phase, but the future will be bright. That future has yet to come.

The "free trade" brand does not seem to have actually improved national economies, only created the illusion that it has. Evidence to date suggests that the global tradeoff of compromising certain freedoms in a society for unrestrained commerce has not paid off economically for poorer countries or, remarkably, even for richer ones. "When some of these highly successful East and Southeast Asian developing countries (e.g., Korea, Malaysia, and Indonesia) liberalized external capital flows and undertook other far-reaching liberalization of measures in the mid-nineties, they were soon plunged into huge financial crises, virtual meltdowns," found Ajit Singh, professor of economics at Cambridge University. By contrast, Singh noted that China and India, with "considerable capital controls" avoided the Asian crisis. "Equally significant, the Latin American countries that have obediently followed the Washington consensus since the late eighties, and liberalized their trading and external capital regimes accordingly, have not fared well either. . . . Their long-term rate of economic growth under this regime has been only 3 percent per annum, compared with almost 6 percent per annum in the dirigiste period of 1950 to 1980."[42] Many in richer countries could justify such world poverty, and even the loss of lower-paying jobs in richer nations, under the illusion that the first-worlders were better off economically for the changes. However, Professor Singh's research shows that richer countries have actually fared worse economically in the corporateer age of the eighties and nineties than during the fifties and sixties "under the 'illiberal' and 'regulated' regime of the social-market economy at the national level and controlled capital movements at the international level."[43] The magic of the invisible hand has prevented many individuals from seeing through their illusions to these facts. "GDP growth in the eighties and nineties in industrial countries has been considerably lower than that achieved in the fifties and sixties," Singh reported. "Economic growth has not only been lowered during the past two decades, it has also been more unstable, i.e., more subject to booms and busts. Productivity growth in the globalization period has been half what it was in the golden age."[44]

If rich and poor people have fared worse under corporate commercial governance, who has benefited? Freer corporations. "The only important gainers are the multinationals and the big financial institutions, which wish to have unrestrained freedom to move capital and goods anywhere and everywhere on the planet, irrespective of the consequences for people," Singh concluded. Those consequences differ nation by nation. However, the general pattern of crippling economic volatility and social upheaval has also included a blow to cultural traditions where a people once defined their own freedom as distinct from other peoples of the world.

Exporting corporateer logic has forced people to develop economically in uniform ways that undermine their unique cultural development and traditions. The messengers and the message of markets have changed how individuals feel about themselves and their world. For example, my colleague Emmy Rhine spent two years in the Peace Corps in villages from Nepal and India to Ecuador and Micronesia. She recalled that often a single television set would be the only modern appliance in a region and the marketing images often made younger generations feel inadequate about their sense of self. Fewer than 8,000 residents lived on the Micronesian island of Yap proper, and the majority had a primarily subsistence, village lifestyle. However, the establishment of a single commercial television channel created a new sense of shame for traditional ways. "The teeth of the Yapese are stained a deep red from years of chewing their beloved betel nut," Emmy explained. "Traditionally, the darkened teeth were a mark of beauty, with the darkest enamel considered the most attractive. Yet huddled in front of a village's single television set, as an advertisement for Colgate's teeth whitening polish flashed across the screen, looks of confusion and shame moved across the attentive faces. They judged themselves harshly in light of this new compelling standard. In this culture where large bodies are the beauty ideal, the children gather around the television and view the diet industry's incessant pitches for wafer-thin beauty. As a counselor at the local high school, I listened as young girls, for the first time in their people's history, cried and called themselves fat."

Diversity may be needed as much for cultural change as for evolutionary development. The more elements in the stock, the richer the soup. Viewing evolution, writer and zoologist Stephen J. Gould wrote that diversity, or variation, has been the essence of excellence as the full house in poker shows the excellence of all parts together. For instance, Gould proved in his book *Full House* that commentators have erroneously focused on the disappearance of the baseball batting average of .400 as a sign of decline in play when in fact there had been all-around improvement in excellence that made its attainment more difficult. While acknowledging the differences between cultural and evolutionary development, Gould offered this about the lessons of evolution for culture: "I think that the Full House model does teach us to treasure variety for its own sake—for tough reasons of evolutionary theory and nature's ontology. . . . Excellence is a range of differences, not a spot. . . . In a society driven, often unconsciously, to impose a uniform mediocrity upon a former richness of excellence—where McDonald's drives out the local diner and the mega–Stop & Shop eliminates the corner Mom and Pop—an understanding and defense of full range as natural reality might help to stem the tide and preserve the rich raw materials of any evolving system: variation itself."[45] Unfortunately, corporate marketing and commerce worldwide has contributed to the homogenization of world culture, reducing the diversity of people, and thus cultural vitality. The assumptions, symbols, logic, and language of corporateers allow for only one truth, a commercial one.

An important indication of the homogenization has been the disappearance of world languages. "There are currently 6,000 languages still spoken in the world, but fewer than 300 of those are spoken by more than a million people and nearly half will be lost by the end of the twenty-first century," noted author Jeremy Rifkin of the homogenizing world culture in *The Age of Access*. "More than 20 percent of the world's population now speaks English, largely because of the hold U.S. media companies enjoy over world cultural commerce. In a century from now, English is likely to be all pervasive."[46] The larger the spectrum of cultural experience and possibility, the freer the individual. When cultural traditions and languages become subsumed by commercial priorities, the possibilities for cultures diminish. Then the potential for the individual's self-exploration and understanding evaporates, too.

The inevitable result of the global reach of the invisible hand's logic, assumptions, and rules is worldwide sanction of exploitation. If corporate commerce determines cultural value, then the worst consumers deserve the worst problems. This perspective was articulated most clearly by Lawrence H. Summers who, as Secretary of the United States Treasury, was said to have pushed Stiglitz out of his World Bank job in 1999 for not being market-oriented enough.[47] Summers, as a World Bank economist himself in 1991, stated simply that the strength of markets should determine the value of societies. Summers argued in the internal memo that begins this chapter for the transfer of waste and dirty industries from industrialized to developing countries. "Just between you and me, shouldn't the World Bank be encouraging more migration of the dirty industries to the LDCs [lesser developed countries]?" Summers wrote. "I think the economic logic behind dumping a load of toxic waste in the lowest wage country is impeccable and we should face up to that. " Summers later said that the memo was meant to be ironic. My colleagues at the Multinational Monitor did not find it so witty and have memorialized the remarks with an annual award, the Lawrence H. Summers Award, for those rivaling its chutzpa.

When the only value is commercial, those who cannot be sold should be forsaken, that which cannot be sold should be forgotten, and that which can be sold should be taken. Such a threat to a free world requires a global rejoinder that reasserts the individual's authority over their society, the corporation, and their freedoms. The next chapter presents a possible response.

PART THREE

COUNTER-CORPORATEERING

COUNTERING CORPORATEERING

Words enter the language or leap to prominence when there is something new to describe; they stick around if there is some continuing reason to describe it.

THE NEW YORK TIMES, FEBRUARY 24, 2002
"WORDS OF 9/11 GO FROM COFFEE SHOPS TO THE DICTIONARIES"

If the market is society, if commerce is culture, then individuals will become shareholders in America rather than citizens of the United States with inalienable rights. Social custom will allow for the individual's freedoms to be rationally, justifiably, and—ultimately—legally bought and sold by others. Confusing the cultural and commercial realms has been a conscious strategy by the corporateer to gain greater power over individuals and society in order to open new markets that trade in the individual's freedoms in their public and private lives. Markets often work well but societies do not when the main goal is to keep corporations awash in money without concern for social costs. Independence, for the individual and the public, must begin in the mind before it can take shape in the body. Borders to protect the individual's self-determination and liberty must be recognized before they can be defended.

Many of the priorities of the corporateer could not have become the duty of society during recent years if not for a potent mythology that the fundamental nature of the corporation has changed to reflect the priorities of people. A drumbeat has exclaimed that corporations have become us and we have become them due to the rise of mutual funds and 401(k)s that have made individuals collectively huge shareholders. "The caricature capitalist is no longer the swag-bellied robber baron of the nineteenth century or the autonomous manager of the twentieth; he is [corporate critic and former labor secretary] Robert B. Reich and the 45 percent of the rest of Americans who own stock," wrote *Atlantic Monthly* senior editor Jack Beatty, who edited a collection of essays on corporate history called *Colossus*. "The capitalist c'est moi! Moral ambiguity should therefore inhibit the sincerity of our indignation at public enemy number one, reminding us that, with management, we shareholders share responsibility for things corporations do that offend our values. . . . The trend toward the democratization of ownership in America has upended the terms of the debate over social responsibility. The corporation is no longer pitched against society; the corporation is society."[1] If we do own the corporation, then it also owns us. Acting against the corporation when it is wrong can be like acting against oneself or a family member, against a cultural taboo. Acting in a social interest can jeopardize an economic one. Commentators like Beatty claim that the individual's failure to check the corporation's abuse is merely a reflection of the public's own greed.

Either naïve or disingenuous, boosters of corporateering ignore the imbalance of power between corporations and the individual. They claim that the power of mutual and pension fund managers can make or break a listless and bloated corporation, in much the same way that corporate raiders working on behalf of such shareholders dismantled inefficient corporations in the 1980s. In the real world, for any individual shareholder to tumble management at a corporation in today's structure is a monumental task. In the rare cases when it happens, the reason is economic losses, not social concern. How then, can the individual hold the corporateer accountable?

What Works and What Doesn't

The successful counter-corporate campaigns I have been involved with or witnessed firsthand have had a few key characteristics in common.

1. They genuinely responded to an existing, broad-based public need. They did not try to change people's minds, but rather they dealt with their widespread problems and focused their convictions on a specific action. The rule of thumb is that if your issue does not poll over 70 percent before you begin, don't bother, because corporations have the money to distort your cause and bring those numbers down quickly. Similarly, if you are canvassing door to door, don't bother arguing with the door of an opponent, move on to find the supporter.

2. They were proactive, rather than reactive. To effectively go after an industry means that, at the very least, it must defend itself, so it cannot take the offensive against you.

3. They required ceaseless repetition of a powerful message that resonated with the public. The drumbeat must draw on the wealth of cultural tradition because it will not have the money behind it that corporations have. The fife and drum minutemen of Harvey Rosenfield's "Voter Revolt to Cut Insurance Rates" passed California insurance reform Proposition 103 because he and Ralph Nader recreated the imagery of the American revolution in California. And who could not agree with the drumbeat in the HMO reform movement, "Doctors, not bureaucrats, should be practicing medicine"? While this became President Clinton's and Vice President Gore's signature sound bite, we actually pioneered the line in California in the ballot initiative campaign Proposition 216 of 1996. A widely felt message has lots of legs.

4. They included unlikely partners who came together despite their differences. Doctors and consumer groups often fight, but the

American Medical Association's endorsement of legal accountability for HMOs was a huge gain for the movement. Likewise, effectively countering corporations requires good corporations to
step forward and endorse reforms.

5. They took advantage of a unique historical moment. Without a
visible electricity crisis in 2001, our consumer group could not
have helped to create and endow with billions of dollars a state
public power authority to act as a fulcrum against supply manipulation by private generators. Only due to a need to renew
mandatory auto insurance laws in California in 2000, a boon for
insurers, could my colleague Doug Heller bootstrap to the legislative reauthorization the nation's first flat-rate, low-cost auto
insurance program for the poor. Like "life-line" telephone service, the life-line auto insurance guarantees a flat premium for
anyone living at or below 250 percent of the poverty level in Los
Angeles and San Francisco.

6. They separated the good from the bad by creating a more even
playing field for the good to profit and the bad to pay. They did
not ruin markets, but improved them. Driving a wedge between
your opponents by recruiting fair corporations for your cause
gives instant credibility to a genuine public interest campaign by
showing it has been "business sanctioned." This is one reason
why corporations generally like to stick together on public policy.
Reaching across conventional battle lines to find allies is often
perceived as a demonstration of broad-based support. The public campaign against Microsoft's anti-trust abuses, the bundling
of its Internet browser, gained steam when Ralph Nader and his
colleagues in Washington, D.C., brought in hi-tech executives to
discuss Microsoft's anti-competitive behavior.

7. They never quit. One of the greatest changes in California history, the tax revolt of Proposition 13 in 1978, which limited resi-

dential property taxes to about 1 percent of a home's sale price, was on the ballot three times before it succeeded. While the tax limits depleted the resources available to public schools and community infrastructure, the initiative represented a sea change in California politics. The initiative mistakenly limited corporations' taxes; however, still untouched today, it has saved homeowners billions and kept seniors in homes that they might have been taxed out of.

8. They had coattails. Politicians want to be with you because they know it will give them political power.

9. They talked about real people, not abstractions or symbols. HMO casualties of the day, restaurant owners who had to close up because their electric bill quadrupled, and low-income families that had to choose between food and mandatory auto insurance were important enough for society to respond to.

10. They used their enemy's own strengths against it, which came from understanding the enemy and forcing its mistakes. For example, Harvey Rosenfield accomplished remarkable political jujitsu when the insurance industry spent so heavily on advertising against his Proposition 103, $80 million, that the public understood clearly which side the insurance industry was on and voted against it. People saw so many anti-103 commercials that they knew it had to be the insurance industry paying for them.

Finding the Bastille

Through the lens of these principles, the paradigms that traditionally have balanced power between the individual and the corporation today lack the critical component of challenging the corporateer at the root of its power—cultural intrusion. The traditional remedy for abusive corporate power had been to increase public regulation of markets.

The public sphere exerted itself to restrain the private sector. The problem in recent years has been that the public and private sectors have become so intermingled that where one begins and the other ends is increasingly hard to say. For instance, it's increasingly difficult to draw lines between the corporations that have come to sponsor politics and the politicians who are sponsored.

Good capitalists want regulation because they want level playing fields on which to compete. Sol Price, the founder of Price Club, later to be Costco, told me, "The capitalist system works better than any other system we've ever created, as far as producing and distributing goods, but if you allow the capitalist system to be in a free market where it can do whatever it wants, then you get into trouble. . . . Capitalism has to have some kind of governmental intervention, and then it's always a question of how much. So, politicians say, 'Okay, you can't, you're not allowed to throw stuff into the river that's going to poison people, you're not allowed to do that, you know.' So, that's always the question, the back and forth thing, within the limits of how much intervention."[2] To me, the question has expanded significantly because advocates are no longer fighting against just the brute force and resources of the corporation but against entrenched cultural assumptions, logic, and customs that have become the brand of the invisible hand. Popular faith in government has continued to dwindle. Exerting the public sphere is no longer enough, because it has become corrupted by the same corporateer assumptions, logic, and strategies that have reduced it and discredited it. The problem has escalated beyond single issues.

A classic expression of how corporateers have changed social customs, traditions, and mores to bolster their status and diminish those of the individual and her society arose within a month after the September 11th attacks. The New York Stock Exchange widely broadcast a television advertisement that equated business with freedom. It suggested that the ring of the stock market bell had replaced that of the liberty bell, and it ended with, "Let freedom ring." The market not only equaled the society but also represented all the fruit of American history back to the first clang of independence. There could be no answer from society to the Exchange's expropriation of freedom's bell because the question of the corporation's appropriate role had not even been asked. The mainstream American vocabulary did not even have the capacity to articulate when the corporation should feel shame or guilt, or see its self-interest more broadly.

Challenging abusive power has required understanding its basis, exposing its fact, then attacking its legitimacy. For example, the corrupt politician could be publicly questioned about whether she represented the constituents who elected her or contributors who benefited from her votes. By contrast, the power of the corporateer resides in elusive cultural assumptions, logic, strategies, and language that have leveraged its unique cultural place. One of the greatest problems facing those challenging corporate power is the amorphous nature of the modern corporation. Unlike the politician, the corporation has no official obligation to serve, nor does it have term limits or face re-election. The corporation resides largely outside the democratic structure of society, even as it influences culture from the inside. It creates its own authority. There is no Bastille to storm, no physical structure to target, no apparent basis for attack. "How do you organize against an ideology so vast, it has no edges; so everywhere, it seems nowhere?" asked global activist Naomi Klein in *The Nation* magazine. "Where is the site of resistance for those with no workplaces to shut down, whose communities are constantly being uprooted? What do we hold on to when so much that is powerful is virtual—currency trades, stock prices, intellectual property and arcane trade agreements?"[3] Klein pointed out that the solution had been to attack symbols, be they brand logos, stock exchanges, or meetings of world leaders. Writing in the wake of the September 11th attacks, she correctly noted the weakness of the strategy. Suddenly, the symbols had become too significant to attack. Symbols are not a foundation for power, but merely reflections of it. Challenging them also attacks all the meaning they hold for a public socialized to accept their significance, rather than propounding simple propositions to which most people would agree, such as, "There should be limits to markets." Attacking the symbol of a successful brand itself is like going after the enemy at the strongest point of defense. In America, the basis of the corporation's power is cultural—part sociological, part psychological, and part political. Brands can be a prison without bars. Pragmatically, if every American decided to boycott the same corporation for the same reason, it would not survive. However, such collective conscious-ness has become exceedingly difficult to achieve, hence the failures of most boycotts since the 1970s, due to the power of the invisible hand's assumptions over the public. The simplicity with which the consumer can simply stop buying has created illusions about the power any indi-vidual consumer really has over the corporation. For instance, even af-ter the scandal over the safety of the Ford Explorer, the brand and the corporation thrived. However, if popular consciousness about the cor-porateer could be awakened, if the invisible hand could be made visi-ble, the means to excise the corporateer from the vital organs of culture would be at hand. Corporateers create their own authority culturally, which means that undermining that ability would undermine their power.

Branding Corporateering

The goal of counter-corporateering is to create competition among corporations based on their respect for the individual's freedom and his culture. If "the market = the society," society can create a market of the corporation's cultural respect of individuals and their traditions. If the corporation's job is to compete, it can compete to be respectful of culture. The strategy uses the corporation's own weight, its throne of competitiveness, against it. If the people, not the corporation, are sov-ereign, then the corporation will compete.

A key principle of corporations' success in and beyond markets has

been to take the weakest claim against a product or service and turn it
into its biggest strength. For instance, the nationwide effort by a few
large telecommunications companies to keep Internet hookups closed
to all other service providers limited choice but claimed it was against
"Forced Access," since it is hard to ever argue against access alone. My
friend and long-time hell-raiser Sara Nichols was fishing around for a
moniker for a slate of corporate accountability legislation championed
by public interest groups that legislators would be scored on. After talking with college friends, who were market research specialists for large
corporations, Sara reported on their tactics:

> They said that the tried-and-true marketing formula was to
> take your most verifiable but least credible promise and use it
> to sell you. An example is "100 percent satisfaction guaran-
> teed." People like this because they think, "I will know if this
> isn't true, how can they lie about a thing like that?" Or,
> "Choosy moms choose Jif peanut butter" (when Jif is very
> high in salt and sugar, so if you were really choosy you'd never
> choose it). Moms know though, if THEY are choosy. And if
> they're choosy and they choose Jif (because it tastes really
> good), then it must be good, because choosy moms choose it.

The brand defines the user, rather than the user making the brand.
Our group of advocates finally settled on "Better Business Scorecard"
(and later, "Alliance for Better Business") because, besides being true,
the term "better business" utilized the branding principle. It defused
our opponents' best argument that we were not reformers but against
business in general. It said we were simply for a certain brand of business—better business—which hardly anyone could argue against.

The blanket objection corporations have to all cultural limitation
is that it stifles competition. If corporateering were to be a cultural
brand, then it would represent a standard by which corporations could
compete culturally and be scored on. The brand would then define the

user by separating the corporateer from the corporation. Polls show that most individuals believe corporations serve a useful commercial purpose, but are quite concerned about what corporations take from them culturally. The lack of public debate about this common concern represents a pressing need. The debate can be sparked by popular acceptance of a new standard. Corporateering is the "Danger: Keep Out" sign that can be hung on social custom, ethics, and mores that the vast majority of people wish to be preserved. It's a word that can point a finger at violations of the cultural trust. Since the corporateer's power springs from assumptions, logic, and language, so must counter-corporateering's. The first level of involvement for an individual is simply to patronize the brand, use the word, spread the standard.

cor•po•ra•teer *v.* to prioritize commerce over culture *n.* One who prioritizes commerce over culture

corporateering: When corporations exceed their traditional role in a marketplace to dominate the cultural sphere and compromise individuals' rights, freedoms, power, and the democratic systems that protect them. The act implies corporations vying with a democratic people for sovereignty over their society and societal rights by redefining the basic rules of society, law, and ethical customs to the detriment of individuals.

Use the word in conversation five times a week for ninety days, or any time the circumstances warrant (daily for me), and see what happens. What's in a word? Word of mouth is the most valued corporate commodity. It can send a film sinking or sailing quicker than the ink can dry on a critic's review.

Corporations spend one trillion dollars per year to buy it. But you've got it, and it's free. It's your mouth and your words, and there are some things that aren't for sale. Use your word of mouth in your social circle to give the gift of boundaries to those you know.

Why does some corporateer call every time we sit down for dinner?

It's corporateering when all I hear is "Mom, why am I too young for makeup?" because the school board bought books sponsored by a cosmetic company. The corporateer does not care what children learn, only what they buy.

I do not support companies that corporateer.

Ralph Nader likes to say that every person can be an epicenter. Her energy and transmissions emit in the culture around her. Nader's epicenter led to federal consumer protection laws and agencies of the 1970s such as the Food and Drug Administration, an air bag in every car, and mandatory seat-belt laws. Ralph was once bumped from a flight by an airline that overbooked. He sued and won for every passenger the right to receive a flight coupon when bumped. A project that Nader inspired with our group created a small band of high-energy volunteers, The Oaks Project, so called for their roots in the community. Each Oak collects one thousand signatures per year for citizen ballot measures and is an epicenter in his or her community. As of this writing, there are about 200 Oaks, but among their successes is the passing of the strongest conflict-of-interest laws in the nation in five California cities through local ballot measures. In San Francisco, Santa Monica, Claremont, Pasadena, and Vista, the small group collected 70,000 signatures for laws in each city that preclude any city official from voting for a benefit for a contractor and then receiving a gift, job, or dollar from them for five years.

I will create the first Circle of Corporateering. I will find 100 opinion leaders—doctors, nurses, lawyers, commentators, politicians—who agree to use the word, vocabulary, and concepts in their circles in conjunction with the release of this book. Readers can add their voices to this circle. In my experience, with regard to the corporation, people tend to exaggerate their own importance, how much their individual experience means to a corporation, and to underestimate their own power, how easy it would be to change things through simple persistence and repetition. Use a word and give culture a means to change. It's critical that our language adapt to facilitate a means to understand the influence of the largest and most powerful modern institution over it.

Of course, counter-corporateering will take more than words. What is the standard for the corporateer?

That is the substantive point society defines from which to push back to protect the individual's freedom. The following standards are merely a beginning template that, from my experiences, seems as good a place as any to begin. They are society's to grow, to change, or to let perish. The indexes to measure corporations today are all economic, but a new scorecard could measure how hard corporations are competing to respect the individual's freedom in his public and private life.

The Corporateer Quotient

While corporations and industries differ greatly, there are some basic premises that make for easy comparison within and across industries. I offer the following "Corporateer Quotient" as criteria to guide the types of questions that the individual should be asking of the corporation and that corporations with a commitment to cultural protection should be asking themselves. Publicly available information from Edgar, the Securities and and Exchange Commission's extensive on-line database, can answer some of these questions (*www.freeedgar.com*). Others require the corporation's cooperation. Whether corporations answer them or not, they are the type of questions that need to be asked, from within and without. Next time a corporation wants to involve you in a purchase, pick a category relevant to you or them and seek an answer. If you find one, you can e-mail it to *quotientanswers @corporateering.org*, where a list of responses will be kept. Just asking the questions enough times will yield attention to them. If enough people do, and the corporation really wants to be intimate with us, then it will have to answer.

Category	Questions
Privacy	Does your corporation sell private information about its customers to other companies without their consent? Does your corporation buy private information from other corporations about individuals that it uses to market to them? Does your corporation seek a consumer's consent before it shares personal information? (The "opt in" system)
Purchasing Influence	What percentage of total expenditures is spent on a) marketing and b) advertising?
Political Influence	What percentage of total expenditures is spent on political contributions and trade lobbying?
Respect for Youth	Does your company advertise in schools or in public school materials?
Legal Rights	Does your corporation require consumers to submit to mandatory binding arbitration agreements as a condition of purchase?
Judicial Independence	Does your corporation contribute for or against the election of judges?
Respect for Home Life	Does your company telemarket its product or service?
Internal Ethics	Does your corporation have an officer dedicated to resolving the ethical disputes of workers?
Dissent	Is there a formal complaint process for workers who have ethical questions about their jobs? Is there a formal policy to protect whistle-blowers from retaliation and to encourage dissent through appropriate channels? May I have a copy?
Public Responsibility	Did the corporation pay federal taxes last year? What percentage of the company's revenue did it pay in federal taxes? (10 percent or more would put it on a par with most individuals.)

Category	Questions
Governance	Are workers represented on the board of directors? Is there a conflict-of-interest code that prevents most board members and their family members from being hired by the corporation? Is the CEO the chairman of the personnel committee or is there an independent board member—who does not work for the company—who oversees the personnel committee? Are the majority of directors on the board public representatives who have no financial ties to the corporation?
Worker Value	What is the ratio of the most highly paid employee to the least-well paid employee? What percentage of all employees are full-time? What percentage of all employees are contract labor?
Accountability	What percentage of revenue was spent defending lawsuits and in legal awards and settlements?
Job Security	What percentage of your workforce has been laid off in the last a) one year b) five years?
Transparency	Will your company make public all legal judgments and settlements against it?
Customer Intimacy	Does your corporation have systems for customer relations management (CRM)? If so, are consumers advised of their rights not to be solicited? Is there a process for allowing customers to "opt out" of solicitations or the sharing of their name and financial information with affiliates?
Health and Safety	Does the corporation have a process for identifying threats within the corporation to the public's health and safety, and resolving them?
Respect for Time	When your company makes a major mistake with regard to a customer, does it have a policy to make the customer whole for excessive lost time? Is there a process for identifying similar mistakes in other accounts?

The fact that none of these questions are trade secrets but so few of the answers are now publicly available shows the need for new public policy. Similar to the greater democratization that the American colonists embraced after their independence from England, the reforms that follow seek to make the corporation more responsive to the individual and to society, as well as to create barriers to corporate intervention or corruption. They are proposals that you can give voice to at the level of policymaking.

A New Corporate Compact

Every large corporation should have an Inspector General (I.G.) or Compliance Officer for Better Business that reports directly to the CEO. Federal government agencies have these posts to prevent against fraud, corruption, and ethical violations. Corporations need them to prevent against this same type of abuse, as well as to avoid violating or offending social custom, law, and cultural values. It is not only in the interest of the individual and the society for the corporation to have an independent post examining its social conduct, but it is also in the interest of "loss mitigation" for the corporation. The I.G./Compliance Officer will protect the corporation against lawsuits by making the company practice deterrence, or at least have an honest debate from within. Frontline employees and middle management often identify troubling trends well ahead of a lawsuit that publicly reveals them, but corporate culture mitigates against the CEO finding out early enough to make a difference.

Recent history has shown that corporate attorneys and auditors are far more worried about retaining their client by using loopholes in the law than about protecting the public interest. The I.G./Compliance Officer should not be from any trade that can be manipulated to suit the needs of profit, but her focus should be entirely in the practical area of where profit motive intersects with the interests of the individual and society. She should be an ethicist. A lot of corporations will no doubt be fearful of looking too closely at themselves, but the history of one of the biggest frauds ever perpetrated against the American taxpayer shows that they should do so now, rather than be sorry later.

Columbia/HCA, once the nation's largest hospital chain and now simply called HCA, defrauded the government by submitting inflated bills—one of the offenses for which, during 2000, it paid $840 million in criminal and civil penalties, the largest health care fraud settlement in American history.[4] On a plane ride over Montana, I happened to sit next to the man who came forward to make the government's case against the company, James Alderson.[5] Alderson told me that the result of the fraud scandal was that most hospitals in America have hired compliance officers to protect against fraud. Every corporation should respect this cautionary tale and get an I.G/Compliance Officer. When whistle-blowers come forward, it's far better for a corporation to have the whistle blown from within than from without. And it could be a sign of social responsibility to the public.

Large corporations should create Customer Associations so that individuals can associate to make the corporation better and more responsible. If corporations are really serious about customer intimacy, then they have to give something back to customers. The idea of a Customer Association is to give any corporation's customers a voluntary way of uniting: by pooling their money to set up a nonprofit watchdog group of experts who protect against corporate abuse. The key is for corporations to include with their bills an opportunity for the consumer to voluntarily join a customer association that will hire professionals to represent their interests vis-à-vis the corporation. The customer would pay a few dollars per year to a new nonprofit entity, independent of the corporation, that would chart the corporation's conduct and inform members of its behavior. This would be like a union for customers. Why would any corporation want one? Good corporations could score points for wanting to have a more equal relationship with their customers, who would then know the give and take of a real relationship. This also could become the equivalent of a Good Housekeeping seal of approval that corporations would utilize in their advertising: "Customer Association Approved." Then it's up to the public to make sure such brands win in markets, even if it means paying a few extra pennies to give them the edge. The voluntary association's board would be elected by the membership and be totally independent of the corporation. The model is based on existing Consumer Utility Boards, or CUBs, that Ralph Nader pioneered. CUBs have saved utility ratepayers billions of dollars. The Illinois Citizen Utility Board, with 200,000 members, has saved Illinois taxpayers more than $3 billion since 1983 by challenging utility rate hikes, and has successfully educated ratepayers on how to save money on services and on conservation issues.

Schools should be free from corporateers. Corporations should respect the ability of children to be educated in an environment dedicated solely to the transmission of cultural values, not commercial ones. This is a pledge corporations should make to individuals. They should have a "Schools Free" policy. They will not market, advertise, or sell products in schools through grades 12, in textbooks, or on commercial television stations directed to schools.

The corporation should let individuals choose, but not force them to accept, binding arbitration as a condition of commerce. Many corporations force a waiver of the Seventh Amendment right to trial. Mandatory binding arbitration favors large corporations that give repeat business to arbitrators. Corporations should not force a consumer to give up his right to trial as a condition of doing business. The corporations that choose not to require mandatory binding arbitration should metaphorically fly the flag "Seventh Amendment Observed."

The Public Sector's Role

All deregulation efforts should be time-limited and subject to renewal. Industries have made very bold promises when lobbying for deregulation, but few of these promises have materialized. The extension of

deregulation of an industry should be contingent on the promised benefits to the individuals and the society materializing. Deregulation legislation should "sunset," i.e., be subject to renewal every five years.
Government has long applied this standard to consumer protection measures and agencies. For instance, state medical boards' legislative autho-
rizations often sunset at given intervals, which requires that the boards
prove that they fulfill a need before being authorized to continue. Even if
deregulation efforts are renewed, the periodic renewal period would offer
an opportunity for amending the terms of unregulated-market and com-
panion measures to help consumers based on lessons learned. Corporations would also have to worry about essentially renewing their charter
periodically and answering public questions with real ramifications. For
instance, our consumer group passed the nation's first flat-rate, low-cost
auto insurance program for the poor in 2000 only because we were able
to hitch its approval to the renewal of the mandatory insurance law in
California, which insurers badly wanted. We were effectively able to leverage the new law as a condition of the old one's extension.

Government should report on customer service and responsiveness.
The government collects enormous economic data about corporations,
but little information on customer service. With a click of their computer
mouse, Americans should be able to find basic information collected by
the U.S. government about the largest corporations in the nation. What
is the average customer wait time on hold? How many customer service
agents serve how many customers? Does the corporation protect privacy,
observe the Seventh Amendment, market in elementary schools? The
American government should have a Department of Corporate Responsiveness whose sole mission is to standardize, disclose, and improve the
responsiveness of corporations across industry. The federal government
does not even have a Department of Consumer Affairs, to respond to the
needs of consumers in markets. A federal Department of Corporate Responsiveness or Consumer Affairs would differ from industry-specific
regulation in that it would create a federal data bank for comparing all

corporations and charting their responsiveness to public concerns. Industries could then be compared to others, and patterns across industry lines could be highlighted and revealed to the public. Is there a better use of taxpayer dollars than to take on a task that the vast majority of Americans would do if they had the power to do it individually?

New standards should value the customer's time so that an individual can recover the cost of their excessive lost time due to a corporation's gross mistake. The law should recognize the value of an individual's "time value." When an individual's payment is late, the corporation charges them a late fee. When a corporation forces an individual to spend hours of her time to fix a mistake she did not make, the corporation should similarly have to pay the individual an error fee that is a factor of the hours that the individual had to spend fixing a problem not of her own making. Government could establish certain guidelines for various industries. The law should develop to recognize that the individual's time is as valuable as the corporation's. The individual's fees and costs associated with unnecessary delays should be valued and compensible through a small claims process that could be administered by mail and telephone through a governmental apparatus or court system, so as not to subsume more of the individual's time. Corporations are guaranteed to make far fewer blatant mistakes if they know that the individual can force them to pay for those mistakes without having to hire a lawyer.

Individual corporate managers should be personally liable for harms their corporations cause that they have personal knowledge of but make no effort to stop. California has led the nation by making it a crime for managers to know about a seriously concealed danger in a product or business practice but to fail to disclose it to employees and the state. There is no equivalent federal law. In fact, when manufacturers sought to force through Congress a bill limiting their legal liability for dangerous and defective products, I worked with Senator Dianne Feinstein's office to propose an amendment similar to California's law holding individual executives accountable. Not surprisingly, the amendment was handily defeated. Even the California law could be expanded to include not just threats to an individual's health and safety but also for intentional violations of other lawful trusts, such as privacy, financial security, good faith, and fair dealing. In response to the corporate scandals of 2002, our consumer group sponsored California legislation that would hold executives personally responsible for knowing about fraud but not coming forward. (It passed both houses of the legislature but was vetoed by Governor Gray Davis.) A key reason for the lack of corporate accountability is that individuals running the corporations are themselves rarely personally liable. To make the corporation more of a human enterprise, individuals within the structure need to know that they can go to jail for not living up to humanity's legal and ethical standards.

A tax levied on corporate advertising could fund a not-for-profit public media sector. If unbiased information is society's most valuable resource, then society has treated it too lightly. A not-for-profit media sector not dependent on contributions from an elite segment of society, or upon corporate advertising dollars, would report on what is far less visible in the rest of the media, including the invisible hand of the corporation. Advertising taxes us all, and taxing excessive spending on advertising by large corporations can provide funds for a not-for-profit media. The alternative, for government to sponsor the sector, has never resonated with Congress or the public. This could also lead to censorship of stories critical of the government's role. Media companies will claim that the downside of taxing advertising is that less advertising will mean fewer resources for the networks to entertain and inform. Sponsorship, they argue, buys what is sponsored. Often the sponsorship corrupts what is sponsored as well. Professor McChesney estimated that a 1 percent tax on advertising expenditures would have generated $1.5 billion in 1997, compared to the $260 million in federal funds for all public broadcasting that year.[6] $1.5 billion could establish a not-for-profit media sector with the sole incentive of telling, not selling. Many European nations have these, though it is the government that funds them directly without any curb to governmental critique, and such independence allows stations like the BBC to produce high-quality programming without compromise. In America, such an alternative media sector would also drive the corporate-sponsored media to compete with it. This competition will improve the quality of commercial programming far more than any unlikely reduction in the amount of advertising will hurt it.

Charge for the airwaves. To create a free commercial-free media sector, the federal government could simply charge a price for the public airwaves that it currently allows networks to use rent-free. In 1997, the FCC similarly gave away broadcast licenses for a new digital television spectrum, although it estimated the value of the licenses to be from $11 billion to $70 billion.[7] $70 billion could pay for a highly impressive public interest media sector. The FCC placed the value of the traditional analog spectrum even higher, at up to $132 billion.[8]

Give broadcasters rental credit for the airwaves if they provide free air time to political candidates who shun campaign contributions. Political contributions from special interest groups have gridlocked the democratic process. However, banning campaign contributions to candidates precludes political challengers from being heard. Providing public financing to candidates can be very expensive for taxpayers. Broadcasters hold public communication frequencies valued at about $200 billion, but pay no rent. In exchange for free rent, broadcasters could be required through Congressional action to provide free air time to political candidates that shun private contributions. I first articulated this idea in a discussion with a Las Vegas taxicab driver. Two months later, in October 2002, U.S. Senators John McCain and Russell Feingold independently introduced legislation to do just this, but it has yet to be given serious consideration.

E-democracy has the power to inform, and government should establish an Internet domain for better business reporting. The Internet has been largely commercialized, but as surfers know, finding the right

Internet site can, with a single click of the mouse, provide a wealth of information that would otherwise take hours, days, or weeks of research. Better business practices can easily be defined by a government that already establishes laws to mandate many of them. There is no central government site listing all the corporations that have broken the law, been convicted, entered into settlements or paid fines. Public interest groups that publicize problems with corporations often face the threat of defamation lawsuits. When government has caught corporate crime, it should report on it so the public knows who and what to look out for. A little information goes a long way. A public sector Internet domain that lists, through a simple name search, the rap sheet of every corporation that has one will arm individuals with the power to see corporateering and avoid becoming a victim of it. Until the public sector develops a better solution, *www.corporateering.org* will seek to piece together key publicly available information and sites.

Whistle-blowers within the corporation need greater protection. Few protections exist for corporate employees that come forward with evidence of serious abuses within a corporation. A comprehensive federal whistle-blower protection act should be legislated to 1) ensure the financial security of those who sacrifice their jobs for society's safety, 2) prohibit retaliation against and harassment of employees that report threats to the public's health and safety, and 3) create a federal whistle-blower protection program (similar to the witness protection program) to support insiders with critical information. No such effective federal law exists.

Corporate welfare programs should be publicly disclosed and time-limited. Under the federal overhaul of public assistance programs in the mid-1990s, public aid for families with dependent children was time-limited. By contrast, a 130-year-old corporate welfare program, the 1872 Mining Act, gave mining corporations federal land for $5 per acre to mine gold, silver, lead, and other minerals without paying any royalty to the federal treasury. Designed to settle the West, the program remains in effect due to millions of dollars in campaign contributions from mining interests that has prevented its repeal. A new law should be enacted requiring legislative reauthorization of all existing corporate welfare programs every year. There should be a lifetime limit on corporate welfare of sixty months—the same lifetime time cap that applies to families in poverty with dependent children who receive public assistance. The American taxpayer is slated to spend more than $394 billion from 2000 until 2004 just on federal corporate tax subsidies.[9] Particularly in time of war, public scrutiny of expenditure of every taxpayer dollar should be a national priority. To promote such public inspection, Ralph Nader has suggested, "Every federal agency could be required to list every program under its purview which confers below-cost or below-market-rate goods, services, or other benefits on corporations. The Security Exchange Act could be amended to require publicly traded corporations to list the subsidies (both by type and amount) they receive from government bodies, and to publish this information on the Internet."[10] To curb corporate welfare at the local level, Nader has recommended that Congress consider requiring such expenditures to be taxed federally.

National referendum, recall, and initiative procedures could counter corporate power. At the turn of the twentieth century, railroad barons controlled the California statehouse, until populist anger swept reformer Governor Hyrum Johnson and a slate of candidates loyal to him into office. Johnson gave Californians the political tools to prevent the railroad companies or any other special interest from putting them in the same situation again: the referendum, the recall, and the ballot initiative. By collecting signatures to put these items on the ballot, voters, through a popular vote, could override legislation (referendum), recall candidates, and directly enact their own laws (ballot initiative). The referendum and recall have been used sparingly, but the ballot initiative, since the tax revolt of Prop 13 in 1978, has been utilized with increasing frequency. Harvey Rosenfield turned the tables on the insurance industry with it, but corporations have also used it to their ends. Often the threat of a ballot initiative on a popular subject has been enough to force good legislation or stop a bad bill, such as the $4 billion legislative bailout of the electric utility Southern California Edison in 2001. Establishing a binding national recall, referendum, and ballot initiative process could take a constitutional convention, depending upon how the Congress interprets its duties. The use of a nonbinding referendum or popular plebiscite would clearly not require such a convention.

Three strikes should apply to corporations, too. If a person can go to jail for life for three criminal convictions, why shouldn't corporations face a similar standard? A corporate death penalty for any corporation convicted of three separate criminal offenses would set a new bar for corporate responsibility and deter the corporate crime waves of tomorrow. Such legislation was introduced in California in 2003 by our Foundation for Taxpayer and Consumer Rights. (The first strike requires that a full-page advertisement be taken out in major newspapers; the second necessitates a fine to the state treasury; the third results in the loss of the right to do business.) Laws could be enacted at the state or federal level revoking the charter of any corporation that proved through its conduct that it was beyond rehabilitation. Trusteeships to take care of laid-off workers could be created. Mostly, however, such laws would provide a deterrent to wrongdoing.

The corporation's legal status as a person must be re-evaluated. Changing the legal fiction that the corporation is a person appears as difficult as unringing a bell. The most effective way to curb the corporation's cultural power would be to clarify that, under the law, the corporation is not a person or entitled to the same legal rights as the individual. Many in modern times have sought the revocation of corporate charters, without success. If the founding fathers saw our society today, however, they would recognize the need for a constitutional amendment to clarify that only individuals are entitled to certain protections under the Constitution.

Changing Individual Consciousness

Blaming the corporation for its cultural dominance is natural, but some of the responsibility also rests with individuals. Corporations communicate with people all the time. "The only communication most people have with a corporation is to send it a check," said my wife, Michelle Williams Court, a civil-rights attorney who spends much of her time corresponding with corporations. People must educate themselves about their rights and start communicating back to the corporation in ways that limit the corporation's cultural grasp. Corporations rely on individuals' ignorance to take advantage of them in markets and beyond. Here are five simple ways to fight back by asserting substantial rights individuals already have, but rarely use.

1. Tell a corporation, "Do not call." Next time a telemarketer calls, just say, "Put me on your do-not-call list." Corporations are required under a federal law called the Telephone Consumer Protection Act to have such lists and to pay $500 every time they call someone on them. If they keep calling, collect $500 for each violation.[11] Many states have also developed "Do not call" lists that individuals can sign up for and corporations have to respect.

2. "Opt out." Send a corporation the following note to inform them that you "opt out" of their system of sharing your private financial information:

   I am asserting my rights under the Financial Services Modernization Act and the Fair Credit Reporting Act to "opt out" of the following two uses of my personal information:

   • Do not disclose personally identifiable information with your non-affiliated third-party companies or individuals.

   • Do not disclose my creditworthiness to any affiliate.

   Further, I request, even though it may not be required by law, that you:

- Do not disclose my transaction and experience information to any affiliate of yours.

- Do not disclose any information about me in connection with marketing agreements between you and any other company.

I would appreciate written confirmation of these requests.

3. Change a corporate contract. Corporations typically require individuals to sign long, standardized contracts that often have restrictive clauses, such as a waiver of the right to trial, in the fine print. Next time you are presented with such a contract, read it and cross out the objectionable provisions before you sign. Individuals have a right to negotiate that they rarely use. A corporation may reject your purchase, or an agent for the corporation may simply ignore the change in order to win your business. I routinely cross out mandatory binding arbitration provisions. In some cases, it works. In others, it doesn't. If it doesn't, you're simply back to making a decision based on the limits of the offer. If it does, you've retained important rights. To help, we have posted standardized contracts for many purchases on *www.corporateering.com*. Try using these contracts in place of the ones corporations offer, and we will see together if we can create a national standard.

4. Stop corporate junk faxers. A federal law makes it illegal to send an unsolicited commercial advertisement to a fax machine from anywhere in the U.S. People who receive junk faxes have the right to recover at least $500 per fax. In most cases, the law authorizes courts to award up to $1,500 per fax. For how to stop junk faxers and a sample complaint, visit *www.consumerwatchdog.org*.

5. Challenge a corporation. When the corporation upsets you, put your gripe in writing to the corporation, to a regulator, and to the media. The corporation may or may not change, but the letter

memorializes your problem. If it is serious enough, the corporation will want to fix it because if they don't they may get sued, and such letters will show that they knew of the problem. If you want to make a corporation nervous, put something serious about it in writing.

The corporation can also be challenged in social discourse. The next section provides a list of words and phrases to help draw useful boundaries between the corporateer and the corporation, the corporation and the individual.

APPENDIX

SPEAKING ABOUT CORPORATEERING

The power of the corporateer over the individual depends on a vocabulary that denies the existence of corporateering. Invisibility is the corporateer's strength, but it can also be its Achilles heel. Making visible the invisible hand and making audible the subliminal voice can undo the source of the corporation's control over individuals and their society—hidden assumptions, logic, and strategies repugnant to most individuals.

The terms that follow represent a vocabulary of illumination, audibility, and, thus, resistance. They are key concepts and effective expressions that will help other individuals see corporateering within the corporation and outside of it. Corporations have almost unlimited sums of money to market their messages. Individuals have the truth. These words and phrases allow individuals to convey the truth of corporateering from their epicenter and change consciousness in their social circle.

Abuse. Corporate abuses, not corporations, should be the subject of criticism. Exposing how corporations exploit the power they hold over individuals resonates with the public. Speaking about corporate abuses faced by real people in daily life connects and unites individuals. *HMO abuse hospitalized my neighbor because the company refused to approve the drug that would have stabilized her and prevented her admission.*

Balance of power. Most real conflicts boil down to this. In any prob-
lematic relationship with a corporation, ask this question: What is the
balance of power and how are corporateers trying to change it to their
advantage? *The real issue is that the financial services industry controls
the balance of power by forcing the individual to specifically "opt out" if
they do not want their personal information shared.*

Bailout. Bailouts are the silver bullet that show the corporation is not
more significant than the individual or the society. Bailouts are not
limited to taxpayer "rescues." The individual bails out the corporation
when she has to spend time fixing a billing error, reversing a service
charge, paying with her stock wealth for a corporation's failure to disclose losses to investors, or writing a check for a second opinion that
the HMO should have paid for. Neither the individual nor the public
should bail out a corporation for its own mistakes. *I had to bail out the
cable company by taking two personal days because the installer didn't
come when he said he would.*

Better business. Good corporations cannot compete in an environment where bad businesses go unpunished. Ending corporateering is
about creating better business practices, not eliminating corporations.
Historically, industry lobbies have stood together under the proposition that all businesses are created equal in their right to be free of accountability to the public. This has hurt good businesses that don't
pollute, don't manufacture dangerous products, and don't invade privacy. Better business protects individuals and *businesses* from corporate
abuses. *Blue Shield took a stand for better business when it broke with the
HMO industry in California and did not require patients to waive the
right to trial in order to receive health coverage.*

Borders, boundaries, and balance. These are the Three B's of better
business. Where does the individual (worker, investor, consumer, citizen) end and the corporation begin? The Three B's: *There should be
boundaries to corporate marketing in schools and the junk food that can be
sold. Without new borders, corporations will continue to invade the indi-*

vidual's privacy. Balance must be established between the public's right to know and the corporation's commercial interest in concealing its problems.

Censorship. Free societies should not have it, but commercial priorities can impose it. Discussing commercial censors is every bit as important for democracy as a dialogue about government censorship. *When CBS would not air controversial reruns of the series* Family Law *because Procter & Gamble, a big advertiser with a $300-million-per-year contract with CBS, objected, commercial censorship trumped the public's right to know.*[1]

Cheating, not competing. Corporateers often cheat rather than compete because it is easier to profit every time the market moves rather than only when the company has the goods to win. *Oil companies would rather cheat than compete, which is why they try to keep independent refiners from entering the market.*

Choice. Choice is what individuals want and corporations purport to grant. But the corporation also takes cultural choices away, such as rights to trial, to speech, and to knowledge. Individual choice is a crucial lever of popular concern in America. *Telecommunication companies take away the individual's choice when they require that broadband Internet connections connect only to one service provider.*

Capturing consciousness. Individuals should value the capturing of consciousness at least as much as corporations. *Television on the elevator inappropriately captures the individual's consciousness in unavoidable public places. I'm troubled that in my son's public school companies like Zapped Me and other corporateers seek to capture his consciousness. When TV advertisers record advertisements louder than the programming, they are seeking to capture the individual's consciousness when they leave the room.*

Economic growth. Rapid economic growth at all costs threatens cultural and economic stability. As the Internet stock bubble proved, rapid growth in one direction is often artificial and necessitates a fall in the other. During the age of the corporateer, it was not enough for corporations to be profitable, they also had to achieve rapid growth in profitability. Within the corporation, growth in profits is the product, not the result of a high-quality product. In society, stimulating economic growth became a standard reason for giving corporations bailouts, subsidies, and new privileges. *The push for economic growth became the corporateer excuse for everything from killing the rain forests of Brazil to disregarding HMO patients' needs.*

Focus and blur. Corporateers have the power to bring into focus commercial benefits and blur cultural losses. *Tobacco maker Philip Morris changed its name to Altria Group in 2003 to focus the public on its philanthropy and blur its unseemly past. A report by the company for the Czech government focused on the fact that tobacco use would save the country's health-care system money, but blurred the reason: Smokers die young.*

For sale. Cultural protections of the individual should not be subject to commercial purchase. *Children's consciousness, private records, the free press, governmental decisions, and naming rights to community institutions should not be for sale to the corporateer.*

Free society. A.k.a. free people, free press, free religion, free speech, etc. *Free societies depend on unrestrained cultural rights and freedoms for the individual, not simply freer commercial choices.*

Globalizing. That the common usage of the word "globalization" represents commercial ends exclusively reflects the degree to which corporateering has turned societies into markets. *We should be globalizing higher standards for labor, the environment, and consciousness about corporateering.*

Homogenization. Milk can be homogenized, but culture should be as diverse as possible to protect the individual and his freedom. *Corporateers hasten homogenization of culture, including the McDonaldization of cities from Omaha to Cancún.*

Individual. Individuals, not corporations, are the subject of the Declaration of Independence, the U.S. Constitution, and the Bible. The corporation is not mentioned at all. *The individual is more important than the corporation, but is not always treated that way.*

Invisible hand. Speaking about the illusions created by the invisible hand will help to make them visible. *What the visible hand of the corporation provides, such as cheaper products, does not excuse what the invisible hand takes, like safety.*

Naming rights. These should belong to parents, not corporations. *Naming rights to civic institutions should not be sold, but reserved for civic heroes.*

Market ≠ Society. The market does not equal the society. The free society is more important than the free market. *Adam Smith did not believe that the market and the society were the same thing, but that the society was more important than the market.*

Privatizing gain/socializing risk. Corporateers socialize risk and privatize gain. *When taxpayers socialize corporate risk by subsidizing the development of a new drug, the pharmaceutical company should not be allowed to privatize all the gain.*

Public. Privatization efforts during the age of the corporateer have made this a dirty word, but where would we be without public bathrooms? After September 11th, popular views about the public sector and confidence in it have changed. In August 2001, prior to the attack, Price Club/Costco founder Sol Price made the following prophecy in response to my query about the lack of public involvement: "You only get the public engaged actively in anything when it becomes significant enough to where it's hurting. Otherwise the public does not engage, and so you never get any great changes until there's some kind of a crisis, either a war or a depression, something like that." The public sector may have a better hope than at any other time in modern history of regaining the public's faith. *Public needs like electricity, natural gas, and water should not be open to manipulation by private corporations.*

Smith, Adam. Don't cede his name to the corporateer. *Adam Smith believed that corporations were anti-competitive forces because they had monopolistic power, and many corporateers today act similarly.*

Spending is not saving. Buying corporate stock is not the same as saving money. *Spending on stock gambles is not the same as saving for your future.*

Sweatshop clothes. Not to be confused with sweatpants or sweatsuits. *I will not allow my family to wear sweatshop clothes because I insist on buying from Worker Safe companies.*

Taxation. Not without representation. The influence of corporate campaign dollars over politics violates the principle for which Americans declared independence. Freedoms, time, energy can be taxed as easily as money and property. *Corporateers tax the individual's freedoms and offer no means for the individual to be represented.*

Welfare. Corporate, that is. U.S. taxpayer dollars spent $1.6 million to promote Chicken McNuggets in Singapore and $11 million for Pillsbury to plug the Dough Boy abroad.[2] Exxon took a $300 million tax deduction for the legal settlement paid for its culpability in the Exxon Valdez spill.[3] *That corporations receive welfare in order to make profits shows their control over society.*

10 LAWS TO COUNTER CORPORATEERING

1. **Freedom of Information Act.** Did you ever wonder about potential government plans to build a nuclear waste site or military installation near your home? Under the Freedom of Information Act (FOIA) you can obtain access to existing government documents pertaining to these and other official matters. Signed into law in 1966 by President Johnson and strengthened in 1974 following the Watergate scandal, the FOIA is a national sunshine law designed to promote accountability and transparency in government. All federal agencies except Congress and the federal judiciary are required to disclose those records requested in writing by any citizen, unless the documents fall under one of nine categories of FOIA exemptions. (Sample FOIA request and appeal letters appear later in this appendix.) States also have similar public records acts.

   RESOURCES: More FOIA information including a listing of "Principal FOIA Contacts at Federal Agencies" is accessible online at *www.usdoj.gov/foia*. A consumer handbook entitled "Your Right to Federal Records Questions and Answers on the Freedom of Information Act" can be found at *www.pueblo.gsa.gov* or by contacting the Federal Consumer Information Center, Dept. WWW, Pueblo, CO 81009; Phone: (888) 878-3256. A second consumer handbook entitled "The Freedom of Information Act: A User's Guide" can be found at *www.citizen.org* or by contacting the Freedom of Information Clearinghouse, PO Box 19367, Washington, DC 20036; Phone: (202) 588-7790.

2. **False Claims Act.** The next time you hear of HMOs committing Medicare fraud, or huge corporations engaging in tax fraud, know that a powerful civil recourse exists against those who seek to rob the public treasury. Dating back to the Civil War, when Abraham Lincoln sought to deter unscrupulous war profiteers from taking advantage of the Union Army, the Federal Civil False Claims Act stands today as a strong deterrent to fraud and a means of recovering huge sums of taxpayer funds through the issuance of severe damages and other stiff penalties.

RESOURCES: For more information about the False Claims Act, visit *www.falseclaimsact.com* or *www.taf.org*, or contact Taxpayers Against Fraud, the False Claims Act Legal Center, 1220 19th Street NW, Suite 501, Washington, DC 20036; Phone: (800) USFALSE.

3. **Qui Tam whistle-blower protection.** If you ever find yourself with direct knowledge of a corporation defrauding the government, you can sue the company under the Qui Tam provision of the False Claims Act to halt the impropriety and share in any financial recovery. Qui Tam—a Latin abbreviation meaning "he who sues for the king as for himself"—is a whistle-blower provision designed to encourage and enable ordinary citizens with knowledge of government fraud to file a suit on behalf of the government. Amended significantly in 1986 to allow for greater ease of public use, hundreds of Qui Tam suits have since been filed, resulting in billions of reclaimed taxpayer dollars.

RESOURCES: Taxpayers Against Fraud, 1220 19th Street NW, Suite 501, Washington, DC 20036; *www.taf.org/taf/*

4. **Consumer Credit Protection laws.** Ever been unfairly turned down for credit or inaccurately billed for more than you owe? Beginning with the Consumer Credit Protection Act (CCPA) of 1968, Congress has enacted a series of laws designed to safeguard consumers from these and other abusive and unfair financial lending practices. **Truth in Lending**—a provision of the CCPA— mandates clear and uniform disclosure by lenders of all credit terms and rates, in order to facilitate ease of comparison by the general public. Similarly, the **Equal Credit Opportunity Act** was designed to prohibit denial of credit based on factors unrelated to creditworthiness such as race, gender, sexual orientation, marital status, and age. Other Consumer Credit Protection laws include the **Fair Credit Billing Act,** the **Fair Credit Debt Collection Act,** and the **Fair Credit Reporting Act.** (See a description of the latter below.)

RESOURCES: Additional information on your credit rights can be found in the Federal Reserve "Consumer Handbook to Credit Protection Laws," accessible on-line at *www.federalreserve.gov* or by contacting Federal Reserve Publications Services, MS-127, Board of Governors of the Federal Reserve System, Washington, DC 20551; Phone: (202) 452-3244 or 3245.

5. **Fair Credit Reporting Act.** If you have opened a bank account, applied for a loan, filed for bankruptcy, leased a car, or been late in paying a bill, there is a file about you full of information gathered and sold by Consumer Reporting Agencies (CRAs). Under the Fair Credit Reporting Act (FCRA) you are guaranteed the right to know what is in your file, to be told of the information used against you, to dispute and have corrected or deleted any inaccurate information, and to seek damages from violators. En-

acted in 1970 and strengthened in 1996, the FCRA mandates legal standards for the collection, use, and transfer of consumer credit and other information in order to ensure the fairness, privacy, and accuracy of information maintained by all CRAs.

RESOURCES: For a summary of your FCRA rights, visit *www.ftc.gov/bcp/conline/edcams/fcra/summary.htm*, and for more FCRA information, go to *www.ftc.gov/bcp/conline/pubs/credit/fcra.htm* or contact the Federal Trade Commission at (877) FTC-HELP.

6. **The Privacy Act.** What does the government know about you . . . and whom can they tell? The Privacy Act of 1974 established for all individual citizens and permanent resident aliens a right of access to their own government-maintained files, and a right to pursue correction of inaccurate information. Further, the Act ordered this personal information to be safeguarded from inappropriate use and unauthorized disclosure, and granted individuals the right to sue the government for statute violations. (A sample Privacy Act request letter appears later in this appendix.)

7. **Unfair or Deceptive Acts or Practices laws.** Have you ever been billed for unsolicited goods or experienced fraud over a commercial service or product? Under laws in all fifty states, abusive and deceptive business practices are illegal and punishable. Known generally as Unfair or Deceptive Acts or Practices laws, these statutes differ in name from state to state, referred to variously as consumer fraud acts, consumer sales acts, deceptive trade practices acts, consumer protections acts, unfair trade practices acts, etc. Together they stand as some of the most important consumer protections and recourses against nearly all forms of corporate deception practices. Find out about the laws in your state by contacting your state representatives, or by visiting your state government's website. (A list of state websites follows.)

8. **Emergency Planning and Community Right-to-Know Act.**
   What precisely are the chemicals used by those factories and
   businesses near your home, and how do they impact your health
   and your environment? Enacted by Congress in October 1986,
   the Emergency Planning and Community Right-to-Know Act
   (EPCRA) was designed to improve public access to information
   about chemical hazards impacting local communities. The Act
   directs the Environmental Protection Agency (EPA) to collect,
   maintain, and make public a record of all chemical polluters. Environmental activists and community leaders employ this vital
   information in their fight against toxic pollution in communities
   across the country.

   RESOURCES: For more information on the EPCRA, go to
   www.epa.gov/ceppo/crtk.html or call the EPCRA Hotline at (800)
   424-9346; TDD (800) 553-7672. For information on chemical
   polluters, visit *www.epa.gov/tri* and the Right-to-Know Network
   at *www.rtk.net*, or contact OMB Watch, 1742 Connecticut Avenue NW, Washington, DC 20009; Phone: (202) 234-8494; *www.
   ombwatch.org*

9. **Community Reinvestment Act.** Your local banks may owe you
   and your neighbors more than you realize. Passed by Congress in
   1977, the Community Reinvestment Act (CRA) was created to
   encourage banks to assist and serve the needs of the local community through such means as providing loans to low- and
   moderate-income people. The Act requires that depository institutions maintain public files, detailing their community service
   plans and practices. These files are frequently accessed by community groups to determine whether local institutions are fulfill-
   ing their promises and obligations.

   RESOURCES: For more CRA information, visit *www.ffiec.gov/
   cra* or call the CRA Assistance Line at (202) 872-7584.

10. **Hazard Communication Standard.** Over 30 million workers in the U.S. are exposed annually to one or more of the 650,000 existing hazardous-chemical products, in addition to hundreds of new products introduced each year, according to estimates by the Federal Occupational Safety and Health Administration (OSHA). Under the Hazard Communication Standard—promulgated in 1983 and modified in 1994—all employees must be provided detailed information of all dangers, and protective measures associated with any potentially harmful chemicals, to which they may be exposed. Further, the Standard requires chemical training programs for these employees, as well as clear and immediate labeling of hazard-carrying containers, and easily accessible safety data sheets.

RESOURCES: More information about the Hazard Communication Standard is available at *www.osha.gov* or by contacting the U.S. Department of Labor, Occupational Safety and Health Administration, 200 Constitution Avenue, Washington, DC 20210; Phone: (800) 321-OSHA

Sample FOIA Request Letter

[Your Name, Address, Daytime Phone]
[Date]

Freedom of Information Unit
[Name and Address of Specific Government Agency]
Re: Freedom of Information Request

Dear Sir or Madam:

Pursuant to the Freedom of Information Act, 5 U.S.C. 552, I hereby request access to (and/or copies of) all records pertaining to _____ [clearly describe the subject or document containing the information that you want, including any pertinent names, places, or dates. Attach any reports, news clips, and/or other documents if you believe they may assist in explaining the information you are seeking].

I am requesting these records _____ [as a representative of the news media, for non-commercial personal use, for an educational institution, etc.].

[If any expenses in excess of $_____ are incurred in connection with this request, please obtain my approval before these charges are incurred.] **OR**

[I request a waiver of fees because my interest in the records is not primarily commercial, and disclosure of the information will contribute significantly to public understanding of the operations or activities of the government because _____.]

I will expect a response within 20 working days as provided by law. If my request is denied in whole or in part, I expect a detailed justification for withholding the records. I also request any segregable portions that are not exempt to be disclosed.

Thank you for your prompt attention to this matter.

Very truly yours,

[Your Signature] [Your Name]

Sample FOIA Appeal Letter

[Your Name, Address, Daytime Phone]
[Date]

Freedom of Information Unit
[Name and Address of Specific Government Agency]
Re: Freedom of Information Request

Dear Sir or Madam:

By letter dated [month day, year], I requested access to _____ [use same description as in request letter]. By letter dated [month day, year], Mr./Ms. _____ of the Freedom of Information Unit [usually] of your agency denied my request. Pursuant to the Freedom of Information Act, 5 U.S.C. 552, I hereby appeal that denial. I have enclosed a copy of my request letter and the denial that I have received.

The denial of my request was improper because _____ [describe why the denial was improper, e.g., why the exemption should not apply in your circumstances].

I expect a response within 20 working days, as the law provides.

Very truly yours,

[Your Signature] [Your Name]

Sample Privacy Act Request Letter

[Your Name, Your Address, Your Daytime Phone]
[Date]

FOIA/Privacy Act Unit
[Name and Address of Specific Government Agency]
Re: Privacy Act Request

Dear Sir or Madam:

Pursuant to the Freedom of Information Act, 5 U.S.C. 552, and the Privacy Act, 5 U.S.C. 552a, I hereby request access to (and/or a copy of) all records pertaining to _____ [clearly describe the subject or document containing the information that you want, including any pertinent names, places, or dates. Attach any reports, news clips, and/or other documents if you believe they may assist in explaining the information you are seeking].

I am requesting these records _____ [as a representative of the news media, for non-commercial personal use, for an educational institution, etc.].

[If any expenses in excess of $_____ are incurred in connection with this request, please obtain my approval before these charges are incurred.] **OR**

[I request a waiver of fees because my interest in the records is not primarily commercial, and disclosure of the information will contribute significantly to public understanding of the operations or activities of the government because _____.]

I will expect a response within 20 working days as provided by law. If my request is denied in whole or in part, I expect a detailed justification for withholding the records. I also request any segregable portions that are not exempt to be disclosed.

Thank you for your prompt attention to this matter.

Very truly yours,

[Your Signature]

[Your Name]

APPENDIX

III

BETTER BUSINESS HEROES

t's important not to forget Enron CEO Kenneth Lay, but it's just as important to remember and encourage executives that have stood for better business. Here is a short list of them.

Aaron M. Feuerstein is owner of Malden Mills, which makes Polartec and Polarfleece outdoor clothing. Malden Mills is the largest employer in one of Massachusetts' poorest towns, Lawrence. After a December 1995 fire destroyed much of his company's factory, Mr. Feuerstein could have retired with around $300 million in insurance payouts or moved the mill south of the border for cheaper labor. Instead, he spent $430 million to rebuild and paid his idled workers for months more than $25 million. By the time the new factory reopened nearly two years later, he had rehired most of his 2,700 employees.

Ray C. Anderson, founder of Interface, Inc. in Atlanta, Georgia. Mr. Anderson revolutionized the carpet and floor-covering industry by acknowledging the environmental degradation from production methods and dedicating his company to reducing waste. Interface hopes to pioneer the model for a "sustainable" corporation, factoring the environmental impact into commercial decisions. For example, Interface is learning to harness solar energy and provide for its raw-material needs by harvesting and recycling carpet and other petrochemical products, while eliminating waste and harmful emissions from its operations. (See *www.interface.com.*)

Sol Price, founder of Price Club warehouse stores, which later became Costco. Mr. Price is considered the father of the large-volume discount industry. He opened his first Fed-Mart in the early 1950s—it was the prototype of today's discount club stores—and then opened his first Price Club in 1976 in a gargantuan warehouse, and revolutionized discount retailing. Mr. Price was one of the first retail business owners to offer medical benefits to his employees, in addition to paying them a living wage. He sold the chain in 1993 to Costco, and he and his wife, Helen, have since dedicated their energies toward philanthropy and working for positive social reforms in the inner city of San Diego and elsewhere.

Ben Cohen and Jerry Greenfield, co-founders of Ben & Jerry's, Vermont's Finest Ice Cream and Frozen Yogurt. These childhood friends started their first store in 1978 in a renovated gas station in Burlington, and their business grew into the popular chain known for its innovative flavors, natural ingredients, and socially conscious business. Ben & Jerry's has treated the community as a co-equal with its commerce: introducing the ice cream industry's first pint container made from unbleached brown kraft paper with a non-toxic printable clay coating; opposing harmful Bovine-Growth Hormones (BGH) in cows and supporting the voluntary labeling of their products to highlight that they are BGH-free; and giving a portion of proceeds from Rainforest Crunch ice cream to rain-forest preservation efforts. Ben and Jerry sold ownership of the company to Unilever in April 2000, but the company claims still to be dedicated to Ben and Jerry's values. Ben & Jerry's gives away 7.5 percent of its pre-tax earnings to support models for social change and creative problem solving, and to help children, disadvantaged groups, and the environment.

Gordon B. Sherman, founder of Midas Muffler Shops. He turned his father's auto-parts business into the famous franchise by providing fast and convenient muffler repairs and replacement. As president of the company, Mr. Sherman made the management of his company more democratic and used proceeds to subsidize social activists Ralph Nader and Saul Alinsky. He joined with a group of businessmen frustrated and disillusioned with the Vietnam War and helped to form the Business Executives Move for Vietnam Peace. He also founded Businessmen for the Public Interest (BPI), an active advocacy organization in Chicago.

MANY BRANDS, ONE CORPORATION: THE TOBACCO COMPANY BEHIND THE CURTAIN

Big corporations often wear many faces to the public. This conceals their true power and reach, and it encourages illusions about how many choices individuals really have. The hocus-focus of tobacco maker Philip Morris's brand list below shows that you should always check the corporation behind the label. Philip Morris changed its name in 2003 to Altria Group—a Latin derivation meaning "high" and suggesting high performance—in order to create an overall brand that distances itself from the smoke.

PHILIP MORRIS COMPANIES, INC. ($80.356 billion in 2000 revenues) Sample of Philip Morris North American Products	
TOBACCO	Marlboro · Virginia Slims · Parliament · Merit · Benson & Hedges · Basic · L&M · Chesterfield · Lark · Cambridge
BEER	Miller Lite · Miller Genuine Draft · Miller Genuine Draft Light · Miller High Life · Miller High Life Light · Milwaukee's Best · Milwaukee's Best Light · Icehouse · Foster's · Red Dog · Southpaw Light · Leinenkugel's · Henry Weinhard's · Henry's Hard Lemonade · Hamm's · Mickey's · Old English 800 · Magnum · Presidente · Sharp's non-alcohol brew
CHEESE	Athenos · Cheese Whiz · Churny · Cracker Barrel · Deli Delux · DiGiorno · Easy Cheese · Hoffman's · Kraft · Philadelphia · Polly-O · Velveeta
DAIRY PRODUCTS	Breakstone's sour cream, cottage cheese · Knudsen sour cream, cottage cheese · Kraft dips · Light n' Lively lowfat cottage cheese
MEALS	Kraft macaroni & cheese and other dinners · Minute · Stove Top · Taco Bell* · Velveeta shells & cheese
ENHANCERS	A.1. · Bull's-Eye · Good Seasons · Grey Poupon · Kraft barbecue sauce, mayonnaise, salad dressings · Miracle Whip · Oven Fry · Sauceworks · Seven Seas · Shake 'n Bake
COOKIES & CRACKERS	Better Cheddars · Cheese Nips · Chips Ahoy! · Handi-Snacks · Honey Maid · Newtons · Nilla · Nutter Butter · Oreo · Premium · Ritz · SnackWell's · Stella D'Oro · Teddy Grahams · Triscuit · Wheat Thins
SNACKS	Corn Nuts · Planters · Claussen
PET SNACKS	Milk-Bone

(continues on next page)

*Licensed Trademark. Distribution agreement signed with Philip Morris Company or subsidiary.

PHILIP MORRIS COMPANIES, INC.	
CONFECTIONERY	Altoids · Callard & Bowser · Crème Savers · Farley's · Gummi Savers · Jet-Puffed · Life Savers · Milka L'il Scoops · Now and Later · Sather's · Terry's · Tobler · Toblerone · Trolli
BEVERAGES	Capri Sun* · Country Time · Crystal Light · Kool-Aid · Tang
COFFEE	General Foods International Coffees · Gevalia · Maxwell House · Sanka · Starbucks* · Yuban
DESSERTS	Baker's · Balance Bar · Breyers yogurt · Calumet · Certo · Cool Whip · Dream Whip · Ever-Fresh · Handi-Snacks · Jell-O · Knox · Light n' Lively lowfat yogurt · Minute · Sure-Jell
CEREALS	Alpha-Bits · Banana Nut Crunch · Blueberry Morning · Cranberry Almond Crunch · Cream of Wheat · Cream of Rice · Fruit & Fibre · Golden Crisp · Grape-Nuts · Great Grains · Honey Bunches of Oats · Honeycomb · Oreo O's · Pebbles* · Raisin Bran · Shredded Wheat · Toasties · Waffle Crisp
MEAT	Louis Rich · Lunchables · Oscar Mayer
MEAT ALTERNATIVE	Boca
PIZZA	California Pizza Kitchen* · DiGiorno · Jack's · Tombstone

*Licensed Trademark. Distribution agreement signed with Philip Morris Company or subsidiary.

GOVERNMENT AGENCIES THAT CAN HELP COUNTER CORPORATEERING

For assistance in determining which federal agency or department to contact regarding a specific inquiry, contact the Federal Consumer Information Center (FCIC) toll free at (800) 688-9889.

Center for Food Safety and Applied Nutrition
Food and Drug Administration
200 C Street SW
Washington, DC 20204
(888) SAFEFOOD (OI&C)
www.cfsan.fda.gov

Consumer Product Safety Commission (CPSC)
Washington, DC 20207
(800) 638-CPSC (Product Safety Hotline)
TDD: (800) 638-8270
info@cpsc.gov
www.cpsc.gov

Department of Education

Office of Public Affairs
400 Maryland Ave SW, Room 7E231
Washington, DC 20202
(202) 401-1576
www.ed.gov

EDGAR: Securities and Exchange Commission (SEC)

450 Fifth Street NW
Washington, DC 20549
(202) 942-7040 (information and complaints)
(800) SEC-0330 (to order publications)
TDD: (202) 628-9039
help@sec.gov
www.sec.gov/edgar.shtml

The SEC requires all public companies (except foreign companies and companies with less than $10 million in assets and 500 shareholders) to file registration statements, periodic reports, and other forms electronically through its database EDGAR. Anyone can access and download this information for free. For a complete list of filings available through EDGAR on-line, go to *www.sec.gov/edgar.shtml*

EPA Headquarters Information Resources Center

Environmental Protection Agency (EPA)
1200 Pennsylvania Avenue NW, Mailcode 3201
Washington, DC 20460
(202) 260-5922 (general information)
public-access@epamail.epa.gov

Federal Consumer Information Center (FCIC)

Dept. WWW
Pueblo, CO 81009
(800) 688-9889 (TTY: 800-326-2996)
www.pueblo.gsa.gov

Federal Trade Commission (FTC)
Consumer Response Center
600 Pennsylvania Avenue NW
Washington, DC 20580
(877) FTC-HELP (877-382-4357)
TDD/TTY: (202) 326-2502
www.ftc.gov
The FTC works to prevent fraudulent, deceptive, and unfair business practices and to inform consumers of ways to help spot, avoid, and stop them. To file a complaint or obtain free information on more than 150 consumer topics, call the number listed above or access the FTC website. Fraud-related complaints are recorded in Consumer Sentinel, a secure, on-line database employed by hundreds of law-enforcement agencies across the country and internationally.

FirstGov
General Services Administration
750 17th Street NW, Suite 200
Washington, DC 20006-4634
www.firstgov.gov
FirstGov is an interagency electronic initiative providing access to more than 51 million web pages from federal, state, local, and tribal governments, the District of Columbia, U.S. territories, and nations around the world.

Government Printing Office (GPO)
Superintendent of Documents
PO Box 371954
Pittsburgh, PA 15250
(202) 512-1800
Toll-free outside D.C.: 1-866-512-1800
orders@gpo.gov
www.gpo.gov

A free catalog of popular titles, including a list of the twenty-four GPO bookstores nationwide, can be obtained by writing to:
Free Catalog
PO Box 37000
Washington, DC 20013

Library of Congress
101 Independence Avenue, SE
Washington, DC 20540
(202) 707-5000
www.loc.gov
The Library has a collection of nearly 121 million items, more than two-thirds of which are in media other than books. These include the largest map, film, and television collections in the world. The Library has twenty-two reading rooms on Capitol Hill and a website designed to serve the public.

National Archives and Records Administration
8601 Adolph Road
College Park, MD 20740-6001
(301) 713-6800
inquire@nara.gov
www.nara.gov

National Health Information Center
Department of Health and Human Services (HAS)
PO Box 1133
Washington, DC 20013-1133
(800) 336-4797
info@nhic.org
www.health.gov/nhic or *www.healthfinder.gov*

U.S. Census Bureau
Department of Commerce
Customer Services
Washington, DC 20233
(301) 763-INFO (Consumer Information Line)
www.census.gov

In addition, an array of state agencies, which can be located through state government websites (listed below), exist to regulate certain industries and enforce certain areas of law, including:

Consumer Protection Offices. Operated variously at the state, county, and city level, Consumer Protection Offices work to protect consumers through addressing and investigating complaints, prosecuting violators of consumer laws, providing educational materials, etc. (See *www.pueblo. gsa.gov.*)

Banking Authorities. In addition to their primary responsibility for regulating state-chartered banks, state Banking Authorities may address complaints regarding other types of financial institutions and provide answers to general financial inquiries.

Insurance Regulators. Agencies exist in each state to regulate various types of insurance, such as auto, health, and home-owner. Among other roles, state Insurance Regulators may provide information on insurers, handle consumer complaints, and prosecute violators.

Secretaries of State. Secretary of State offices provide publicly accessible information regarding topics such as elections, campaign finance, lobbyists, and voter registration. These offices also provide official, business, and commercial codes and records required to be filed with the office.

Securities Administrators. State Securities Administrators enforce state laws covering all types of securities including commodities, stocks, real estate, mutual funds, and more.

Utility Commissions. State Utility Commissions regulate rates and services for such vital consumer necessities as electricity, gas, water, transportation, and/or telephones.

For information on finding these agencies in your area, contact the Federal Consumer Information Center (FCIC) toll-free at (800) 688-9889.

Official Home Pages for All U.S. States

Alabama: *www.state.al.us*
Alaska: *www.state.ak.us*
Arizona: *www.state.az.us*
Arkansas: *www.state.ar.us*
California: *www.ca.gov*
Colorado: *www.colorado.gov*
Connecticut: *www.state.ct.us*
Delaware: *www.delaware.gov*
District of Columbia (Washington, D.C.):
  www.washingtondc.gov
Florida: *www.myflorida.com*
Georgia: *www.state.ga.us*
Hawaii: *www.state.hi.us*
Idaho: *www.state.id.us*
Illinois: *www.state.il.us*
Indiana: *www.state.in.us*
Iowa: *www.state.ia.us*
Kansas: *www.accesskansas.org*
Kentucky: *www.kydirect.net*
Louisiana: *www.state.la.us*
Maine: *www.state.me.us*
Maryland: *www.state.md.us*
Massachusetts: *www.state.ma.us*
Michigan: *www.michigan.gov*

Minnesota: *www.state.mn.us*

Mississippi: *www.ms.gov*

Missouri: *www.state.mo.us*

Montana: *www.state.mt.us*

Nebraska: *www.state.ne.us*

Nevada: *silver.state.nv.us*

New Hampshire: *www.state.nh.us*

New Jersey: *www.state.nj.us*

New Mexico: *www.state.nm.us*

New York: *www.state.ny.us*

North Carolina: *www.nc.gov*

North Dakota: *discovernd.com*

Ohio: *www.state.oh.us*

Oklahoma: *www.state.ok.us*

Oregon: *www.oregon.gov*

Pennsylvania: *www.state.pa.us*

Rhode Island: *www.state.ri.us*

South Carolina: *www.myscgov.com*

South Dakota: *www.state.sd.us*

Tennessee: *www.state.tn.us*

Texas: *www.state.tx.us*

Utah: *www.utah.gov*

Vermont: *www.state.vt.us*

Virginia: *www.vipnet.org/cmsportal*

Washington: *access.wa.gov*

West Virginia: *www.state.wv.us*

Wisconsin: *www.wisconsin.gov/state/home*

Wyoming: *www.state.wy.us*

WHAT IS YOUR TIME WORTH?

orporations often do not respect the value of their customers'
time. Individuals can waste hours fixing a corporate mistake.
Should the corporation have to repay individuals when they
waste an excessive amount of their time? The chart below shows just
how valuable the individual's time actually is, based on her or his annual salary.

Your Annual Salary	Lost Dollars				
	In 30 minutes	In one hour	In four hours	In eight hours	In 25 hours
$ 15,000	3.25	7.50	30.00	60.00	187.50
$ 20,000	5.00	10.00	40.00	80.00	250.00
$ 30,000	7.50	15.00	60.00	120.00	375.00
$ 42,000	10.50	21.00	84.00	168.00	525.00
$ 54,000	13.50	27.00	108.00	216.00	675.00
$ 66,000	16.50	33.00	132.00	264.00	825.00
$ 80,000	20.00	40.00	160.00	320.00	1,000.00
$ 95,000	23.75	47.50	190.00	380.00	1,187.50
$ 110,000	27.50	55.00	220.00	440.00	1,375.00
$ 150,000	37.50	75.00	300.00	600.00	1,875.00
$ 300,000	75.00	150.00	600.00	1,200.00	3,750.00
$ 500,000	125.00	250.00	1,000.00	2,000.00	6,250.00
$ 750,000	187.50	375.00	1,500.00	3,000.00	9,375.00
$ 1,000,000	250.00	500.00	2,000.00	4,000.00	12,500.00

NOTES

CHAPTER 1: SEEING CORPORATEERING

1. Leslie Savan, *The Sponsored Life* (Philadelphia: Temple University Press, 1994), p.1.
2. Gordon Fairclough, "Dying Early Saves Money, Tobacco Company Says," *Wall Street Journal*, July 12, 2001.
3. Norihiko Shirouzu, "Ford Paid Its CEO Nasser $12.1 Million in 2000," *Wall Street Journal*, April 11, 2001.
4. Kenneth R. Weiss, "College Freshmen Rate Money as Chief Goal," *Los Angeles Times*, January 22, 2001. p. A1.
5. Richard Stevenson, "Pondering Greenspan's Next Moves," *The New York Times*, March 21, 2000, p. C1.
6. Joseph Kahn, "Trying to Turn Stocks into a National Pastime," *The New York Times*, October 28, 1999.
7. Businessweek/Harris Poll cited in cover story, "Too Much Corporate Power," *Businessweek*, September 11, 2000.
8. Jeremy Rifkin, *The Age of Access: The New Culture of Hypercapitalism Where All of Life Is a Paid-For Experience* (New York: Jeremy P. Tarcher/ Putnam, 2000), p.171. Rifkin is the president of the Foundation for Economic Trends in Washington, D.C. Kevin J. Clancy and Robert S. Schulman—respectively chairman and CEO of Copernicus: The Marketing Investment Strategy Group, Inc. in Westport Connecticut—interviewed marketing directors for their 1994 book *Marketing Myths That Are Killing Business*. They write, "During the last two decades, corporations have been shifting money they spend on advertising to buyer and trade promotion and to sports and event marketing—all questionable

activities masquerading as clever marketing tools. The ratio, which was roughly two-thirds advertising/one-third promotion, is now three-quarters promotion/one-quarter advertising." Kevin J. Clancy and Robert S. Shulman, *Marketing Myths That Are Killing Business* (New York: McGraw-Hill, Inc., 1995) p.171. While statistics about corporate advertising expenditures are readily available, statistics about total corporate marketing expenditures are rare. Inserting known advertising expenditures from 2001 into the formula presented by Clancy and Shulman, however, produces overall marketing expenditures by American corporations of nearly $1 trillion domestically and $1.84 trillion internationally.

9. Robert Coen, "Bob Coen's Insider Report," McCann-Erickson World Group, December 2001. Coen is a premier business forecaster and charter of advertising spending. Also see similar early data from Naomi Klein, *No Logo: Taking Aim at the Brand Bullies* (New York: Picado, 1999), pp. 8, 11.

10. *No Logo*, p. 9.

11. *The Age of Access*, p. 171.

12. About 100 television advertisements per day cited by Leslie Savan, *The Sponsored Life* (Philadelphia: Temple University Press, 1994), p. 1.

13. Dianne Levin, Ph.D. "Marketing Harms Children," Fact Sheet from Judge Baker Children's Center at Harvard/Wheelock College, presented at press conference protesting Golden Marble Awards, New York, NY, September 14, 2000.

14. Naomi Klein, *No Logo: Taking Aim at the Brand Bullies* (New York: Picador, 1999), p. 21.

15. Ibid., p. 20, citing Shultz's book *Pour Your Heart into It* (New York: Hyperion, 1997), p. 5.

16. William E. Schmidt, "A Growing Urban Fear: Thieves Who Kill for 'Cool' Clothing," *The New York Times*, February 6, 1990.

17. "Abandon the prison of your couch. Leave the answering machine in charge. And go. Go to the places the road maps leave empty. Find dirt. Find elevation. Find fingerholds. Find happiness. Roll down Mother Nature's washboard welcome mat. Stop not because a sign told you to, but because your eyeballs made you. Get out into the air no one else breathes, and wonder, in awe, why no one else is there. Nissan Xterra. Everything you need, and nothing you don't" from *www.nissanusa.com/vehicles/ModelHomePage/0,,20460,00.html*

18. Graphic "Warm Fuzzy Feelings," with Steve Lohr, "Few Computer Users Give Microsoft a Positive Rating," *The New York Times*, August 2, 1999, p. C1. Research by Susan Fournier, associate professor at Harvard Business School.

19. Russell Mokhiber, *Corporate Crime and Violence: Big Business Power and*

the Abuse of the Public Trust (San Francisco: Sierra Club Books, 1988), p. 227. Remarkably, the convicted companies were each fined only $5,000; the convicted individuals were each fined $1; no one was sent to jail.

20. Roland Marchand, *Creating the Corporate Soul* (Berkeley: University of California Press, 1998) pp. 130–163.
21. Ibid., p. 139.
22. Ibid., p. 140.
23. Ibid., pp. 142–45.
24. Ibid., p. 155.
25. Much of it produced in *Anderson v. General Motors,* Los Angeles Superior Court, which led to a $4.9 billion verdict against General Motors, recognized as the largest personal injury verdict ever. Ann W. O'Neill, Henry Weinstein, Eric Malnic, "GM Ordered To Pay $4.9 Billion In Crash Verdict," *Los Angeles Times,* July 10, 1999, p. A1. Jury foreman Coleman Thorton stated, "GM has no regard for the people in their cars, and they should be held responsible for it."
26. E. C. Ivey, Advance Design, "Value Analysis of Auto Fuel Fed Fire Related Fatalities," Internal Memo, June 29, 1973.
27. *Anderson v. General Motors,* Los Angeles Superior Court.
28. Ann W. O'Neill, Henry Weinstein, Eric Malnic, "GM Ordered to Pay $4.9 Billion In Crash Verdict," *Los Angeles Times,* July 10, 1999, p. A1.
29. Myron Levin, "Engineer's Memo Returns To Haunt GM," *Los Angeles Times,* April 30, 2001.
30. Notes made by a pharmaceutical company employee produced in the Rezulin Multi District Litigation, Southern District of New York, Judge Kaplan, MDL #1349, provided by attorneys for plaintiff.
31. Cover story, "Why Service Stinks," *Businessweek,* October 23, 2000; Edmund Sanders, "System Lets Banks Identify Most Profitable Customers," *Los Angeles Times,* July 21, 2000.
32. *Businessweek,* October 23, 2000.
33. *The American Heritage Dictionary of the English Language, Third Edition* (Boston: Houghton Mifflin Company, 1992), p. 454.

CHAPTER 2: REMOVING ACCOUNTABILITY TO THE INDIVIDUAL

1. Richard N. Current, T. Harry Williams, Frank Freidel, Alan Brinkley, *American History: A Survey, Volume I. To 1877, Seventh Edition* (New York: Alfred A. Knopf, 1987), p. 40.
2. Charles Derber, *Corporation Nation: How Corporations Are Taking Over Our Lives and What We Can Do About It* (New York: St. Martin's Press, 1998), p. 124.
3. Ibid., p.125, citing Richard Grossman, Program on Corporations, Law and Democracy (*www.poclad.org*), pamphlet *Taking Care of Business.*

Grossman's original source is John W. Cadman, *Corporations in New Jersey* (Cambridge, Massachusetts: Harvard University Press, 1949) p. 76.

4. Ibid.

5. John Balzar, "The Gilded Age Goes On and On," *Los Angeles Times,* June 15, 2001, opinion commentary.

6. R. R. Palmer, Joel Colton, *A History of the Modern World, Sixth Edition* (New York: Alfred A. Knopf, 1984), pp. 570–571.

7. Carl Mayer, "Personalizing the Impersonal: Corporations and the Bill of Rights," *Hastings Law Journal,* Volume 41, March 1990.

8. *People v. North River Sugar Refining Corp.,* 24 N. E. 834 (1890), cited by Richard Grossman, "Can Corporations Be Accountable?" Program on Corporations, Law and Democracy (*www.poclad.org*), June 1998.

9. Carl Mayer, "Personalizing The Impersonal: Corporations and the Bill of Rights," *Hastings Law Journal,* Volume 41, March 1990, p. 578.

10. "Joined by the insurance and securities industries, banks launched an aggressive national lobbying campaign this year to defeat privacy reform bills in California and about two dozen other states that sought to adopt tighter rules than those approved last year by Congress," Edmund Sanders of the *Los Angeles Times* eulogized in the spring of 2000. Edmund Sanders, "Panel Defeats Bill to Boost Privacy Rights," *Los Angeles Times,* April 25, 2000, p. A1.

11. California Assembly Judiciary Committee Analysis, AB 1707, March 27, 2000, citing letter of opposition from financial services industry, p. 15.

12. Ibid., p. 16.

13. Edmund Sanders, "Panel Defeats Bill to Boost Privacy Rights," *Los Angeles Times,* April 25, 2000, p. A1.

14. John C. Jeffries, Jr. *Justice Lewis F. Powell, Jr.* (New York: Macmillan/ Charles Scribner's Sons, 1994), pp. 188–193.

15. Lewis F. Powell, Jr., "Attack on American Free Enterprise System," confidential memo to Mr. Eugene B. Sydnor, Jr., Chairman, Education Committee, U.S. Chamber of Commerce, August 23, 1971.

16. On every major issue that consumer advocates like myself across the nation confront, the Business Roundtable surfaces as the major opponent with the money and power to make pro-consumer reforms difficult and corporate-backed legislation, no matter how unreasonable, possible.

17. Ralph Nader, *Crashing the Party* (New York: Thomas Dunne/St. Martin's, 2002), p. 21.

18. Ibid., p. 29–30.

19. Adolf A. Berle, *Power* (New York: Harcourt, Brace, and World Inc, 1967), p. 27.

20. James A. Smith, *The Idea Brokers* (New York: The Free Press, 1991), p. xvi.

21. Dan Morgan, "Think Tanks: Corporations' Quiet Weapon," *Washington Post,* January 29, 2000, p. A1.
22. Sheldon Rampton and John Stauber, *Trust Us, We're Experts* (New York: Jeremy P. Tarcher/Putnam, 2002), p. 306; citing Tom Brazaitis, "Big Think Tanks Lead the Charge in Washington," *The Plain Dealer* (Cleveland), December 19, 1999, p. A1.
23. Charles Derber, *Corporation Nation* (New York: St. Martin's Press), 1998, p. 11.
24. For example, the titans of health care are Aetna, CIGNA, United Healthcare, Foundation Health Systems, PacifiCare, Kaiser, and WellPoint; of auto makers are General Motors, Ford Motor Company, Toyota, Honda, and DaimlerChrysler; of air travel are American Airlines, United Airlines, Delta Airlines, Northwest Airlines, Continental Airlines, U.S. Airways, and Southwest Airlines; of food are Philip Morris Companies, Inc., ConAgra, H. J. Heinz & Company, Nestlé USA, and General Mills.
25. Robert B. Reich, "Corporate Power in Overdrive," *The New York Times,* March 18, 2001.
26. The series can be viewed and read at *www.pbs.org/wgbh/commandingheights/lo*
27. Research by Sarah Anderson and John Cavanagh of the Institute for Policy Studies, Multi-National Monitor, June 1999. Measuring Gross National Product (GNP) against gross revenues.
28. Charles Gay, "Corporate Goliath," *Multi-National Monitor,* June 1999. Exxon Mobil, GM, Ford, Mitsui, DaimlerChrysler, Mitsubishi measured by gross corporate revenue. The gross revenue of the top fourteen American corporations is greater than the United States government's budget.
29. Robert Pear, "Bush Rolls Back Rules on Privacy of Medical Data," *The New York Times,* August 10, 2002, p. A1.
30. William Greider, *Who Will Tell the People: The Betrayal of American Democracy* (New York: Touchstone, 1993), pp. 109–113.
31. Ibid.
32. Robert B. Reich, "Corporate Power in Overdrive," *The New York Times,* March 18, 2001.
33. *Crashing the Party,* p. 32.
34. *etext.virginia.edu/jefferson/quotations/*; University of Virginia.
35. James Madison, *Writings* (New York: The Library of America, 1999), p. 762.
36. Ibid.

CHAPTER 3: THE LOGIC OF MAKING CORPORATIONS
COUNT MORE THAN INDIVIDUALS

1. Kristi Turnquist, "Competition Drives Advertisers to Get Offbeat," *The Plain Dealer,* August 25, 2000, p. 4C.
2. Constance L. Hays, "Variable-Price Coke Machine Being Tested," *The New York Times,* October 28, 1999.
3. Adam Clymer, "Lawmakers Are Pouring Their Politics Straight," *The New York Times,* July 1, 2002.
4. Stephen Labaton, "AT&T's Acquisition of MediaOne Wins Approval by F.C.C.," *The New York Times,* June 6, 2002, p. A1.
5. Stephen Labaton, "AOL Time Warner Gain Approval For Huge Merger," *The New York Times,* December 15, 2000, p. A1. As a condition of the merger, the Federal Trade Commission required AOL Time Warner to open up each of its cable systems to at least three competing Internet providers.
6. Although I am not an AT&T cable customer, my telephone answering machine recorded the following computerized message on Monday, October 14th, at 5:36 P.M. "AT&T BroadBand Cable Customer: We are calling to announce that beginning August 13, 2002, AT&T BroadBand will be offering our cable Internet service [in your area]. . . . If you need more information about system requirements, or pricing for our cable Internet service, please call 1-866-279-2744."
7. Public Citizen, "Chronology of Firestone/Ford Knowledge of Tire Safety Defect," Washington, D.C.
8. G. William Dauphinais and Colin Price, Price Waterhouse, *Straight from the CEO: The World's Top Business Leaders Reveal Ideas That Every Manager Can Use* (New York: Simon & Schuster, 1998), p. 251.
9. Milt Freudenheim, "A Merger of Health Insurers: Managed Care Empires in the Making," *The New York Times,* April 2, 1996, p. D1.
10. Editorial, "When Big Is Good," *The New York Times,* April 3, 1996.
11. Letter by Bruce V. Vladeck, Administrator, Department of Health and Human Services, to Dr. Gordon Schiff, Department of Medicine, Cook County Hospital, October 21, 1994.
12. Based on HMOs' medical loss ratios in California and the nation as filed with government agencies.
13, Jamie Court and Francis Smith, *Making a Killing: HMOs and the Threat to Your Health* (Monroe, Maine: Common Courage Press, 1999). *www. makingakilling.org*
14. Associated Press, "U.S. Healthcare Chief Will Get $1 Billion," June 15, 1996.
15. Milliman & Robertson guidelines. Milliman & Robertson, Inc., reproduced by Kaiser Permanente Northern California Region under licens-

ing agreement with Milliman & Robertson, Inc.; complete set of guidelines. Modified 10/14/96.

16. *Wall Street Journal* quote cited by Steffie Woolhandler and David Himmelstein in "The National Health Program Slideshow Guide," Physicians for a National Health Program, Harvard Medical School/The Cambridge Hospital, 2000.

17. Chrysler, in the end, made money for the public because the government was issued stocks as security.

18. For more detail on the scandal, see William Greider, *Who Will Tell the People: The Betrayal of American Democracy* (New York: Touchstone Books, 1993), p. 60–78.

19. David Cay Johnston, "Study Finds That Many Large Companies Pay No Taxes," *The New York Times*, October 20, 2000, p. C2; David Francis, "More Firms Find Tax Loopholes," *The Christian Science Monitor*, October 20, 2000. p. 1.

20. Citizens for Tax Justice Press Release, "Less Than Zero: Enron's Income Tax Payments, 1996–2000."

21. David Cay Johnston, "Study Finds That Many Large Companies Pay No Taxes," *The New York Times*, October 20, 2000, p. C2; David Francis, "More Firms Find Tax Loopholes," *The Christian Science Monitor*, October 20, 2000. p. 1.

22. Tax Report: "Taxing Factlets," *Wall Street Journal*, April 3, 2002, p. A1.

23. The United States ranks 37th out of 191 countries for "overall health system performance"; 72nd for "level of health"; and 1st for "health expenditures per capita," according to *The World Health Report 2000,* "Health Systems: Improving Performance," World Health Organization, Geneva, Switzerland June 21, 2001; p. 155. Full report accessible on-line at: *www.who.int/whr/2001/archives/2000/en/index.htm*

24. "We want customers to be aware that they have more options than ever before to take charge of their energy expenses, but that the choice is in their hands," said Pam Fair, vice president of customer services at SDG&E. Sempra Energy press release, PR Newswire, May 5, 2001. The utility hedged its bets in this statement, however, warning, "Because summer is traditionally a time of high energy use, we want all our customers to understand the dynamics of the new deregulated market, so they will be better prepared when electricity commodity prices fluctuate."

25. "California businesses and residents paid $10.9 billion more for electricity last summer than the year before, with much of the money flowing to out-of-state energy firms. One of them, Houston-based Reliant Energy, saw its wholesale energy profits jump 600% during that time, with about $100 million coming from California." From: Nancy Vogel, "How State's Consumers Lost With Electricity Deregulation," *Los Angeles Times*, December 9, 2000, p. A1. Other companies also saw huge increases: NRG's

3rd Quarter 2000 profits rose 221%, AES Q3 2000 profits jumped 131%, Duke Energy's wholesale energy profits climbed 374% for the year.

26. Foundation for Taxpayer and Consumer Rights Report, "Hoax: How Deregulation Let the Power Industry Steal $71 Billion from California," January 17, 2002, p. 6; Greg LaMotte, "San Diego at Center of California Deregulation Dispute," CNN.com, December 20, 2000.

27. According to the California Independent System Operator (the state's grid manager) peak demand was down 5% in July 2000, from July 1999 and down 1% in August 2000.

28. From Monthly and Annual Transition Cost Filings with the California Public Utilities Commission for PG&E and Southern California Edison, as compiled by The Utility Reform Network.

29. Kevin Yamamura and Emily Bazar, "Employees: Power Supply Held Down," *Sacramento Bee*, June 22, 2001.

30. "Monthly Calendar of Daily Maximum Prices," Consortium for Electric Reliability Technology Solutions (CERTS) Market Pricing Resource Site, updated June 11, 2001.

31. Richard W. Stevenson, "Enron's Trading Gave Prices Artificial Lift, Panel Is Told," *The New York Times*, April 12, 2002.

32. Ibid.

33. KPMG LLP, *Report on Southern California Edison's Solvency and Liquidity Concerns*, January 29, 2001, p. I5.

34. Dan Morain, Chris Kraul, Mitchel Landsberg, "Deepening Crisis Raises Specter of Power Rationing," *Los Angeles Times*, December 21, 2000, p. A1.

35. Data from California Independent Systems Operator, California Power Exchange; and the "Monthly Calendar of Daily Maximum Prices," Consortium for Electric Reliability Technology Solutions (CERTS) Market Pricing Resource Site, updated June 11, 2001.

36. California Public Utility Commission decision #88-01-063, Condition 12, January 28, 1988.

37. Emily Bazar, "Davis consultants had contract with Edison," *Sacramento Bee*, June 22, 2001.

38. Peter G. Gosselin and Jennifer Warren, "Deal Could Cap Electricity Rates—But At A Price," *Los Angeles Times*, January 11, 2001," p. A1.

39. Associated Press, "Text of Governor Davis' State of the State Address," January 8, 2000.

40. Nancy Vogel, "PUC Plans $5 A Month Electricity Rate Hike: Angry Utilities Say It's Not Enough And Warn of Blackouts," *Los Angeles Times*, January 4, 2001. p. A1.

41. Goldman Sachs was a banker for the state's largest utility, involved in energy trading and the owner of a company that sold natural gas to power generators.

42. Credit Suisse/First Boston, Paul Patterson, analyst, "US Economics

Comment: A Very Brief Note on California," January 18, 2001; Miguel Bustillo, "Wall Street Firm's Web Site Calls Blackouts A Tactic To Raise Rates," *Los Angeles Times,* January 15, 2001, p. A19.

43. G. William Dauphinais and Colin Price, Price Waterhouse, *Straight from the CEO: The World's Top Business Leaders Reveal Ideas That Every Manager Can Use* (New York: Simon & Schuster, 1998), pp. 251–252.

44. Paul Krugman, "Power and Profits," *The New York Times,* January 24, 2001, p. A19.

45. Carrie Peyton, "Edison Pact Could Point Way for PG&E," *Sacramento Bee,* October 12, 2001, p. A3.

46. Mark Z. Barabak, "Most Californians Think Electric Crunch Is Artificial," *Los Angeles Times,* January 7, 2001, p. A1.

47. Jenifer Warren, "Power Shortage Not Real," *Los Angeles Times,* June 28, 2001, p. A1.

48. George Orwell, "Politics and the English Language," 1946, reprinted in: George Orwell, *A Collection Of Essays* (San Diego: A Harvest Book, 1981).

49. Ibid.

50. "Positive Thoughts Regarding the Eight Hour Discharge," Kaiser Permanente Los Angeles Sunset Facility, in conjunction with "Guidelines for Early Homecoming Program," June, 1995.

51. Literature from "Hands Off the Internet" campaign packet distributed in Los Angeles.

52. Albert Dunlap, *Mean Business* (New York: Fireside/Simon & Schuster, 1996), p. xii. Ironically, the SEC sued Dunlap over massive financial fraud in March 2001 for his leadership at Sunbeam; Dunlap settled for $15 million with shareholders alleging fraudulent accounting practices at Sunbeam under his leadership. Sunbeam was forced to restate six months worth of financial statements before Dunlap's departure, which helped put it into Chapter 11 bankruptcy. From: Thomas Mulligan, "Xerox Agrees to Record SEC Fine," *Los Angeles Times,* April 2, 2002.

53. David Korten, *When Corporations Rule the World* (San Francisco: Berret-Koehler/Kumarian Press, 1996), p. 40.

54. Ralph Nader and Wesley J. Smith, *No Contest: Corporate Lawyers and the Perversion of Justice in America* (New York: Random House, 1996), p. 264. See Chapter Four for more detailed statistics.

55. Paul Vitello, "Just What Drug Makers Ordered?" *New York Newsday,* June 25, 2002, p. A8.

56. Robert C. Goizueta, "Why Shareowner Value?" The CEO Series, Business Leaders: Thought and Action, Center for the Study of American Business, Washington University in St. Louis, February 1996, Series No. 13.

57. G. William Dauphinais and Colin Price, Price Waterhouse, *Straight from the CEO: The World's Top Business Leaders Reveal Ideas That Every Manager Can Use* (New York: Simon & Schuster, 1998), pp. 20–21.

CHAPTER 4: CAPTURING JUSTICE, EDUCATION, AND COMMUNITY

1. Constance Hays, "Commercialism in U.S. Schools Is Examined in New Report," *The New York Times,* September 14, 2000, p. C1.
2. "State common law causes of action arising from the improper processing of a claim are preempted." From: *Pilot Life Insurance v. Dedeaux.*
3. Nathan Weber, "Product Liability: The Corporate Response," Research Report #893, The Conference Board (1987) cited in a report by Megan Mulligan and Emily Gottlieb, edited by Joanne Doroshow, "Lifesaver: CJ&D's Guide to Lawsuits That Protect Us All," (2002 Supplement) Center for Justice and Democracy, New York, NY. *http://centerjd.org*
4. *Gryc v. Dayton-Hudson Corp,* 297 N.W.2d 727 (Minn. 1980), cert denied, 449 U.S. 921 (1980), cited in "Lifesaver" report, p. A11.
5. "Lifesaver" report p. A28.
6. Ibid., p. A34.
7. Robert Pear, "Patients' Rights Pick Up Momentum In 2 Senate Votes," *The New York Times,* June 27, 2001, p. A1.
8. Editorial, "An Inflammatory Fire Strategy," *The New York Times,* August 26, 2002.
9. Maura Dolan and Myron Levin, "Smokers May Sue For Fraud," *Los Angeles Times,* August 6, 2002.
10. Since insurance industry lawyers prevailed on the U.S. Supreme Court in 1987 (*Pilot Life Insurance v. Dedeaux*), 180 million Americans with employer-based insurance could not recover a dime in damages when denied medically necessary treatment by an HMO or insurer, no matter how serious the injury or egregious the wrongdoing.
11. California's Medical Injury Compensation Reform Act or MICRA of 1976 limits both the contingency fees an attorney can earn in a medical negligence case and the damages a victim can recover. Joanne Doroshow, J.D., of the Center for Justice and Democracy, who works with malpractice victims and attorneys for injured consumers in New York, confirms that a similar contingency fee cap exists in that state.
12. Jeri Mellon, "Keating's Revenge," *The New York Times,* December 15, 1995, Op-Ed page.
13. *Olsen v. Sharp Rees–Steely Medical Group et al.* San Diego Superior Court, Case No. 666808.
14. Letter to the Editor, *San Diego Union Tribune,* May 20, 1995.
15. Ralph Nader and Wesley J. Smith, *No Contest: Corporate Lawyers and the Perversion of Justice in America* (New York: Random House, 1996), p. 264.
16. Ted Rohrlich, "We Aren't Seeing You In Court," *Los Angeles Times,* February 1, 2001, p. A1.
17. *No Contest,* p. 264–266.
18. *No Contest,* p. 264.

19. William Glaberson, "US Chamber Will Promote Business Views in Court Races," *The New York Times*, October 22, 2000, p. 22.
20. John Restrup, "Bigger Business Role in Judicial Elections Stirs Controversy," *Liability & Insurance Week*, November 6, 2000 (JR Publishing, PO Box 6654, McLean, Virginia, 22106).
21. Ibid.
22. U.S. Chamber of Commerce Press Statement, "U.S. Chamber Cheers Victory in Mississippi Case—Fifth Circuit Court Upholds Free Speech Rights in Judicial Races," April 5, 2002.
23. John Restrup, "Bigger Business Role in Judicial Elections Stirs Controversy," *Liability & Insurance Week*, November 6, 2000 (JR Publishing, PO Box 6654, McLean, Virginia, 22106).
24. Ibid.
25. Center for Justice and Democracy, and Public Citizen, "The CALA Files: The Secret Campaign by Big Tobacco and Other Major Industries to Take Away Your Rights," November 2000; *www.citizen.org*
26. Ibid.
27. Reynolds Holding, "Judges' Action Casts Shadow on Court's Integrity," *San Francisco Chronicle*, October 9, 2001.
28. Reynolds Holding, "Can Public Count on Fair Arbitration?" *San Francisco Chronicle*, October 8, 2001.
29. Ibid. Holding further reports that a 1997 study revealed that "employees won only 16 percent of their cases against repeat players, defined as employers in arbitration at least twice a year. But the employees won 71 percent of their cases against non-repeat players. Even when employees beat repeat players, the employees generally won no damages, the study found."
30. The American Arbitration Association, the largest association of arbitrators in the nation, recommends this cost-sharing approach in most cases.
31. Reynolds Holding, "Millions Are Losing Their Legal Rights," *San Francisco Chronicle*, October 7, 2001.
32. *Nida Engalla et al. v. The Permanente Medical Group, Inc.*, California Supreme Court, No. S-04881-1, 1997.
33. Diane Levin, Ph.D. "Marketing Harms Children," Fact Sheet from Judge Baker Children's Center at Harvard/Wheelock College, presented at press conference protesting Golden Marble Awards, New York, NY, September 14, 2000. Other estimates differ, because of the imprecision of calculating purchases made as opposed to purchases influenced, though all estimates are significant. "There are approximately 37 million children in America," the authors of *Children First! A Parent's Guide to Fighting Corporate Predators* wrote in 1996. "They represent an attractive and lucrative market that is worth well over $150 billion annually

and is growing rapidly." (Corporate Accountability Research Group, PO Box 19312, Washington, DC 20036). The Wheelock College numbers represent a consensus among academics from across the country who gathered at the Manhattan protest of the Golden Marble awards.

34. Lenore Skenazy, "TV Ads Aimed at Kids: A $12B Warp Machine," *New York Daily News,* September 13, 2000, citing Diane Levin, Professor at Wheelock College.
35. Julie Marquis, "Eating Habits Puts Teens at Risk, Study Says," *Los Angeles Times,* June 14, 2000, p. A1.
36. Fact Sheet, "Marketing to Children: A Call to Action," Save Children from Advertising (The SCAM project), Judge Baker Children's Center, Boston; *www.jbcc.harvard.edu*
37. Ibid.
38. Jeff Leeds, "Surgeon Gen. Links TV, Real Violence," *Los Angeles Times,* January 17, 2001, p. A1.
39. Doreen Carvajal, "Major Studios Used Children To Test-Market Violent Films," *The New York Times,* September 27, 2000, p. A1.
40. Ibid.
41. Constance Hays, "Commercialism In U.S. Schools Is Examined in New Report," *The New York Times,* September 14, 2000, p. C1.
42. Ibid.
43. Ibid.
44. David D. Kirkpatrick, "Snack Foods Become Stars of Books for Children," *The New York Times,* September 22, 2000, p. A1.
45. Statement of Allen Kanner, Ph.D. Berkeley, Wright Institute, "The Commercialization of Childhood: A Protest of the Golden Marble Awards," at Manhattan protest of Golden Marble Awards, September 14, 2000.
46. Ibid.
47. Linda Coco, *Children First! A Parent's Guide to Fighting Corporate Predators* (Washington, D.C.: Corporate Accountability Research Group, 1996), p. 6.
48. Ibid.
49. Lenore Skenazy, "TV Ads Aimed at Kids: A $12B Warp Machine," *New York Daily News,* September 13, 2000.
50. Barbara Meltz, "Consumer mania: Creating Kids Who Are Hip To Hype," *The Boston Globe,* September 14, 2000.
51. Professor Dianne Levin, Testimony Before the Senate Committee on Commerce, Science and Transportation, "Marketing Violence to Children," Federal News Service, May 4, 1999.
52. Statement of Allen Kanner, Ph.D. Berkeley, Wright Institute, "The Commercialization of Childhood: A Protest of the Golden Marble Awards," at Manhattan protest of Golden Marble Awards, September 14, 2000.

53. Constance Hays, "Commercialism in U.S. Schools Is Examined in New Report," *The New York Times,* September 14, 2000, p. C1.
54. *No Logo,* pp. 117, 129.
55. Juan Williams, "Naming Rights of Buildings Such as Stadiums, Arenas, Hospitals and Schools," *Talk of the Nation* (National Public Radio), March 5, 2001, 2 P.M. E.S.T.
56. Ibid.
57. Julie Edelson Halpert, "Dr Pepper Hospital? Perhaps, For A Price," *The New York Times,* February 18, 2001, Section 3, p. 1.
58. Commercial Alert Press Release, "Nader Criticizes Smithsonian Head for Proposed Naming Rights Deal with General Motors," July 19, 2001. In the 1930s and '40s the world's largest interurban electric transportation systems in over 100 U.S. cities from New York, Philadelphia, and St. Louis to Los Angeles, San Francisco, and Salt Lake City were destroyed in a systematic corporate-collusion scheme led by General Motors to make way for today's automobile homogenization of American transportation.
59. Juan Williams, "Naming Rights of Buildings Such as Stadiums, Arenas, Hospitals and Schools," *Talk of the Nation* (National Public Radio), March 5, 2001, 2 P.M. E.S.T.
60. Mathew McAllister, *The Commercialization of American Culture* (Thousand Oaks: Sage, 1996), p. 177.
61. David D. Kirkpatrick, "Many Words From Our Sponsor; Fay Weldon Produces a Novel Commissioned by a Jeweler," *The New York Times,* September 3, 2001.
62. Raffi Cavoukian, "Yes, We Have No Advertising," *Toronto Globe & Mail,* June 9, 2000, reprinted by Commercial Alert, June 19, 2000; *www.commercialalert.org*
63. David W. Dunlap, "City Officials Tell Microsoft to Get Its Butterfly Decals out of Town," *The New York Times,* October 25, 2002.
64. Robert D. Putnam, *Bowling Alone* (New York: Simon & Schuster, 2000), p. 60.
65. Putnam's term "social capital" has caught on like wildfire with charitable foundations and the intellectual community. This shows how commercial concepts, such as "capital," have been far easier to grasp and relate to for societal leaders and opinion makers. When individuals discuss expending their political capital or seeing the value of their stock to their employer go up, there is an implicit commercial standard that is being applied to a social relationship. Individuals conduct themselves based on gaining or losing worth, rather than on growing socially, intellectually, or emotionally.
66. *Bowling Alone,* p. 283.
67. Ibid., pp. 27–28.
68. Ibid., p. 25.

CHAPTER 5: WORKERS OF THE WORLD INCORPORATE

1. Michael Moore, *Downsize This!* (New York: Harper Perennial, 1997), p. 155.
2. Charis Conn and Lewis H. Lapham, *The Harper's Index, Volume 3* (New York: Franklin Square Press, 2000), p. 128.
3. Ibid., p. 132.
4. G. William Dauphinais and Colin Price, *Straight from the CEO: The World's Top Business Leaders Reveal Ideas That Every Manager Can Use* (New York: Simon & Schuster, 1998), pp. 20–21.
5. Ibid.
6. Ibid., p. 17.
7. Ibid., p. 21.
8. Tom Peters, *The Circle of Innovation* (New York: Vintage Books, 1999), p. xvi.
9. Ibid., p. 155.
10. Ibid., p. 124.
11. Ibid., "destroy" pp. 35, 69, 71; "forget" pp. 75, 77, 79, 81, 83, 89, 90, 93, 95, 96, 99, 101, 103, 107, 109, 111, 112, 114, 119, 120; "cannibalize" pp. 84, 121.
12. Melinda Ligos, "Job Contracts With Noncompete Teeth," *The New York Times,* November 1, 2000, p. G1; Sean Schultz, "Temp Services Come to The Beauty Biz," *Green Bay Gazette,* October 8, 2002; Bernard Stamler, "How Long Is The Reach Of Your Former Employer?" *The New York Times,* February 11, 2001.
13. Norihiko Shirouzu and Jon E. Hilsenrath, "A Debate On Deflation Simmers, Auto Makers Live the Experience," *Wall Street Journal,* November 21, 2001, p. A1.
14. Tom Peters, *The Circle of Innovation* (New York: Vintage Books, 1999), pp. 190, 246.
15. See "Surprise, You're on Corporate Camera," The United Electrical, Radio and Machine Workers of America website: "In 1990 according to one survey about 8 million workers were subject to some form of electronic surveillance by their employers. In 1996 the number had risen to 20 million workers, and this is just based upon the employers who admit to spying on their workers. In a 1993 survey of large corporations 22 percent admitted they spied on their workers with some form of electronic surveillance and never told the workers they were being monitored." *www.ranknfile-ue.org/stwd_corcam.html*
16. *The Circle of Innovation,* p. 8.
17. Ibid., p. 24.
18. The Federal False Claims Act rewards those who uncover fraud against the federal government.

19. The California legislature modestly extended it in 2000 due to new evidence.

20. Declaration of Jo Ann Lowe in opposition to motion for preliminary injunction, *Julie O. Houg v. Allstate Insurance Company,* Superior Court for the State of California for the County of Los Angeles, Case No. BC 142582 August 25, 1997, p. 3.

21. Ibid., p. 4.

22. Ibid., pp. 5–9.

23. Ibid., p. 8.

24. Ibid., pp. 9–11.

25. Ibid., p. 12.

26. Author interview with David Grant in Louisville, Kentucky, September 12, 2001. The name is fictitious because the expert believes that if a security expert's identity is revealed then their tactics will be as well.

27. Author interview with Dr. Linda Peeno at her home in Louisville, Kentucky, September 12, 2001. Other quotes from Peeno from interviews on this day unless otherwise noted.

28. Linda Peeno, "Managed Care Ethics: The Close View," The U.S. House of Representatives Committee on Commerce, Subcommittee on Health and Environment, May 30, 1996.

29. Linda Peeno, Testimony to California Assembly Committee on Health, April 15, 1997.

30. Layoffs: U.S. Airways—11,000 (24% of workers); Continental—12,000 (21%); United—20,000 (20%); Northwest—10,000 (19%); American—20,000 (15%); America West—2,000 (14%). From the *Wall Street Journal.*

31. After receiving bad publicity, some of the airlines changed their minds, but their initial ignorance of the inappropriateness of the act demonstrates the point.

32. Mike Fish, CNN.com, "Airport Security: A System Driven by the Minimum Wage": "According to reports submitted to Congress, security screeners are generally paid at or near minimum wage to serve as, in many cases, the last line of defense for safe air travel"; *www.cnn.com/ SPECIALS/2001/trade.center/flight.risk/stories/part1.mainbar.html*

33. Christopher Oster, "Insurance Companies Benefit from September 11, Still Seek Federal Aid," the *Wall Street Journal,* November 15, 2001, p. A1.

34. Ibid.

35. "Hardening Markets Likely To Get Harder," *Smart's Insurance Bulletin,* September 21, 2001, p. 3.

36. Richard Stevenson, "Divided Senate Takes Up Stimulus Bill Today," *The New York Times,* November 13, 2001.

37. Paul Krugman, "Taking Care of Business," *The New York Times,* October 28, 2001.

38. Public opinion polls cited by Charles Derber in *Corporation Nation,* p. 94.

39. Interview with Hughes, August 1, 2001, at his corporate headquarters in Los Angeles.

CHAPTER 6: INDEBTED TO THE CORPORATION

1. Richard Stevenson, "Uncle Sam Learns Thrift While America Spends," *The New York Times,* July 4, 1999.
2. According to CardWeb.com, reported by Leslie Ernest, "More Debt Fewer Pay Checks Spell Trouble For Economy," *Los Angeles Times,* October 5, 2001, p. A1.
3. Ibid.
4. Louis Uchitelle, "Equity Shrivels as Homeowners Borrow and Buy," *The New York Times,* January 19, 2001, p. A1.
5. Garth Turner, "Home Equity Debate Heats Up Again," *London Free Press* (Sun Media Corporation), May 20, 1999.
6. Louis Uchitelle, "Equity Shrivels as Homeowners Borrow and Buy," *The New York Times,* January 19, 2001, p. A1.
7. Leslie Ernest, "More Debt Fewer Pay Checks Spell Trouble for Economy," *Los Angeles Times,* October 5, 2001, p A1.
8. Daryl Strickland, "Home Buyers Turning To Interest-Only Loans," *Los Angeles Times,* August 20, 2002, p. C1.
9. Stanley A. Brown, PriceWaterhouse Coopers, *Customer Relationship Management* (Ontario: John Wiley & Sons, Canada, Ltd, 2000), pp. 57–60.
10. Ibid.
11. Charis Conn and Lewis H. Lapham, eds., *Harper's Index, Volume 3* (New York: Franklin Square Press, 2000), p. 122.
12. Different versions of the legislation passed both the United States Senate and House of Representatives, but at the time of publication, had not reached President Bush's desk.
13. Glenn H. Thrush, "Saving Your Way Into Debt," *The New York Times Magazine* (Sunday), October 15, 2000, p. 106.
14. Ibid., p. 107.
15. Ibid., p. 108.
16. Jeff Turrentine, "Investing Is the New Spending," *The New York Times Magazine* (Sunday), October 15, 2000, p. 21.
17. Ibid.
18. Kathy Kristoff, "Decades-Low Interest Rates Take a Toll on Savers," *Los Angeles Times,* November 22, 2001.
19. Editorial, "Disinformation On Wall Street," *The New York Times,* April 11, 2002.
20. Patrick McGheehan, "Merrill Lynch Under Attack as Giving Tainted Advice," *The New York Times,* April 9, 2002.

21. William Greider, "Father Greenspan Loves Us All," *The Nation*, January 1, 2001.
22. Ralph Nader, *Cutting Corporate Welfare* (New York: Seven Stories Press, 2000), p. 71.
23. Alan Cowell, "Can The IMF Tame the Beast," *The New York Times*, October 14, 2001, Section 3, p. 5.
24. John Balzar, "They Bet Against America," *Los Angeles Times*, September 19, 2001, Commentary.
25. For example, Enron created a complex energy trading system, but did not own very many energy generation plants. This allowed it to artificially inflate the price of electricity in California by having each of its subsidiaries bid up the price of energy against each other, artificially inflating a product it did not even generate.
26. Bill Goldstein, "Word for Word: When Greed Was A Virtue And Regulation The Enemy," *The New York Times*, July 21, 2002.
27. Tom Brokaw, "The Informant: Company Executive Mark Whiteacre Helps the FBI by Going Undercover," *Dateline* (NBC), September 10, 2000, 7 P.M. E.S.T.
28. The informer, Mark Whiteacre, was the subject of a book by Kurt Eichenwald entitled *The Informant* that showed that Whiteacre had his own credibility problems, although the evidence he taped was solid enough for ADM to admit its guilt.
29. Reported in *Consumer Reports* magazine, October 1993; cited in *Physician* for a National Health Program Slide Show 2000, Harvard Medical School, authored by Dr. David Himmelstein and Dr. Steffie Woolhandler.
30. See Harvey Rosenfield, "Auto Insurance: Crisis and Reform," The University of Memphis Law Review, Volume 29, Number 1, Fall 1998.
31. Robert McChesney, *Corporate Media and the Threat to Democracy* (New York: Seven Stories Press, 1997), p. 22.
32. Ibid.
33. Martin Smith, "Dot Con," *Frontline* (PBS), January 24, 2002. This excellent report of the phenomenon (transcript available at *www.pbs.org*) explained that the seeds of the problem began when broker commissions were deregulated on May 1, 1975. Since commissions went down, the brokerages looked for profit elsewhere. "These institutions, once primarily thought of as brokerage houses, used to make their big profits by offering advice to clients on what stocks to buy or sell and then charging commissions on those transactions. But when deregulation forced commission rates to drop, they began to rely more on money they made from investment banking. In the '80s, it was mergers and acquisitions. Then, in 1995, along came the Netscape initial public offering, or IPO. The company was less than 18 months old, had little revenue and no profits. Its debut would change everything."

34. Louis Uchitelle, "3 Americans Awarded Nobel for Economics," *The New York Times,* October 11, 2001.

35. Peter Gosselin, "Three Americans Share Nobel Economics Prize," *Los Angeles Times,* October 11, 2001, p. C1.

36. Ibid.

37. Adam Smith, *An Inquiry into the Nature and Causes of the Wealth of Nations,* Edwin Cannan, ed. (Chicago: University of Chicago Press, 1976), vol. I, p. 69.

38. Ibid., p. 138.

39. Ibid., p. 477.

40. David C. Korten, *The Post-Corporate World* (San Francisco: Berrett-Koehler Publishers, Inc. and Kumarian Press, Inc., 1999), pp. 38–39.

41. Memo from J.S. Morisson, "SPU Meeting January 26, 1982/SPU Discussion Outline," January 14, 1982. Internal ARCO document.

42. Cited as exhibit in letter to Federal Trade Commission Chairman Robert Pitofsky, May 30, 1997, by Edward Rothschild, Citizen Action; Marc Cooper, Consumer Federation of America; Michael Shame, Utility Consumer Action Network; David West, Washington Citizen Action; Jim Driscoll, Arizona Citizen Action. Presented by Automotive Trade Organization and California Service Station and Automotive Repair Association to California Attorney General's Taskforce on Gasoline Pricing, February 9, 2000.

43. Memo from J.S. Morisson, "SPU Meeting January 26, 1982/SPU Discussion Outline," January 14, 1982. Internal ARCO document.

44. Melita Garza, "Gas Prices Look Stable," *Chicago Union-Tribune,* June 12, 2001. Marathon Ashland Petroleum LLC acknowledged that it was the company discussed. The FTC report stated that an unidentified company had "increased summer-grade RFG [reformulated gas] production substantially and, as a result, had excess supplies of RFG available and had additional capacity to produce even more RFG at the time of the price spike. It thus found itself with considerable market power in the short term. This firm did sell off some inventories of RFG, but acknowledged that it limited the magnitude of the response because it recognized that increasing supply would push down prices."

45. Neela Banerjee, "Fears, Again, of Oil Supplies at Risk," *The New York Times,* October 14, 2001, Section 3, p. 1. In 1980, OPEC accounted for 62% of all U.S. imports. Data from Energy Information Association.

46. Liz Pulliam Weston, "Credit Card 'Gotchas' Bleed Customers With A Thousand Cuts," *Los Angeles Times,* January 21, 2000 p. C1.

47. Seth Schiesle, "Charges From Calling Cards Often More Than Expected," *The New York Times,* February 15, 2001.

48. Greg Winter, "What Keeps A Bottom Line Healthy? Weight Loss," *The New York Times,* January 2, 2001, p. A1.

49. Robert H. Frank, "Why Living in a Rich Society Makes Us Feel Poor," *The New York Times Magazine* (Sunday), October 15, 2000, p. 62.

50. Ibid.

51. Charis Conn and Lewis H. Lapham, *The Harper's Index, Volume 3* (New York: Franklin Square Press, 2000), p. 122.

52. Ibid.

53. Ibid., p. 35.

54. Ibid., p. 129.

CHAPTER 7: SELLING THE FREE PRESS AND THE PUBLIC INTEREST

1. Robert Scheer, "Extra! Extra! Read Less About It," *Los Angeles Times*, April 24, 2001, commentary, p. B9.

2. Interview with Foner in his office at Columbia University, New York City, September 15, 2000.

3. Such a change could only occur when the notion of the press as a public sphere of interest was undermined by the so-called "privatization" movement of the post–Cold War world, and when, in the legal system, the modern corporation hitched its "private" speech rights to the individual's.

4. *Debate on the Constitution: Federalist and Anti-federalist Speeches, Articles, and Letters During the Struggle over Ratification, Part One* (New York: Library of America, 1993), p. 95.

5. Ibid., p. 77.

6. Robert McChesney, *Corporate Media and the Threat to Democracy* (New York; Seven Stories Press, 1997), p. 6.

7. Since "what bleeds leads," and "what thinks (often public interest matters) stinks."

8. Brooks Jackson, "Doctors Make Washington House Call to Support HMO Reform," *Inside Politics* (CNN), June 23, 1998, 5:23 P.M. E.S.T.

9. Ben Bagdikian, *The Media Monopoly* (Boston: Beacon Press, Sixth Edition 2000), p. viii.

10. Ibid.

11. Ibid., p. 10.

12. Jack Beatty, *Colossus: How The Corporation Changed America* (New York: Broadway Books, 2001), p. xv.

13. Ibid.

14. Ibid.

15. Ibid., p. xiv.

16. Ralph Nader, *Cutting Corporate Welfare* (New York: Seven Stories Press), p. 50; citing Robert Pepper, Chief FCC Office of Plans, letter to Senator Joseph Lieberman, September 6, 1995.

17. Operating in the "public interest" has been redefined under the new logic to mean advancing the "private interest" (public interest = private

interest). Such leases are technically granted for eight years, but are automatically renewed. The leases also include the new digital spectrums for high-definition television. *New York Times* columnist William Safire called broadcasters "spectrum squatters" because the leases were granted with the understanding that broadcasters would develop and mass market high-definition television, which they have yet to do.

18. Stephen Labaton, "Media Companies Succeed in Easing Ownership Limits," *The New York Times,* April 16, 2001, p. A1.

19. Ibid.

20. Seth Schiesel, "FCC Rules on Ownership Under Review," *The New York Times,* April 3, 2002, p. C1.

21. Yochi J. Dreazen, "FCC's Powell Quickly Marks Agency As His Own," *Wall Street Journal,* May 1, 2001.

22. David Welna, "Senate Commerce Committee Hearing On Rules Restricting Media Consolidation," *Morning Edition* (National Public Radio), July 18, 2001, 10:00 A.M. E.S.T.

23. Ibid.

24. Jim Lehrer, "Megamerger Masters," *NewsHour with Jim Lehrer* (PBS), January 12, 2000.

25. Jeff Greenfield, "Millennium 2000: Media in the New Century," CNN Live Event/Special, January 2, 2000.

26. Ibid.

27. "AOL To Lay Off 1,700 Workers," NewsHour Online (PBS), August 22, 2001. Another 2,400 positions were eliminated in January.

28. Ray Suarez, "Newsmaker: William Kennard," NewsHour with Jim Lehrer(PBS), and NewsHour Online, January 12, 2001.

29. Ray Suarez, "AOL–Time Warner Merger," NewsHour with Jim Lehrer (PBS), and NewsHour Online, January 10, 2000.

30. Ibid.

31. A web search found 0 references to "cross ownership" from 1996 to 2001 on CNN.com but found 69 of those references in *The New York Times.*

32. Robert Scheer, "Extra! Extra! Read Less About It," *Los Angeles Times,* April 24, 2001, Commentary, p. B9.

33. A Time.com search found 0 references to "open access/forced access" from 1993 to 2001.

34. Felicity Barringer, "18 CNN Journalists Protest Departure of Chief Counsel," *The New York Times,* July 27, 2001.

35. Ibid.

36. Jim Rutenberg, "CNN Aims At Young Viewers As It Revamps News Format," *The New York Times,* August 15, 2001, Section 1, p. 1.

37. Thompson left in March 2002, with CNN sources suggesting that the daily news business was too rigorous for her. Financial Desk: "CNN

Headline News Anchor Says She'll Leave Network," *The New York Times,* March 15, 2002, p. C2.

38. Elizabeth Jensen, "Headline News Faces Criticism For Channeling Viewers," *Los Angeles Times,* August 20, 2001.

39. From January 1998 to January 1999, reported by Jim McConville, "Cable Ratings Get Boost From Impeachment," Crain Communications Inc., Electronic Media, February 19, 1999 p. 34.

40. While CNN has a relatively small overall market share, its nonstop coverage is watched religiously by opinion leaders and decision makers in a way that fuels their fire for issues and alters their sense of proportion about what is reasonable and important. The traction an issue gets on a network like CNN feeds the attention that policymakers and opinion leaders will give it as much as it reflects it.

41. Ben Bagdikian, *The Media Monopoly* (Boston: Beacon Press, Sixth Edition, 2000), p. xxxiv. Unfortunately, as Bagdikian points out, National Public Radio has had to take on more commercial sponsorships and has adopted shortened, standard formats due to commercialization within its ranks. Still, its programming is far superior to the commercial product in the length of its reporting and focus on key national decisions that have no hook to sell products, such as the insider view on debates in Washington, D.C.

42. Robert McChesney, *Corporate Media and the Threat to Democracy* (New York: Seven Stories Press, 1997), p. 24.

43. Jim Lehrer, "Megamerger Masters," NewsHour with Jim Lehrer (PBS), January 12, 2000.

44. Bill Carter, "CBS Is The Odd Man Out As ABC Woos Letterman," *The New York Times,* March 1, 2002, p. A1.

45. Ibid.

46. Ted Koppel, "Network News Is Serious Business," *The New York Times,* March 5, 2002, Op-Ed, p. A23.

47. Mike Davis, *City of Quartz* (New York: Vintage Books, 1992), p. 100.

48. Trudy Lieberman, "The Truth About Censorship," *Columbia Journalism Review,* May/June 2000.

49. Ibid.

50. "Reheated Disney/ABC To-Do," *New York Daily News,* November 13, 1998, p. 134.

51. Reed Irvine, "As ABC's Story On Disney's Pedophile Problem Gets Spiked," Insight on the News, New Worlds Communications, December 28, 1998. Reed Irvine is chairman of Accuracy in the Media, a Washington, D.C.–based media watchdog group.

52. Trudy Lieberman, "The Truth About Censorship," *Columbia Journalism Review,* May/June 2000.

53. Ibid.

54. Neil Hickey, "Coping With Corporate Mergers," *Columbia Journalism Review,* March/April 2000.
55. Trudy Lieberman, "The Truth About Censorship," *Columbia Journalism Review,* May/June 2000.
56. Downsizing in newsrooms, particularly foreign newsrooms, is noted by media critics Ben Bagdikian (*Media Monopoly,* pp. xxix–xxx), Robert McChesney (*Corporate Media Culture and the Threat to Democracy,* pp. 26–27) and Pew's survey ("Time-starved reporters say they simply do not have the opportunity to follow up on important subjects." *people-press.org/reports/display.php3?PageID=218*). Those of us in the consumer advocacy community have noted the dramatic downsizing during the last ten years in newspapers across America.
57. Trudy Lieberman, "The Truth About Censorship," *Columbia Journalism Review,* May/June 2000.
58. Ibid.
59. Elizabeth Jensen, "Headline News Faces Criticism For Channeling Viewers," *Los Angeles Times,* August 20, 2001.
60. Jim Rutenberg, "ABC–CNN Talks Could Leave CBS the Odd Network Out," *The New York Times,* October 28, 2002.
61. Ibid.
62. Ben Bagdikian, *The Media Monopoly* (Boston: Beacon Press, Sixth Edition, 2000), pp. xxv–xxvii.
63. Ibid., p. xxv.
64. Ibid., p. xxvii.
65. Having spent much time in newsrooms across California and the nation, this observation is a personal one, but also backed up by Bagdikian, McChesney, and conversations with more than a dozen journalists I frequently deal with.
66. Sheldon Rampton and John Stauber, *Trust Us, We're Experts!* (New York: Jeremy P. Tarcher/Putnam, 2001), p. 23.
67. Ibid., p. 22.
68. Dean Murphy, "What Cost $75 More Than Manhattan," *The New York Times,* April 14, 2002.
69. Henry Waxman, "Did NBC Make Call With Welch In the Backfield?" *Los Angeles Times,* August 13, 2001, Commentary. NBC initially called the election for Gore, as did the other networks.
70. Ibid.
71. "Rep. Waxman Knows Better," *Los Angeles Times,* August 9, 2001.
72. Henry Waxman, "Did NBC Make Call With Welch In the Backfield?" *Los Angeles Times,* August 13, 2001, Commentary.
73. Robert Fisk, "Terror in America," *The Nation,* October 1, 2001.
74. Peter Jennings, "Answering Kids' Questions, An ABC Special," ABC News, September 15, 2001.

75. Jeff Leeds, Paul Brownfield, "After The Attack: Pop Culture Takes A Serious Reality Check," *Los Angeles Times,* September 18, 2001, p. A1.

CHAPTER 8: GLOBAL CORPORATEERING

1. Lawrence Summers, "Let Them Eat Toxics; Memo From World Bank Economist," *Harper's Magazine,* May, 1992.
2. After the internal World Bank memo was uncovered, Summers claimed that his remarks were meant to be ironic.
3. African Growth and Opportunity Act or NAFTA for Africa (AGOA), Agreement on Agriculture (AoA), Conformity Assessment Body (CAB), General Agreement on Tariffs and Trade (GATT), General Agreement on Trade in Services (GATS), Generalized System of Preferences (GSP), International Monetary Fund (IMF), International Organization on Standardization (ISO), Multilateral Agreement on Investment (MAI), North American Free Trade Agreement (NAFTA), Organization for Economic Cooperation and Development (OECD), Transatlantic Economic Partnership (TEP), Trade-Related Investment Measures (TRIMs), Trade-Related Aspects of Intellectual Properties (TRIPs), and World Trade Organization (WTO).
4. Jamie Court, "The Trade Pack Threatens Sovereignty of California," *San Francisco Chronicle,* November 24, 1994.
5. Lori Wallach and Michelle Sforza, *Whose Trade Organization* (Washington, D.C.: Public Citizen, 1999), pp. 12, 13, 19.
6. Ibid., p. 12.
7. Ibid.
8. Ibid., p. 52.
9. Ibid., p. 100.
10. Ibid., pp. 100, 119.
11. Ibid., p. 12.
12. Ibid.
13. Public Citizen Fast Track Fact Sheet, October 2001; *www.citizen.org*
14. Public Citizen Global Trade Watch, "Harmonization Handbook: Accountable Governance in the Era of Globalization, the WTO, NAFTA, and International Harmonization"; *www.citizen.org*
15. Ibid.
16. Ibid.
17. Ibid.
18. Public Citizen Global Trade Watch, "The Coming NAFTA Crash: The Deadly Impact of Secret NAFTA Tribunal's Decision To Open U.S. Highways To Unsafe Mexican Trucks," February 2001. Press Release confirming ruling February 7, 2001.
19. Public Citizen Global Trade Watch, "Harmonization Handbook: Ac-

countable Governance in the Era of Globalization, the WTO, NAFTA, and International Harmonization"; *www.citizen.org*

20. William Greider, "The Right and US Trade Law: Invalidating the 20th Century," *The Nation,* October 15, 2001.

21. Cases discussed in "NAFTA Chapter 11 Investor-to-State Cases: Bankrupting Democracy," Public Citizen Global Trade Watch.

22. William Greider, "The Right and US Trade Law: Invalidating the 20th Century," *The Nation,* October 15, 2001.

23. Ibid.

24. Ibid.

25. Charis Conn and Lewis H. Lapham, eds., *The Harper's Index, Volume 3* (New York: Franklin Square Press, 2000), p. 134.

26. Cited in *Downsize This!* p. 127, and *No Logo,* p. 372.

27. Bloomberg News, "It's A Rich Deal After All For Eisner," *The Montreal Gazette,* February 26, 1996, p. D2; "Meaty Choices," *St. Petersburg Times,* March 10, 1997, p. 3D.

28. Paul Feldma, Patrick J. McDonnell, and George White, "Thai Workers Sweatshop Probe Grows," *Los Angeles Times,* August 9, 1995, p. A1.

29. "Meaty Choices," *St. Petersburg Times,* March 10, 1997, p. 3D.

30. William Greider, "Global Agenda," *The Nation,* January 31, 2000.

31. Ibid.

32. Ralph Nader, *Cutting Corporate Welfare* (New York: Seven Stories Press, 2000), p. 36.

33. Rick Brooks, "Big Incentives Won Alabama A Piece Of The Auto Industry," *Wall Street Journal,* April 3, 2002, p. A1.

34. Charis Conn and Lewis H. Lapham, eds., *The Harper's Index, Volume 3* (New York: Franklin Square Press, 2000), p. 121.

35. Greg Palast, "The Globalizer Who Came In From The Cold," *The Observer* (London), October 10, 2001.

36. Ibid.

37. Institute for Policy Studies and Sustainable Energy and Economy Network, "Institute for Policy Studies uncovers $7 billion in public assistance for Enron's global operations," Press Release, March 22, 2002. Report is "Enron's Pawns: How Public Institutions Bankrolled Enron's Globalization Game"; *www.seen.org*

38. Ibid., discussed in "Enron's Pawns."

39. Greg Palast, "The Globalizer Who Came In From The Cold," *The Observer* (London), October 10, 2001.

40. Ibid.

41. Ibid.

42. Ajit Singh, "Free Trade and the 'Starving Child' Defense: A Forum," *The Nation,* April 24, 2000.

43. Ibid.

44. Ibid.
45. Stephen Jay Gould, *Full House: The Spread of Excellence from Plato to Darwin* (New York: Harmony Books, 1996), pp. 228–229.
46. Jeremy Rifkin, *The Age of Access,* p. 185.
47. Louis Uchitelle, "World Bank Economist Felt He Had to Silence His Criticism or Quit," *The New York Times,* December 2, 1999, p. C1; also Peter Gosselin in the *Los Angeles Times,* October 11, 2001.

CHAPTER 9: COUNTERING CORPORATEERING

1. Jack Beatty, *Colossus: How the Corporation Changed America* (New York: Broadway Books, 2001), p. xxii.
2. Author interview with Sol Price, La Jolla California, August 9, 2001.
3. Naomi Klein, "Sign of the Times," *The Nation,* October 22, 2001, p. 16.
4. Kurt Eichenwald, "HCA To Pay $95 Million in Fraud Case," *The New York Times,* December 15, 2000, p. C1. The penalty was one in a series totaling $840 million during 2000.
5. Kurt Eichenwald, "He Blew The Whistle And Health Care Giants Quaked," *The New York Times,* October 18, 1998.
6. *Corporate Media and the Threat to Democracy,* p. 67.
7. Ralph Nader, *Cutting Corporate Welfare* (New York: Seven Stories Press, 2000), p. 48.
8. Ibid., p. 50.
9. Ibid., p. 77.
10. Ibid., p. 119.
11. 47 CFR 64.1200; 16 CFR 310—Code of Federal Regulations.

APPENDIX I: SPEAKING ABOUT CORPORATEERING

1. Bill Carter, "CBS Drops Reruns as Advertiser Pulls Commercials," *The New York Times,* August 17, 2001.
2. Michael Moore, *Downsize This!* (New York: HarperPerennial,1997), p. 52.
3. Ibid.

INDEX

ABOUT THE AUTHOR

Jamie Court is executive director of the nonprofit Foundation for Taxpayer and Consumer Rights, based in Santa Monica, California (www.consumerwatchdog.org). A pioneer of the HMO patients' rights movement, Court has also led efforts to reform energy companies, property casualty insurers, the financial services industry, and other major American corporations. He is co-author, with Francis Smith, of *Making a Killing: HMOs and the Threat to Your Health* (Common Courage Press).

THE FOUNDATION FOR TAXPAYER AND CONSUMER RIGHTS

This book is a project of the Foundation for Taxpayer and Consumer Rights (FTCR). FTCR is a tax-exempt, nonprofit organization deploying an in-house team of public interest lawyers, policy experts, strategists, public educators, and grassroots activists to advance and protect the interests of consumers and taxpayers. FTCR's day-in, day-out consumer protection and advocacy work embraces a wide variety of issues affecting the daily lives and pocketbooks of millions of Americans from patient protection to insurance reform to corporate accountability.

If you would like to receive free e-mail alerts from FTCR, or for more information, please contact:

Foundation for Taxpayer and Consumer Rights
1750 Ocean Park Blvd, Ste 200
Santa Monica, CA 90405
Phone (310) 392-0522
www.consumerwatchdog.org

To join FTCR's Circle to Counter Corporateering, visit:
www.corporateering.org